Remembering my father's

... urging ...

of the ... my ...

Mr. Farnum's in... a

& accepted it.

A vacancy occurring

corps of teachers, I began

~~as a teacher~~ in de...

six months before my ...

from College, keeping up ...

studies, & reciting daily ...

A.m, and from p.m

I entered the prof

deaf-mute instruction

~~an instructor of the deaf~~

thusiasm, and with an

ambition to do more ...

interesting class of prison

~~to teach them~~

the Principal, a s...

It was therefore with

interest ~~that~~ I soon

History of the
College for the Deaf
1857–1907

by
Edward Miner Gallaudet

1. Edward Miner Gallaudet writing at his desk, ca. 1907.

History of the
College for the Deaf
1857–1907
by
Edward Miner Gallaudet

Lance J. Fischer and David L. de Lorenzo
Editors

WITH A FOREWORD BY EDWARD C. MERRILL, JR.

GALLAUDET COLLEGE PRESS
WASHINGTON, D.C.

Gallaudet College Press, Washington, DC 20002
Published 1983
Printed in the United States of America

Library of Congress Cataloging in Publication Data

Gallaudet, Edward Miner, 1837–1917.
History of the college for the deaf, 1857–1907.

Includes index.
1. Gallaudet College—History—19th century.
I. Fischer, Lance J., 1949-__ __. II. De Lorenzo,
David L., 1952-__ __. III. Title.
HV2530.G33   1983   371.91'2'09753   83-14211
ISBN 0-913580-85-6
ISBN 0-913580-89-9 leatherbound

Gallaudet College is an equal opportunity employer/educational institution. Programs and services offered by Gallaudet College receive substantial financial support from the U.S. Department of Education.

The Story of the origin
and growth of the
College for the Deaf
at Washington, D.C.,
now called Gallaudet College,
in honor of Thomas H. Gallaudet,
begun by Edward M. Gallaudet
in the winter of 1895 - 6.

Contents

Part Five: Preparing for the Future, 1887–1907

Appendices: Extracts from Annual Reports

Index

Illustrations

Chronology

1857   Columbia Institution for the Deaf and Dumb and the Blind incorporated on two acres of land donated by Amos Kendall.

Amos Kendall appointed Edward Miner Gallaudet as superintendent of the new institution.

1858   Exhibition of pupils' work held at the old hall of House of Representatives.

Edward Miner Gallaudet wed Jane Melissa Fessenden.

1860   Civil War began.

1861   Kendall Green became a military camp.

1864   Enabling Act, giving collegiate powers, passed in Congress and approved by President Abraham Lincoln.

E. M. Gallaudet and Amos Kendall disagreed over college regulations, curriculum, and diplomas.

Thirteen acres of land adjacent to the institution purchased.

1865   Blind pupils transferred to Maryland Institution at Baltimore.

1866   Fredrick Law Olmsted presented plan for arrangement of college buildings and grounds.

Melville Ballard of Maine became first graduate with B.S. degree.

Jane Melissa Fessenden Gallaudet, Gallaudet's wife, died.

1867   Gallaudet toured Europe, examining all methods of teaching the deaf.

Senator Washburne of Illinois began his opposition to the college.

1868   Gallaudet called a conference of principals of regular institutions to discuss education for the deaf.

E. M. Gallaudet wed Susan Denison.

1869   Graduation of first regular class from collegiate department.

Amos Kendall died.

1870   Directors, with $5,000 on hand, purchased 81 acres of adjoining property for $85,000 from Amos Kendall's estate.

1871   Main central building (Chapel Hall) dedicated with President Grant
in attendance.

       Mortgage on Kendall Green paid off with $70,000 appropriation
from Congress.

1872   Gallaudet given a year's leave of absence due to illness.

1874   Gallaudet purchased personal library of Dr. Charles Baker of
England for the college.

       Construction of the college building (College Hall) began.

1876   E. M. Gallaudet, students, and faculty members visited the
Centennial Exhibition in Philadelphia.

1877   Gallaudet's mother, Sophia Fowler Gallaudet, died.

1878   President and Mrs. Hayes visited the campus to celebrate
completion of the college building (College Hall).

1880   Gallaudet attended the Milan Congress.

       Construction of gymnasium completed.

1882   President Arthur visited Kendall Green on 25th anniversary of the
institution.

1886   Gallaudet attended Convention of American Instructors of
the Deaf at Berkeley, California.

       Gallaudet gave testimony on the education of the deaf before
a Royal Commission in England.

       Women admitted to the college.

1889   Thomas Hopkins Gallaudet statue unveiled.

1891   Alexander Graham Bell opposed E. M. Gallaudet over proposed
establishment of the Normal Department.

       Baltimore and Ohio Railroad's plan to lay tracks through Kendall
Green defeated.

       Gallaudet, accompanied by his son Denison, addressed Congress
of Deaf-Mutes of Great Britain and Ireland on combined
system of educating the deaf.

       Normal Department inaugurated.

1894   Collegiate department of institution renamed Gallaudet College.

1895   Boys' dormitory for Kendall School, designed by Olof Hanson,
completed.

1897   Gallaudet, with his son Edson, visited numerous cities in Europe
to discuss methods of teaching the deaf with professionals
and educated deaf adults.

1898   New legislation overcame Interior Department's threat to exercise
control over college disbursements.

1900   Gallaudet and Professor Fay attended the International Congress
in Paris.

1903   Gallaudet's wife, Susan Denison Gallaudet, died.
1905   Colored deaf children transferred to the Maryland School for
        Colored Deaf-Mutes in Baltimore.
        Gallaudet delivered an address in Germany at unveiling of a
        monument to Moritz Hill, an educator of the deaf.
1906   President Theodore Roosevelt visited Kendall Green on
        Presentation Day.
1907   Institution commemorated 50th anniversary.

Foreword

Edward Miner Gallaudet and his father, Thomas Hopkins Gallaudet, held degrees from Yale University. His mother, who was deaf, held no college degree. With a father who established and directed the first permanent public school for deaf children in the United States and with a deaf mother, it is not surprising that young Gallaudet saw the need for deaf persons to have access to higher education. When Amos Kendall invited Edward Miner Gallaudet to consider a position at a school for the deaf which he was establishing in Washington, D.C., Edward Miner Gallaudet formulated a mission which shaped his life. He wrote the following:

> I visited Washington at once and had satisfactory interviews with Mr. Kendall. I unfolded to him my plans for a college and said that if he and his associates in the management of the proposed institution would support me in these plans, I would accept their offer. They met my overtures with alacrity, pleased with the idea of having what they had conceived of as no more than a small local school, grow ultimately into an institution of national importance and influence.

Amos Kendall and Edward Miner Gallaudet became close friends in spite of a large difference in their ages. They met on June 13, 1857, when Gallaudet was 20 years old and Kendall was already 68 years of age. The young man with a vision and the older statesman made a remarkable team as they pursued the common goal of establishing and operating a college for the deaf in Washington, D.C.

This handwritten manuscript provides a unique historical perspective of an important development in the history of education in the United States. The account is the story of the establishment of a college, but it is also a vivid description of the times, of the personalities of prominent

[xv]

persons then serving in Congress and the Federal Government, of the struggle for funding, and of the effort to acquire public understanding of the needs of deaf people and the mission of the institution.

The vision shared by Edward Miner Gallaudet and Amos Kendall has now served deaf Americans for 120 years. The alumni of the College have demonstrated the validity of this vision, for these deaf individuals have become well-educated persons fully capable of independent thought, employment in a variety of occupations and professions, and contributors to the society at large.

This is a story written by the aging hand but clear mind of a great humanitarian about one of the noblest educational ventures in the history of the United States.

EDWARD C. MERRILL, JR.

Preface

The following account is a history of the first, and still only, liberal arts college primarily for deaf persons in the world. This college is now known as Gallaudet College. The original manuscript, from which this book was derived, was handwritten by the founder and first president, Dr. Edward Miner Gallaudet, who began work on the history in the winter of 1895. Dr. Gallaudet was unable to complete the manuscript, and it has been left unpublished until now. The history is a personal account of his work as the first superintendent of a small school for deaf children established by Amos Kendall which grew into a nationally and internationally recognized college for the deaf. The history gives his insights into the problems and frustrations encountered as he built the institution from a student body of five to a college responding to the special needs of deaf persons. Dr. Gallaudet discusses his decision to become a teacher of the deaf as well as his acceptance of the superintendency of the Columbia Institution for the Deaf and Dumb and the Blind. He details the issues and debates in Congress regarding federal support for the establishment and funding of the college.

Along with Alexander Graham Bell, Dr. Gallaudet is considered one of the most significant leaders in the history of education of the deaf in America. Dr. Gallaudet's 53-year career in the field of deafness has no equal. He introduced a combined system which integrated oral methods into the strictly manual residential schools in the United States; he advocated the use of manual methods of instruction when most of the world changed to oral instruction; and he brought about the establishment of the Normal Department, a graduate training program for teachers of deaf children, at Gallaudet College.

Dr. Gallaudet's history demonstrates not only the difficulty of establishing and furthering the goals of the college, but it reaches a deeper level

as an account of his character and genius. He often makes personal statements on events and personalities that influenced him which cannot be
found elsewhere. It is hoped, that from the publication of this work, Dr.
Gallaudet's own place in history may be better appreciated and his contributions more fully understood. Its publication represents an attempt to
provide a basic document on the history of the deaf community in the
United States, a history which has not been fully researched, analyzed,
nor interpreted. Perhaps this book will provide the catalyst for further
research on this topic.

Historical editing is a tedious process when attempting to provide an
exact reflection of a hand-written, unpublished manuscript. The editors
have tried to make the following account what Dr. Gallaudet would have
published if he had been able to do so. Dr. Gallaudet provided satisfactory
biographical information on the prominent individuals mentioned in the
history. The editors did not feel it necessary to add to his work in this
regard or to expand the history with footnotes on now obscure individuals.

Throughout the book, Dr. Gallaudet has referred readers to other
sources where further information can be found. He cites mainly the
annual reports of the institution, all of which he wrote himself each year.
The reports by Dr. Gallaudet pertaining to the inauguration of the college,
the first commencement exercises, the European system of instruction,
and Frederick Law Olmsted's letter on the plans for the campus were
added to the book as appendices because of their significant impact on
the history of the college. All other citations, in spite of their wealth of
information, were not included due to the sheer volume of the material
involved. Interested researchers will be able to acquire copies of this
material by contacting the Gallaudet College Archives.

The editors were guided by a self-imposed rule that this should be
Dr. Gallaudet's history. However, some changes had to be made because
there exist two copies of the history, one at the Gallaudet College Archives,
another at the Library of Congress Manuscript Division. The manuscript
copy at Gallaudet College is believed to be the original draft. It is written
entirely in Dr. Gallaudet's hand and contains original correspondence from
Amos Kendall. The manuscript copy at the Library of Congress, however,
is much more formal. It is written in a secretarial hand and contains few
spelling or other errors. Approximately the first third of this copy had
been corrected by Dr. Gallaudet, as can be seen by his notations in the
margins. It is believed this copy was to have been the final draft but was

left unfinished due either to his ill health or death. This manuscript copy provided the basis for the history recorded herein.

When questions arose regarding wording, grammar, etc., in the latter two-thirds of the manuscript, the first third of the manuscript, and the original draft were looked to as arbitrators. Proper names have been capitalized where appropriate. Modern monetary symbols rather than those of the nineteenth century were used. Other changes are indicated in brackets ([   ]). Both manuscripts lacked chapter separations; therefore, the editors divided the text with imposed chapter titles. As well, a chronological table and an index have been added. Photographs were also inserted in the book to enhance visually the historical narrative.

Dr. Gallaudet's title, *History of the College for the Deaf, 1857–1907*, has been retained. This title helps distinguish the manuscript from other personal diaries and memoirs kept by Dr. Gallaudet.

The Gallaudet College Archives contains nearly all of Dr. Gallaudet's papers, correspondence, and photographs relating to the administration of the institution. These papers are open to the public without restrictions. The National Archives and Records Service in Washington, D.C., holds all legislative records such as the Enabling Act and other public laws which allocated funding and defined the legal standing of Gallaudet College. The Smithsonian Institution Archives contains mainly the correspondence between Dr. Gallaudet and Joseph Henry, the Secretary of the Smithsonian. The Library of Congress Manuscript Division has in its custody the majority of Dr. Gallaudet's personal papers.

The editors thank both the Gallaudet College Archives and the Library of Congress for their invaluable assistance. They also wish to express appreciation to the Laurent Clerc Cultural Fund whose financial assistance made this work possible.

PART ONE
Prologue
ca. 1847–1857

THE COLLEGE FOR THE DEAF at Washington has been so much a part of my life that in attempting to give the history of the one, I must, in a measure at least, tell the story of the other. So I shall hope, for this reason, to be excused for the autobiographical coloring the following narrative will often exhibit, which certainly has not been of my choosing.

The idea that I might someday be a teacher of the deaf was suggested to my mind for the first time by my father when I was about twelve years of age.

I was then attending the high school in Hartford and was at least two years in advance in my studies of most boys of my age. This was largely due to the fact that until I entered the high school, at eleven, I had been taught wholly at home under my father's immediate supervision. My eldest sister, Sophia, had been my teacher, but I recited to my father nearly every day and was stimulated to my diligent study by his interesting and inimitable ways as an instructor. My father never allowed me to be engaged with my lessons more than three hours a day, but during that period not a moment was wasted.

When I became a high school boy, my father began to talk with me as to my future career, and I remember as though it were yesterday the occasion when he suggested that perhaps I might like to take up the work which had engaged the energies of his early manhood. He spoke at some length of the joy he had in doing what he believed was his Master's work when he labored for the deaf [and] said he believed I would never be sorry if I carried out his suggestion.

I was much impressed by his words and his manner but replied I was sure I should be a business man and roll up a great fortune. My father

[3]

said he hoped I would go through college, but I assured him I had no ambition in that direction and was impatient to enter upon a business life as soon as I had completed my course in the high school.

He was amused at my earnestness and said laughingly, "Well, Eddy, perhaps you will be a business man, but never be a banker; his work is narrowing." I do not remember that my father ever spoke to me again of teaching the deaf. He was seized with a mortal illness just as I was completing my high school studies, and at his death in September 1851, I found myself compelled to provide for my own support and so was forced into the business life I desired.

Within a week of my father's death, I was offered a clerkship in a bank and, in spite of his warning, closed with the offer.

I had not been in the bank a year, however, before I felt the truth of his words, which I often called to mind. At fifteen my mind began to crave a pabulum of a higher order than the counting of bank bills and the reckoning of discounts. I began to lament sincerely that my father had not lived to send me to Yale College as was his purpose.

At sixteen, though my success in business was marked and I had bright prospects of rapid promotion, I had made up my mind to secure a college training and was studying with a view of entering Trinity College as soon as circumstances would permit.

At seventeen I entered the junior class of that institution with a definite purpose never to return to a business life. I was thankful, however, to have had the training I had secured from my three years in the bank, which proved the greatest help to me in the work on which I was to enter later.

During my first year in college, the principal of the school for deaf-mutes in Hartford, then the Reverend W. W. Turner, proposed that I should become an instructor in that school on leaving college.

Remembering my father's earnest words urging me to make the teaching of the deaf my life work, I regarded Mr. Turner's invitation as providential and accepted it.

A vacancy occurring in the corps of teachers, I began work in December 1855, six months before my graduation from college, keeping up my studies and reciting daily at 6 a.m. and 4 p.m.

I entered the profession of deaf-mute instruction with enthusiasm and with a strong ambition to do more for the interesting class of persons, of

2. *Edward Miner Gallaudet was 20 years old when he became superintendent of the Columbia Institution for the Deaf and Dumb in 1857.*

which my mother was one, than merely to teach them or to become the principal of a school.

It was therefore with alert interest that I soon learned from one of my fellow teachers, Mr. Jared A. Ayres, then the instructor of the high school in the Hartford school, that suggestions had been publicly made looking to the establishment of a college for the deaf. Mr. Ayres and I had many talks on this subject and agreed to organize the college as soon as a millionaire could be found to endow it.

During my first year's connection with the Hartford school, I was subjected on two occasions to very unjust treatment at the hands of the Board of Directors.

This made me unwilling to continue permanently in their employ, and in the spring of 1857 I found the definite purpose of preparing myself for the ministry. Not having money enough to meet the expense of my theological education, I accepted an offer from Mr. A. G. Hammond, formerly a Hartford banker, to take a position with him in a Chicago bank at a salary which enabled me to carry out my purpose within a few years.

I resigned my position as an instructor and was preparing to go to Chicago when I received the following letter.

Washington May 14th, 1857

Mr. Edward M. Gallaudet.

Dear Sir: Your name has been furnished me as one well qualified to take charge of and build up an Institution for the instruction of the Deaf and Dumb and the Blind in the District of Columbia, recently incorporated by an Act of Congress.

This Act allows out of the Public Treasury $150 per annum for every indigent pupil belonging to the District and permits the reception of pupils from all parts of the United States. A two acre lot of ground with a house of respectable size has been presented to the institution and the liberal disposition of our citizens as already evinced, leave no doubt that it will receive ample support. It may be safely estimated that this District will furnish twenty Deaf and Dumb pupils and ten Blind, and as the adjoining State of Maryland has no Institution, considerable accessions may be expected from that quarter. Indeed, no doubt is entertained that as soon as a suitable Superintendent and good permanent teachers can be secured, more pupils will be offered than we can at present accommodate and that the aid of Congress will be successfully invoked to furnish us with a suitable building.

Much, however, will depend on the ability and skill with which the Institution may be managed in the outset. Several persons have applied or been recommended for the position of Superintendent, but they are all strangers to me and the importance of the station admonishes against a hasty selection. When your name was first mentioned, your age appeared to constitute a serious objection, but it has been materially modified by information contained in a recent letter from Mr. I. L. Peet of the New York Institution. He mentions also that you have a mother who would probably accompany you and assist you by her counsel and efforts. With our limited accommodations, a considerable family who could render no service in the Institution, constitutes a serious objection to some of those who have been recommended; but we trust the time is not distant when our accommodations will be enlarged.

Thinking it probable that you may be inclined to take charge of this Institution at a moderate rate of compensation at first, relying upon the success of your own management to make it worthy of our Republic and secure an ample reward to yourself. I write this letter for the purpose of eliciting your views on the subject.

We have five mutes under temporary teachers and expect the number to be increased in a few days. This with other circumstances renders it very desirable that we shall as soon as practicable procure a Head for the Institution.

I expect to be at the Astor House in New York on the 20th inst. where please address me.

With great Respect
Your Obt Servt.
Amos Kendall
Prest. Columbia Institution
for the Deaf & Dumb & Blind

Hartford Ct.

I showed the letter to my friend Mr. Ayres and asked him if he did not think it would be possible to develop the proposed school for the deaf at Washington into a college under the patronage of the Federal Government. Mr. Ayres was enthusiastic over the idea and advised me to accept Mr. Kendall's offer, assuring me that it gave me a rare opening to do a most important work for the deaf of the whole country.

I replied to Mr. Kendall as follows:

Hartford, May 18th, 1857

Hon Amos Kendall
Prest of Columbia Inst
for Deaf & Dumb & Blind

Dear Sir: Your favor of the 14th Inst. was duly received, and the honor conferred upon me by the request that I would

3. *Amos Kendall, founder and first superintendent of the Columbia Institution.*

consider the subject of becoming the Superintendent of your Institution is fully appreciated.

Before I can come to any final decision in my own mind whether I shall be willing to undertake the duties of so arduous and important a post, I shall, of course, wish to know somewhat more in detail, than I do now, the conditions of the Institution at present, its plans and prospects for the future, and particularly what amount and kind of labor would be required of me and what salary could be afforded.

The work of enlightening the minds of Deaf-Mutes, begun by my deceased father in America, occupies a warm place in my heart, and when an enlarged field is opened to me for use-fulness, like the one you now propose, my inclinations lead me to embrace the opportunity offered and to labor zealously to the extent of my strength and ability.

If, therefore, the arrangements that are yet to be made known to me should meet my views, as I doubt not they may, both myself and my mother would think quite favorably of the position under consideration.

If a personal interview between us should be considered desirable, I should be very glad, sir, to see you at my home No. 97 Main St., at any time it would be convenient for you to visit me, or I would see you in New York if you should prefer it.

> Very respectfully,
> Your obt servt
> *E. M. Gallaudet*

After a few days I received the following reply to my letter:

> *Philadelphia, May 23d, 1857*

Mr. E. M. Gallaudet

Dear Sir: The state of my health and of the weather pre-vented my anticipated visit to New York and your letter of the 19th inst. has been forwarded to me here.

In reference to the condition of our institution and its plans and prospects for the future, I have little to add to my former letter. We have just organized under an Act of Congress mak-ing provisions for indigent pupils in the District of Columbia, but as to plans pertaining to the accommodation of the pupils and their instruction, we look for the counsel and assistance of the person whom we may employ as Superintendent. There are now five mutes under teachers employed temporarily and the number may be increased to about twenty as soon as we have a Superintendent and regular teachers. We contemplate the instruction of the Blind also of whom a class of about ten may be made up.

These estimates refer to materials in the District of Colum-bia alone; but no doubt is entertained that as soon as our Insti-tution has acquired reputation it will receive large accessions from the adjacent States.

At present, however, we confine our views to the District. The services wanted of you are as follows:

To advise as to the repairs, alterations and additions necessary to prepare the house now owned by us for the accommodation of the Institution.

To employ the necessary teachers, digest plans for instruction and superintend the teachers.

To provide suitable food and raiment for the children and employ servants and laborers, the means being furnished you.

In fine, to perform every executive duty indoors and out as well as to advise the Board of Directors in reference to the regulations necessary to be adopted and the proper measures to advance the interests of the Institution.

The Board have no doubt of a liberal support from their fellow citizens; but do not wish to appeal to them until they are prepared to say who is their Superintendent and that they are ready to receive pupils. To obviate any difficulty which may be apprehended from want of funds, I will guarantee the payment of your salary for the first year.

As to the amount of salary, we shall wish you to be entirely satisfied. I learn that the salary of the Pennsylvania Institution here is $1600. As our Institution is comparatively so much smaller and in its infancy, we suppose the salary should be considerably less, but if, under your management, it should expand so as to be of national importance, a commensurate increase of salary may be expected. It is desirable, however, that you should name the lowest amount of salary for the present which will be satisfactory to you.

Please write me at Washington on receipt of this; or, if you incline to go on at once, you and your mother will find a welcome at my house until arrangements can be consummated. We live over a mile from the Depot; but if informed of the time of arrival, will meet you there with conveyances for yourselves and baggage.

With great respect
Your Obt Servt
Amos Kendall

97 Main St, Hartford, Ct

And in response to this letter I wrote Mr. Kendall as follows:

Hartford 25th May 1857

Hon Amos Kendall

Dear Sir: Your favor of the 23rd inst. is received. Before it arrived I had written to you at Washington fearing, as I did not hear from you, that you were detained from coming to New York.

The contents of your letter are of such a nature as to leave very little doubt in my own mind that we can easily consummate satisfactory arrangements in regard to the Superintendency of the Columbia Institution.

I shall be happy, sir, to accept of your kind invitation to your house at Washington and have made my plans to leave here tomorrow and New York at six o'clock on Wednesday evening in the train that will be due at Washington at six o'clock Thursday morning.

My mother will not accompany me as she is just about making a visit to her children in New York. She will however be ready to cooperate with me in my labors as soon as the Institution is prepared to commence operations.

Very respectfully
Your obedient servant
E. M. Gallaudet

I visited Washington at once and had satisfactory interviews with Mr. Kendall. I unfolded to him my plans for a college and said that if he and his associates in the management of the proposed institution would support me in these plans, I would accept their offer. They met my overtures with alacrity, pleased with the idea of having what they had conceived of as no more than a small local school, grow ultimately into an institution of national importance and influence.

PART TWO

The Seed Is Planted

1857–1867

I

The School at Kendall Green
1857–1860

THE INSTITUTION WHICH I was now called upon to organize had come into a corporate existence under the patronage and guiding hand of Mr. Kendall, who gave the following account of its inception in a public address delivered on the occasion of the inauguration of the college of 1864:

Ladies and Gentlemen. About eight or nine years ago, a man appeared in this city having in charge a number of deaf and dumb children whom he exhibited to the citizens, asking contributions to aid him in establishing an institution for the instruction of that class of unfortunates in the District of Columbia, including also the blind. He excited much sympathy among our citizens, and succeeded in getting up a considerable school.* Professing a desire to make it permanent, he solicited a number of citizens to act as trustees, and a board was formed composed of Rev. Byron Sunderland, D.D., James C. McGuire, D. A. Hall, W. H. Edes, Judson Mitchell, and myself. But the board was barely organized when it discovered that the objects of the individual in question had not been understood, and that he was unfit to be intrusted with the management of such an institution. The question for the consideration of the board was, whether they should abandon the enterprise, or proceed under the discouraging circumstances then existing. The tender of a house and lot adjoining the city limits, previously made, was repeated, and, actuated by sympathy for these children of misfortune, the board resolved to proceed, relying for support upon the liberality of their fellow-citizens and Congress.

In the meantime rumors of the ill-treatment of the pupils in the deaf and dumb school by their teacher reached the public authorities, and at the instance of the district attorney, my name was used as their next friend

---

*This individual was Platt H. Skinner.

[15]

in a legal process to test the truth of these rumors. They were proved to be true by abundant testimony, and the court directed such of them as belonged to the District of Columbia to be restored to their parents. There were among them, however, five deaf-mutes who had been brought from the state of New York, having no parents, or none who seemed to care what became of them. These were bound to me as their guardian by the orphans' court, and formed the nucleus of our institution. And now I am most happy to present you with three of my wards, all well advanced in moral and intellectual culture, one of them the young lady whose beautiful composition on Florence Nightingale has been read in your hearing.

The following remarks of Mr. James C. McGuire, at a meeting of the board held after Mr. Kendall's death, throw additional light on the early history of the institution.

Mr. McGuire then gave an account of Mr. Kendall's connection with the Deaf and Dumb Institution, and said:

His [Kendall's] active mind and generous heart seemed to be always anxious for occupation in some enterprise for the good of his fellow-creatures.

It happened that circumstances associated me with him in connection with an incident that first excited his sympathy in behalf of that disabled class for which this institution was established. A despicable wretch, in wandering over the earth, had fortunately, as it turned out, made Washington his home, where he got possession of a building in the First Ward and fenced it in like a sort of prison, with a high board fence. He then hunted up all the deaf and dumb children in the community, got them in his possession, and took them to his building, pretending to call it a school for them. He would then take them about the city and exhibit them for money. A washerwoman from Georgetown, engaged in my household, informed some of my family that her son was a pupil of this man, and that in visiting him she said that the children in this so-called school were treated with cruelty, almost starved to death at all times, and thrown aside with neglect and brutal inhumanity when they were sick.

Happening to meet Mr. Kendall a day or two after hearing of the account given of this establishment, I stated to him what I had learned, and he at once, with his prompt and characteristic decision of purpose, said, "Let us go and see how this is." On this suggestion we went at once, and finding the gate at the entrance locked and barred, we broke it open and entered the building. The miserable sight cannot be described; it was heart-sickening. Two of the unfortunate children lay sick on a pallet, moaning most piteously. Unable to help themselves, it was evident from their horrid condition that their wants had not been attended to, probably for days. Mr. Kendall's generous nature was deeply moved. He called the man to account for the condition of the children, and the treatment they received at his hands. He promised reform. There seemed no remedy for the evil except through the man himself. But this remedy was not given, and his promise of reformation was not observed. But a philanthropist, who was in earnest to do good, had witnessed himself the suffering that cried for aid, and did not rest contented with an unperformed promise of amendment. Mr. Kendall went to work, and by the aid of the law and courts of the District, obtained possession of the children and took them to Kendall Green, and there himself became their guardian and their teacher, and that was the commencement and the foundation of this Institution for the Deaf and Dumb.

What he has done for it since, we all know. Originating in his kindness and philanthropy, he nurtured it by his charities until the day of his death, and still nurtures it by those charities since he is gone.

It has been said (continued Mr. McGuire), "Beware of the man of one book." In the proper sense of this saying, Mr. Kendall was a man of one book. When interested in any subject or enterprise, it engrossed all the faculties of his mind, and he concentrated upon it all the force and vigor of his thought. He grappled it with such intellectual vigor, and such intensity of feeling, that he could not separate himself from it. It went with him wherever he went, and spoke out in any conversation he had, however brief. When the opposition to the Bank of the United States was at its height, and Mr. Kendall believed that it was endeavoring to control the political affairs of the country, he became profoundly interested in arresting the peril which he believed threatened the nation from that institution. This subject then engrossed all his thoughts and feelings, and was with him everywhere and speaking in every conversation.

Talk of any subjects, however interesting, and as soon as courtesy would permit he would recur to the matter with which his mind was struggling.

So was it with him when that other great question of his day, the tariff, was exciting the country. He seized upon it; he took it to his mind and made it the food of his thoughts. And when, retired from public life, he entered upon the telegraph enterprise, he seized that as he had done the great political question.

I was (said Mr. McGuire) at a dinner party with several gentlemen, among whom was Mr. Kendall, at the time he was so much interested in

the telegraph. I offered a wager that before we separated he would introduce the subject of the magnetic telegraph. I had scarcely offered the
wager before he started the subject, much to the amusement of those who
heard the wager proposed.

And thus it was with him in the great enterprise of his philanthropy,
the Institution for the Deaf and Dumb. Deeply interested in ameliorating
the condition of this afflicted class of humanity, he was perpetually de-
vising means and contrivances to accomplish the design of his benevolence.

Mr. Kendall did not possess what is commonly understood, as a bright
and sparkling mind, nor had he a quick appreciation of passing events—
he was too much absorbed for that; but his mind was strong—it was
powerful. It seized hold of a subject with a vigorous and unrelaxing grasp,
and mastered whatever it seized. The rays of his thought were concentrated upon any subject to which they were directed, and by their intensity
penetrated it in every direction.

After a short stay in Hartford, I was again in Washington on the 13th
of June [1857], ready to organize the new institution.

Mr. Kendall's personality and the way he met me and treated me
impressed me greatly. At this time he was about seventy years of age with
hair and side whiskers perfectly white. He looked frail in body but had
brilliant vivacious blue eyes and an unusually fresh complexion. His manner to me was most courteous and cordial. I seemed to win his confidence
completely. He told me that not withstanding my youth the internal
management of the new institution would be entirely in my hands; that
he believed in the one man in power; and that if I was not capable of
managing the institution thus, I would have to give way to someone who
was. This did not frighten me for I was possessed of a fair amount of self-
confidence.

I had been told that Mr. Kendall would be a hard man to please, but
I did not find him so. My habit was to be frank and discreet and to be
"sure I was right" before I "went ahead."

Mr. Kendall's family received me very cordially and made me welcome
in their home until the institution was in readiness to be occupied.

I have a vivid remembrance of the outlook from Mr. Kendall's mansion
with the Capitol a mile and a third away. The morning of my arrival I
took a long gaze over this outlook and said to myself, "For how many
years will this be my house prospect?" I surely did *not* think it would be
forty.

The five deaf children referred to in Mr. Kendall's address already quoted had been for some weeks under the care of Mr. J. Orville Olds and Miss Alice Adams, occupying one of the dozen cottages which Mr. Kendall had built to be rented on the southern end of Kendall Green.*

My first work was to put in order for occupancy the house Mr. Kendall had presented to the institution together with one belonging to his son-in-law, Mr. William Stickney, which the directors had rented.

These two houses stood on adjoining lots of two acres each, fronting on Boundary Street (now Florida Avenue) opposite the northern end of Eighth Street East. Mr. Stickney's house contained about ten rooms, and the house donated by Mr. Kendall had nine. Both houses were of wood, loosely built, and far from comfortable in very cold weather.

My mother assumed her position as matron on the 13th of July, bringing with her from Hartford a very competent white woman named Sarah Grady, who had served in our family for many years as cook. Mrs. Maria M. Eddy, formerly of Worcester, Massachusetts, was appointed assistant matron and instructor of the blind and joined me on the 18th of June.

Mr. James Denison of Vermont, a young man of just my own age, was appointed instructor of the deaf. Mr. Denison became very deaf from the effects of scarlet fever at six years of age and his education was mostly conducted in the American School for Deaf-Mutes at Hartford, Connecticut. He had been teaching the deaf in the Michigan State School for about six months before coming to Washington. I had known him as one of the pupils in the Hartford School when I was a teacher there. He began his duties on the 1st of August.

Our little school at Kendall Green was opened during the last week in June with nine deaf-mutes and five blind pupils. These with my three assistants and three servants made a family of twenty-one persons for whose care I was responsible, and I will remember the patriarchal feelings with which I assumed the reins of government.

The presence of my dear mother and of good Mrs. Eddy, both women of sixty and each of unusual beauty, gave an air of dignity and distinction to the establishment, which were, for the time being, lacking in its very youthful male officials.

---

*The names of the children were John Quinn, Ann Szymanoskie, Isaac Winn, William Blood, and James Henry.

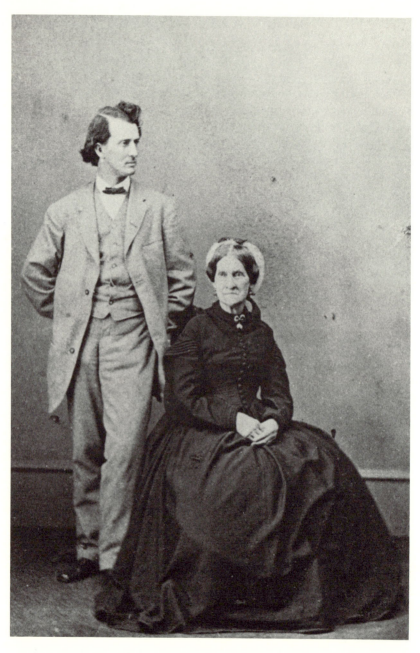

4. E. M. Gallaudet and his mother, Sophia Fowler Gallaudet.

Early in the year 1858 it seemed desirable to excite the interest of Congress and the public in the institution by giving an exhibition of the progress of its pupils. Accordingly, a request was made of the House of Representatives for the use of the old hall out of which it had just moved.

The exhibition was given on the evening of January 21st, and it is of interest to record the fact that since the hall was emptied of its furniture a few days later, our exhibition was the last public meeting held in this historic chamber. The *Washington Union* of the next day contained the following notice of the exhibition:

Interesting Exhibition
The noble old hall of the House of Representatives was lighted up last evening, and at an early hour every seat upon the floor was occupied and the galleries were crowded. It was the first public exhibition of the pupils of the Columbia Institution for the Instruction of the Deaf and Dumb and the Blind, who entered at the appointed hour neatly dressed and took seats around the Speaker's rostrum. Hon. Amos Kendall, President of the Institution took the Chair, and, by his invitation, the Honorable Jacob Thompson, Secretary of the Interior, took a seat at his side. Among the large audience there were many members of Congress, clergymen, and distinguished citizens, with several deaf-mutes, who kept their fingers busily occupied with their pantomime comments on the scene.

E. M. Gallaudet, Esq., the Principal of the Institution, delivered a brief, sensible, and eloquent address. He reviewed the gradual creation of institutions for the education of the deaf and dumb, and of the blind, in the various states, and then urged the claims of the institution here, which has been forwarded, and sustained, by individual liberality, and now asks the aid of Congress.

Vocal and instrumental music followed, after which the deaf-mutes gave representations of various passions, sentiments, etc., in obedience to the signs of their perceptor. A little fellow's personification of a snow storm was very comical, and a young girl's idea of an angel was extremely touching. Exercises on the blackboard followed, in which some of the pupils evinced great proficiency in their studies.

The blind children contributed plaintive yet expressive music, read from the books printed in relief for their use, and added to the interest of the occasion. The exhibition can but add to the deep sympathy already felt for the institution, of which we shall soon have more to say.

Mr. Harry C. Sherman, since distinguished as one of the prominent organists and musical leaders of Washington, assisted at this exhibition as a very young man by playing accompaniments for the blind children as they sang.

The provision made by Congress in the charter of the institution for the support and education of the indigent deaf and blind children of the District was found to be quite inadequate to meet this expense, and one of the objects of the exhibition was to induce Congress to increase its appropriation.

A petition for such an increase from the directors was favorably considered by the House Committee on the District of Columbia, and on February 3rd, 1858, Hon. Sidney Dean of Connecticut, then chairman of the committee presented the following report to the House:

The Committee for the District of Columbia, to whom was referred the petition of the directors of the Columbia Institution for the Instruction of the Deaf, Dumb, and Blind and also sundry citizens of the District of Columbia, asking aid from Congress to carry on the institution, have had the subject under consideration and by laws to report,

That the institution was incorporated by Congress at their last session, and the act of incorporation made provision for the payment out of the treasury $150 per annum for the maintenance and tuition of each deaf and dumb or blind pupil properly belonging to the District of Columbia, whose parents or guardians were pecuniarily unable to give them the advantages of such an institution.

The institution thus organized commenced first with five pupils, which number has since been increased to seventeen, and a further increase of the numbers to twenty five is anticipated within a year while the number of the class of unfortunate persons who will need the benefits of this institution will be fifty or more within a few years. Of the seventeen pupils now in the institution, fifteen were supported by the government and two by their parents. Two things are obvious to your Committee:

First, that such an enterprise could not be started without pecuniary grants from some sources, and those not meager or stinted. A few of the citizens of the District have contributed liberally for this purpose; but the burden has borne hard upon the few who have struggled nobly to give it a hopeful commencement. It is, however, embarrassed with a portion of the outlay absolutely essential to its first successful operation, which the subscription of the citizens was not sufficient to meet.

Second, the sum of one hundred and fifty dollars is not sufficient to feed and clothe a pupil, and even when the parents or guardians furnish the necessary clothing it leaves but a small surplus to meet the payment of salaries and other necessary expenses. To meet the deficiency but two sources are open to the directors. The one is by soliciting subscriptions from the benevolent. That source, always uncertain, has, however, during the late financial trouble, become wholly unavailable. The other alternative was to petition Congress for the necessary aid. This the petitioners have done. It is the opinion of your committee that it will be very difficult for the directors to carry on this institution, even in a crippled and inefficient condition, without some aid from the government. This object is one which commands the sympathy of the civilized world.

This is seen in the liberal endowments and assistance which have been granted similar institutions in Europe, and among the different states in our Union.

The Congress of the United States manifested their appreciation not long after the introduction of the system of mute instruction into this country, by a generous donation of lands to the American Institution at Hartford, Connecticut, and of which that institution has accumulated a fund of about $300,000. Grants of land have also been made by Congress to the deaf and dumb as well as the insane asylum of Kentucky, and the same body has also provided most liberally by the insane of this District. Many of the states have also made ample provision for the instruction of these unfortunate classes of their population by the construction of buildings and a per capita allowance for indigent pupils, besides making annual appropriations to pay salaries and meet contingencies.

The amount allowed last year for board, tuition, and clothing in the New York Institution for the Deaf and Dumb was $180 for each pupil, in addition to which the legislature makes a regular appropriation of $5,000 per annum. Pennsylvania, Maryland, Ohio, Virginia, Indiana, North Carolina, Michigan, Texas, and perhaps other states have institutions for the instruction of the deaf and dumb, or of the blind, or both, which have been established and are supported, in whole or in part, by appropriations from state treasuries.

The Committee can not recommend Congress to be less mindful of that unfortunate class of our fellow beings within this jurisdiction than are the legislatures of the several states enumerated. Your committee are informed that the average cost of supporting deaf, dumb, and blind pupils in the principal state institutions, including the salaries of superintendent, matrons, and teachers, and all contingencies does not vary much from $200 each. When the number of pupils is small, the cost of each must, of course, be greater for the expenses do not increase in the same proportion as the number of pupils increases.

The directors of the Columbia Institution ask an annual appropriation of $3,000 in addition to the per capita allowance now provided for, in order to pay up arrearages, and place the institution upon a sure footing;

and with this the directors pledge themselves to meet all its current expenses without calling upon Congress for further aid.

Your Committee are of the opinion that such an amount is reasonable, and should be granted. They, therefore, report a bill authorizing the payment of the amount requested, limiting it, however, to a term of five years. The Committee have also thought proper to introduce a section placing the deaf, dumb, and blind children of persons in the military and naval service of the United States on the same footing in relation to this institution as the deaf, dumb, and blind of the District of Columbia.

All of which is respectfully submitted.

The bill reported by Mr. Dean passed the House and Senate without opposition and was signed by President Buchanan on May 29th, 1858.

This act fully committed Congress to the support of the institution, relieving the minds of its friends of all anxiety as to the deaf and blind of the District.

The action of the directors in placing the institution under the charge of a very young and unmarried man had been criticized in some quarters.

Feeling solicitous to do all I could to better my position with the critics, I was married in July 1858 to Miss Jane Melissa Fessenden, of Hartford, Connecticut, whom I had known from my boyhood and brought her to Kendall Green before the opening of our second school year. The house in which the officers of the institution lived was handsomely, fully painted in honor of the coming of my young bride. Rooms for our use were tastefully papered and were most comfortably furnished by my wife's father, Mr. Edson Fessenden.

During the year 1858–59, the increasing number of pupils crowded our two small buildings, and efforts were made to secure aid from Congress for the erection of more suitable quarters. The condition of the Federal Treasury was, however, unfavorable to the success of the application, and Mr. Kendall, with a generous spirit worthy of all praise, offered to erect at his own expense a substantial brick building.

I took great pleasure in making the plans for this new house, putting them in such shape with my own hands as to render the services of an architect unnecessary. Mr. Kendall placed these plans in the hands of a builder, an old and valued friend of his, Mr. Charles F. Wood. After Mr.

Wood had reported that he would erect the building for $8,000, Mr. Kendall said to him in my presence, "You may go ahead," and that was the contract for the erection of the building.

The work was done in a most satisfactory manner by Mr. Wood, and his faithfulness is attested by the excellent condition in which the building may be found after thirty-five years of constant use.*

This building was connected by a corridor with the frame house originally donated by Mr. Kendall. Before the winter of 1859–60 set in, the institution gave up Mr. Stickney's house, which had been rented since the summer of 1857, and was comfortably accommodated in its own premises.

It may be interesting for me to mention, at this point, some of the surroundings of the institution. Twenty-five acres of Kendall Green nearest to Boundary Street were then (1859) cut up into a dozen two-acre lots, on each one of which was a frame house painted on its front side and whitewashed on the others. Around each lot was a rather high whitewashed picket fence, and a lane separated the six lots on Boundary Street from those north of them. There were a good many trees planted, mostly poplars, and these were protected by slotted tree-boxes, whitewashed like the fences. The aspect of the place was unspeakably ugly—more like a great stockyard than anything else I can think of.

Mr. Kendall told me that the cottages were built by contract, that the contractor swindled him badly, and that the whole arrangement was a great disappointment to him which can be easily believed.

Of course, back of this huddle of rough cottages and whitewashed fences, Mr. Kendall's mansion and surrounding ground presented a pleasing relief to the eye.

Between Kendall Green and the Government Printing Office hardly a house had been built in 1857. The square opposite the Printing Office on H Street was a great truck garden belonging to the owner of the Metropolitan (then Brown's) Hotel.

The only streets open for driving northeast were North Capitol and H. From the latter at Delaware Avenue, an ungraded and ungravelled road led along that avenue to M Street and out M Street to Kendall Green.

---

*The building was later attached to the Primary Department Building (old Fowler Hall) in 1866 but subsequently destroyed in 1916 to make way for the new Fowler Hall.

A few of the squares bordering on the roads were enclosed and cultivated, but most of the ground formed open commons, well grassed, on which cows, horses, goats, and geese grazed freely.

Though it was quite a drive in the country to Kendall Green, there were more than a few visitors. Mrs. Toucey, the wife of the Secretary of the Navy and an old Hartford friend of my mother's, was an occasional visitor as also was Mrs. Ledgard, the daughter of the Secretary of State, General Cass.

Gail Hamilton (Mary Abigail Dodge), also an old Hartford friend, was fond of walking to Kendall Green from Gamaliel Bailey's home on C Street, where she was governess, and more than once had as an escort Senator John P. Hale.

Mrs. Walter R. Johnson and her sister Miss Donaldson, at whose home Sumner and other anti-slavery men were frequent visitors, were great friends of Mrs. Eddy, our assistant matron, and in the pleasant spring and autumn weather would often call on their way to the woods beyond where they loved to gather flowers and leaves.

Many of the residents in Washington took an active interest in the young school, prominent among whom was Mrs. David W. Mahon who often called, bringing acceptable evidence of her kindly feelings towards the children.

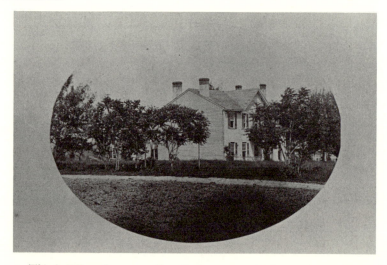

5. *This building, known as Rose Cottage, was the first residence of the Columbia Institution.*

6. *Building erected and presented by Hon. Amos Kendall to the Columbia Institute for the Deaf and Dumb, 1859.*

7. *Amos Kendall's mansion at Kendall Green, just north of the institution.*

II
"Our Plan for a College"
1860–1864

IN 1859 THE LEGISLATURE OF MARYLAND passed a law providing for the maintenance and tuition of deaf-mute children in the Columbia Institution, having no school within her own borders. This action was of importance to our enterprise in several ways, especially because it assisted in making a proper classification of our deaf pupils.

In securing this action I had some interesting experiences at Annapolis, among which I may record a providential meeting of Mr. Denison of Baltimore, who was an important member of the Appropriations Committee of the House, chairman I think, and who kept himself much out of the way for the purpose of avoiding those who had designs on the State Treasury. I had tried in vain to secure an interview with him for several days and was on the point of leaving my room at the hotel for another effort when I dropped on my knees and prayed that I might find him. I had not walked two squares when I met him. I introduced myself, stated my errand in Annapolis, and secured his cordial cooperation within ten minutes.

Early in 1860 I learned that a fund of about $5,000 was in the hands of an organization called Washington's Manual Labor School and Male Orphan Asylum, which had never gone into operation. My grandfather Peter Wallace Gallaudet, who died in Washington in 1843, had borne a prominent part in the founding of this association, which, since his death, had done nothing but take care of the small fund it had raised before he died. As there seemed little prospect of the school's organization, I suggested to its Board of Management that they ask the authority of Congress to dissolve their corporation and make over its funds and effects to the Columbia Institution, in which the income of the fund would be of material aid in teaching manual labor to the pupils.

[28]

My suggestions were acted on favorably. Congress passed such an act as was desired in June 1860, and our institution received a fund from which an income of some $300 a year has been derived and used to aid industrial education.

The years 1860 and 1861 brought stirring experiences to me and exciting times to the institution.

The coming on of the Civil War stirred me greatly. A distant prophecy of it came to me sometime in 1860 in a way worthy of record here. At that time Senator Albert G. Brown of Mississippi was chairman of the Senate Committee on the District of Columbia and on my invitation made a visit to the school. I remember calling for him at his lodgings in an open jump-seat wagon, the only conveyance belonging to the institution, driving Brent, the first horse I ever purchased, which I took as an eleven-year-old when he was twenty-one, but a good horse all the same.

Governor Brown wanted to bring with him a friend from Vicksburg, a Mr. Adams, editor of a paper in that city. The conversation of the men, as we drove to Kendall Green, soon disclosed the fact that Mr. Adams was strongly opposed to disunion while Mr. Brown was a pronounced secessionist. And the latter gave as a reason why disunion was sure to come that for years the youth of the South had been brought up to hate the North, while the youth of the North had been taught to despise the South. This conversation made a great impression on me, as also did certain private utterances of Mr. Seward, whom I knew well, and on whom I called occasionally.

At this period the attending physician of the institution was Dr. Alex Y.P. Garnett, a Virginian and a son-in-law of Governor Henry A. Wise. He had been also my family physician from the opening of the institution.

In October 1859 I had occasion to call him in to prescribe for me, I being at the time in quite a depressed condition of the nervous system, growing out of the pressure of my many cares and responsibilities and the callow state of my physique, I then being twenty-two.

When Dr. Garnett reached the institution and my room where I was suffering, without waiting to find out what ailed me, he broke out into an excited account of John Brown's raid at Harper's Ferry which had occurred the day before. I think he must have talked for thirty minutes before he asked my why I had sent for him. And he had something of a task to quiet me down.

When the war actually opened in 1861, Dr. Garnett remained in Washington for a time and talked very freely with me about the situation of affairs. One day making a professional visit he told me he had been looking over some of the New England, New York, and Pennsylvania regiments that just reached Washington. With an exclamation more emphatic than elegant he said, "If the North can raise an army of men like those I have seen today, the South will have a poor show to win."

Shortly after this, in great depression, Dr. Garnett left Washington, took up his residence in Richmond, and before long became the Surgeon-General of the Confederate Army. When he went away, he left his practice in the hands of Dr. N. S. Lincoln, declaring that he would resume it in a few months. It was ten years or more before he returned to Washington, and not until 1885, when Dr. Lincoln voluntarily gave up his position as attending physician to the institution, did Dr. Garnett resume his old place at Kendall Green.

In the summer of 1861 when my eldest child was born, a very interesting colored woman, Eliza Freeman by name, came to nurse my wife. Mrs. Freeman was born a slave in North Carolina and was understood to be the natural sister of Bishop-General Polk. She had purchased her freedom some years before and had lived much in the most cultivated families. While she was nursing my wife, she talked much of the war and of slavery. She maintained stoutly that the war would not be a short one, that there would be many lives sacrificed, and that the armed contest would continue until every slave in the land was free. This she said in July 1861.

During that first summer of the war, Kendall Green and its vicinity grew to be a military camp. Regiments were located all about us on the commons, and part of our building was occupied as a hospital for the several months of our vacation. More than three thousand men drew all the water they had from a well on our premises.

I may be permitted to record here that it was a severe trial to me not to volunteer for service in the army. My desire to do so was intense, and I could have had an important position in a Connecticut regiment for the asking. My best friends, however, believing that I had a mission to fulfill for the deaf and that if I left my place at the head of the school for the deaf and blind, the college for the deaf might not be started, advised me

8. Army camp near Kendall Green during the Civil War.

strongly to remain in the work to which I had devoted myself. I can say, with truth, that I did so with great reluctance. I wanted to fight for my country.

During the continuance of the war, a great wagon camp was established within five hundred yards of Kendall Green. To this [camp] the Potomac water was brought by a special pipe, and I succeeded in having a connection with this made, bringing the aqueduct water to our own buildings.

During the years 1860 and 1861, the increase in the number of our pupils was so considerable that the building erected by Mr. Kendall in 1859 became crowded. Congress was appealed to, and efficient aid in securing an appropriation of $9,000 to add to our buildings was rendered by my old Hartford friend, Senator James Dixon, who was on the District Committee. This appropriation, together with an increased amount for salaries, etc., was passed March 15th, 1862, and before autumn of that year an important addition to the house built by Mr. Kendall was made.

In my report for that year, I made the first public allusion to our plan for a college, urging upon Congress the propriety of its establishment at the Federal Capital.

By what seemed a special providence, Mr. Kendall, in drafting the Act of Incorporation, provided for the admission of deaf and blind children "of teachable age" as beneficiaries of the United States in the institution but set no limit of time or age at which they must be discharged, as is usual in the state schools for the deaf. So with our pupils from the District of Columbia we had the material for beginning a college, and we were authorized to keep them as beneficiaries of the government as long as we could teach them anything. Thus without intending to do so, Mr. Kendall had secured a very important provision of law for the starting, at least, of a college for the deaf.

It seemed clear to my mind that if action of Congress could be secured, authorizing the Columbia Institution to confer collegiate degrees, the way would be fully open for the development of a college within it.

So early in 1864 without consulting Mr. Kendall or the other directors, I drew up a bill, modelled after one giving power to confer degrees to Columbian College,* and placed it in the hands of Senator James W. Grimes of Iowa, then the chairman of the Committee on the District of Columbia.

I explained my plans for a college for the deaf to Mr. Grimes and secured his friendly interest in the scheme. Senator Grimes secured favorable action on the part of his committee without difficulty and reported the bill to the Senate.

On the 15th of March 1864, Mr. Grimes succeeded in having the bill taken up in the Senate when the following debate occurred:

Mr. HALE of New Hampshire. I wish the chairman of the Committee on the District of Columbia who reported that bill would explain the necessity for conferring this power on the Deaf and Dumb Asylum. It seems to me rather an extraordinary one. It is to confer degrees like other colleges, I believe.

Mr. GRIMES of Iowa. I do not know that there is any necessity for the passage of that bill at all. It is done at the instance of the trustees and superintendent of this institution in this District who desire that they should have permission to confer upon the deaf and dumb and the blind pupils who may graduate at their institution, and who are to go out into the world and become instructors of the deaf and dumb and the blind, a diploma. That, I believe, is the full scope of the bill and the object of the

---

*This is now George Washington University.

persons who desire its passage. It is to allow the trustees of this institution to confer a degree, whatever they may determine the title of it to be, that will indicate that they have passed through a course of thorough education at this institution.

Mr. HALE. As it is explained I have not the slightest objection to it in the world; but it struck me that the bill read a little broader than that. I would be obliged to the Secretary if he would read it again.

The Secretary read the bill as follows:

> Be it enacted, etc., that the Board of Directors of the Columbia Institution for the Instruction of the Deaf and Dumb and the Blind be, and they are hereby authorized to grant and confirm such degrees in the liberal arts and sciences to such pupils of the institution or others—

Mr. GRIMES. I move to strike out the words *or others*. I was not aware that those words were in the bill.

> The amendment was agreed to and the Secretary continued reading: who, by their proficiency and learning or other meritorious distinction, they shall think entitled to them, as are usually granted and conferred in colleges, and to grant to such graduates diplomas or certificates, sealed and signed in such manner as the Board of Directors may determine, to authenticate and perpetuate the memory of such graduation.

Mr. GRIMES. I am satisfied that I was in error in agreeing to strike out the words *or others*. I do not know why this institution or any educational institution designed for the use of the deaf and dumb should not have the privilege of conferring a degree upon an experienced educationist in the particular department, in New Hampshire or in Iowa or elsewhere, as well as upon the pupils of the institution in the District. I do not think any disadvantage can result from the passage of the bill. It is not intended to confer degrees upon anybody except those who are themselves deaf and dumb or who are the instructors of deaf and dumb people.

Mr. ANTHONY of Rhode Island. It ought to say so.

Mr. HALE. I think it ought to say so. The bill as it now stands would empower this institution for the education of deaf-mutes to confer degrees in the arts and sciences the same as Harvard University or Yale College. It seems to me that it should not be done, that it is lessening the thing altogether. They might have an appropriate diploma, indicating that they have passed through the regular order of education [prescribed] by such an institution. I think it would be very well and have no doubt it would be proper. I do not stand here as a particular advocate for degrees in the arts or sciences or for colleges, but the community have supposed that there was some character attached to such degrees, and if there is, it seems to me we should not confer this power on this institution, so that a degree from this deaf and dumb institution should have the same rank and standing as a degree from the highest and oldest colleges and universities in the land.

Mr. ANTHONY. If I understand the bill correctly, it would enable this institution to confer the degree of Doctor of Laws or Doctor of Divinity. I think that would make the thing more ridiculous than it is now, which is hardly necessary. If they were to confer some degree appropriate to the institution upon the deaf and dumb, it would be very proper. But I do not think it is necessary to pass this bill. I suppose they can confer a degree of Doctor of Laws if they choose without a legislative act. I suppose any institution or any voluntary body of men can do it. I think the bill had better be recommitted to the Committee on the District of Columbia to report on the nature of the degree they shall be authorized to confer; and if the chairman will agree to it, I will make that motion.

Mr. GRIMES. I am not very familiar with this business of degrees. I never was in possession of one myself, and I never believed that they conferred upon those gentlemen who were in possession of them any particular merit or distinction. I know that institutions in my country without any particular standing as scholastic institutions confer degrees; but the world judges the graduates by their success afterwards, and not by the fact that they happen to have a degree on parchment. I would not object myself to this institution having the power to confer any kind of degrees. I do not suppose anybody would be injured by conferring that power upon them, although that is not the design of the act; and I do not think there is any possibility or probability of degrees being conferred upon anybody else except upon the pupils of the institution or occasionally upon some person who is distinguished as an educationist of persons who are afflicted by the loss of their sight or articulation.

I do not think it is a very important matter, and I do not care whether it is recommitted or not. I never imagined that it was of any particular advantage to the institution that the bill should be passed. When it was brought to me by the gentlemen who have charge of this institution, I saw no objection to it. There was not a member of the committee to whom it was referred who had any objection to it; and I have failed thus far to hear any substantial objection, except that possibly they may confer degrees like Harvard or Yale colleges. Suppose they do. What harm is going to be done to anybody? Is anybody going to employ a deaf-mute or a man who has not the power of utterance and give him any greater confidence because he has a diploma from this deaf and dumb asylum than they would if he had not one? Would not a man's credentials, if his character be good, be worth just as much without a diploma from this deaf and dumb asylum as with it? I beg pardon of the Senate for occupying its time on such a subject.

Mr. ANTHONY. I move that the bill be recommitted. I think the object of this bill is a very good one indeed, but I do not think the object is expressed in the bill itself. I think it will rather make the institution ridiculous to give it the power to confer literary or scientific degrees, whereas I think it would be very proper to confer some degree that may be framed and invented for the deaf and dumb, and the blind.

The VICE PRESIDENT. The Senator from Rhode Island moves to recommit the bill to the Committee on the District of Columbia.

The motion was not agreed to.

Mr. HALE. There is no provision that the degrees they shall confer shall be on the deaf and dumb and the blind. I move to insert these words before the word *pupils*.

Mr. CLARK. I desire to inquire of my colleague and of the other Senators who oppose this bill if their opposition is not a little captious. Pray, sir, what is the objection to this seminary having the power to confer a degree as a matter of compliment on somebody who was not educated there if they choose to do it and the man chooses to take it? Take the case of a man who happens to be an educator of the deaf and dumb, not deaf or dumb himself, but a man who could talk and who could listen, and this institution, for the purpose of complimenting him for his skill and faithfulness in educating the deaf and dumb or for some other purpose, chooses to confer a degree upon him and he is willing to receive it—pray what is the objection. I do not think there is any danger of making the whole thing ridiculous, as suggested by the Senator from Rhode Island. I think we may as well trust this matter in the hands of these people who educate the deaf and dumb as anybody else. I do not believe that they will abuse it. I can hardly conceive how it can be abused. I think we had better allow this institution and the gentlemen who are engaged in this good work to issue these degrees, and if anybody chooses to receive them, and receive them as a compliment, let him have them.

The bill was reported to the Senate as amended.

The VICE PRESIDENT. The question is on concurring in the amendment made as in the Committee of the Whole to strike out the words *or others*.

Mr. GRIMES. I withdrew that amendment afterwards.

The VICE PRESIDENT. It was put to the Senate and agreed to but can be disagreed now.

The amendment was non-concurred in.

The bill was ordered to be engrossed for a third reading, was read the third time, and passed. The bill soon after passed the House without discussion, and on the 8th of April it became a law by the approval of President Lincoln.

Writing these lines on the 7th of April 1896—thirty-two years ago, lacking a single day, from the date of the approval of the act—and reflecting on the part I took in securing the passage of this law, I can regard my course in asking it as nothing else than an illustration of *monumental cheek*. Pardon the slang—for polite language is inadequate.

I was a youngster of twenty-seven, at the head of a little school of deaf and blind children in which no word of Latin, Greek, or any language but English had ever been taught. Arithmetic had not been completed. No higher mathematics had been touched, no science taught.

But the *purpose* to establish and develop a college for the deaf was within my breast, and I felt that the best way of securing the support of Congress and the public for such an institution was to secure full collegiate *powers* at the outset. And so I went ahead with the enthusiasm and fearlessness of youth.

When Mr. Kendall learned of the passage of the bill authorizing us to confer degrees, he was pleased but remarked he hoped I was not going too fast. My reply was, "You must remember, Mr. Kendall, I am here to get upstream and move forward; if you think my rate of speed too high, you must put on the brakes for that is the province of the directors." He laughed and said he believed he could trust me. And it was not long before he proved his confidence in me by a proposal which surprised me beyond measure.

It was soon decided by the directors to inaugurate a collegiate department with suitable public exercises,* and Mr. Kendall informed me that he wished to have me inaugurated on this occasion as president of the institution in all its departments, including the corporation and the Board of Directors.

I remonstrated and said I should be satisfied to be made president of the college and would prefer to have him president of the corporation and board. But he insisted that in view of the important work about to be

---

*[Footnote by E.M.G.] These exercises took place on the 28th of June 1864, and a full account of them is printed in the Seventh Annual Report of the Institution. [See Appendix A.]

9. E. M. Gallaudet in 1864.

taken up by the institution, it would be better that the man whom the world would look to as the head of the institution should be clothed with all possible dignity.

Mr. Kendall was so positive in this that I was compelled to yield, and measures were taken to so change the constitution of the institution as to make the president of the corporation ex officio principal of the institution. At the same time the number of directors was increased from five to six, so that Mr. Kendall could remain in the Board of Directors without displacing any of his old friends. These changes were made, and I was duly elected president of the corporation at a meeting held on the 22nd of June 1864.

It seemed really unfitting to me that I, then only twenty-seven, should be made the presiding officer of a body in which I was by several years the youngest member and in which these were men fifty years my senior. But I accepted the situation and tried to discharge my duties in the board with modesty.

As I look over the years that have passed and remember that before I was thirty I had to "call to order" grave senators, and even the Chief Justice of the United States, I wonder that they did not rebel against their youthful presiding officer. And, indeed, Chief Justice Chase did on one occasion break out on me in a way that was embarrassing.

We were considering the purchase of a piece of ground for which we had not the money to pay in full. I suggested that we might take a deed, pay what we had, and give a mortgage in the land purchased to secure the balance due. And I urged that the corporate rights conferred on the institution by Congress made such a transaction possible. The Chief Justice contended that the institution had no power to mortgage its property. When I expressed surprise at this and asked if the possession of full corporate powers did not give the right to mortgage the property of the corporation, the Chief Justice broke out on me saying, "I do not know anything about law at all, I suppose."

Naturally this ended the discussion, but within three years from that time when the institution purchased eighty acres and more of the heirs of Mr. Kendall, I signed, by order of the board, a mortgage to secure notes to Mr. Kendall's heirs amounting to $80,000.

And I may as well record the fact here, that not very long after the meeting at which Chief Justice Chase expressed his views as to the power of the institution to execute a mortgage, he resigned his position as director, informing Dr. Sunderland that it was not agreeable to him to continue a member of a body of which he was not the head.

On the 9th of November 1864, an event of great personal interest to me occurred, viz., the birth of a son. Two little daughters had already made us glad—Katherine, born June 25th, 1861, and Grace, born December 27th, 1862. It was especially pleasing to me that a son should arrive within a few weeks of the opening of the college. My own name was given him with the family name of a very intimate friend, LeBaron.

The first months of the college brought serious embarrassments and anxieties. We were fortunate in securing as our first professor, Mr. Richard S. Storrs, whose high scholarship and several years experience as a teacher in the Hartford School for the Deaf made him most valuable.

In full accord he and I matured plans for suitable courses of study for the college and the years leading up to it. But Mr. Kendall, to my great astonishment, met these plans with a most pronounced opposition. He offered a scheme of regulations to the board, the adoption of which would have made the college the laughingstock of all educated men. These regulations he allowed to lie over, and I was at my wits end to secure their defeat, for the board was dominated by Mr. Kendall, with the exception of Dr. Sunderland who was not afraid to oppose him. I tried at first to convince Mr. Kendall of the superiority of my plans. But he grew only the more set in his way. He wrote me a long letter, which must be somewhere among my papers but which I have not been able to find, in which he likened me to a pettish child with a new doll, saying that no sooner had I secured the coveted prize, than I was preparing to pull it to pieces.

Professor Storrs, with whom I took counsel in this emergency, said he saw but one thing for us both to do and that was to resign and give up the college. I assured him I had not come to Washington for any such thing and at once began to pray and work for a deliverance.

By a strange providence just at this time, two of our directors died. Neither of them was a highly educated man, and both were special friends of Mr. Kendall. I was prompt in suggesting men to succeed them and was fortunate in hitting Mr. Kendall's fancy. Hon. Benjamin B. French, then Commissioner of Public Buildings and Grounds, and Hon. Solomon P. Chase, Chief Justice of the United States, were the men I proposed, and they were elected without delay. I at once confided to them both my difficulty with Mr. Kendall and received assurances of their approval.

But I took another important step. I submitted my plan of organization to Professor Joseph Henry, then secretary of the Smithsonian Institution, than whom no higher authority among educated men could be found. I told Professor Henry of the attitude Mr. Kendall had taken and requested him to give me his views in writing.

Within a few days I received the following from him, which I held in readiness to present to our board whenever Mr. Kendall should ask for action on his proposed regulations:

Mr. Gallaudet having submitted to me, for examination, his proposed plan for an extended course of study to be adopted by the Columbia Institution for the Deaf and Dumb, and after having given it due attention, I beg leave, at his request, to offer in regard to it the following remarks.

The general plan proposed embraces three courses: the first, including the studies of the first seven years; the second, those of the two next years; and the third, those of the following, and if successful the latter may be extended to four years. The studies of these several courses are so arranged as to form together a graduated system from the first elements of instruction, through the intermediate branches, to the subjects of a full collegiate course. These three courses or departments as here proposed, appear to me necessary in furnishing a properly graduated and a sufficiently extended course to meet the present demands of the Deaf and Dumb. It has been abundantly proved by experience that as a class they have excellent mental capacities and [they] are susceptible of high mental and moral development.

It will most probably be found in practice that the larger portion of the pupils will stop at the end of the second course if not at that of the first; but this should not discourage the establishment of the third course. For if but one-tenth of the pupils should be able to enjoy the advantages of the higher course, the influence of these on the deaf and dumb, as a class, and on the public generally in their behalf, would be highly beneficial.

The third or collegiate department should be in reality what its name imports, that is, it should be able to afford the pupils all the facilities required for as full mental culture as their capacity will enable them to acquire. But in order to do this, the student should be well prepared to enter upon its studies and hence the necessity of the intermediate, or academic course, in which they may receive the preliminary instruction.

If this plan of a college course cannot be fully carried out, I would advise that it be not attempted and that the name be not adopted; since a government institution, to which the eyes of the whole country are turned, should not set the example of holding out expectations which cannot be realized. The Columbia Institution should be a model for the imitation of all similar establishments, and not only do good service by the effect it produces on its own pupils, but also on the deaf and dumb generally, in elevating the standard and improving the methods of their education.

Not only have the general features of the proposed plan been well considered, but also all the details. The several steps of the course have been judiciously arranged, and the studies well selected to insure the desired effect. I hope the plan will be adopted in full and that proper exertions will be made to obtain the means of carrying it into operation. I am sure it would be productive of good in greatly increasing the means of enjoyment and much extending the sphere of usefulness of a class of persons who call forth, in their deprivation, our warmest sympathies and claim, in their behalf, our most strenuous efforts.

In conclusion it may be important for me to state that the Smithsonian Institution affords unusual facilities for the study of different branches of science, and that as the director of this establishment I am authorized to say in behalf of the Board of Regents that these facilities will always be free to the pupils of the Columbia Institution.

Joseph Henry
Smithsonian Institution,
Nov. 16th, 1864.

Extract from proposed report, giving President Gallaudet's plan of organizing the college:

We desire especially that students who may be thinking of a collegiate course of study should clearly understand the amount of time and labor that is involved in it; and a little consideration of the subject cannot fail to show them there is no magic in the word *college* which can confer added worth or dignity upon a merely academic course of study pursued under that imposing name; and that the coveted diploma will be significant and valuable only as it certifies to a laborious course of advanced study. Nor can they fail also to see that such a course cannot immediately succeed the primary course, i.e., the ordinary course of deaf-mute institutions, which corresponds very nearly to a common school education.

The student cannot expect to step at once from the common school into the college. It must be admitted that an intermediate course of academic study is properly made the indispensable introduction for deaf-mutes, as well as for others, to a worthy collegiate course. But just here we seem to encounter a difficulty. The majority of deaf-mutes in our country have hitherto had no favorable opportunity for engaging in this academic course. The high classes of our two oldest institutions alone offer facilities for it, and these facilities are usually sought only by their own graduates. How then shall the college course be made practicable for the many graduates from the primary departments of other institutions? It can evidently only be by an academic department in connection with its collegiate department, which shall offer to all, facilities for the essential preliminary training. This the Columbia Institution has decided to establish in connection with its collegiate department for the benefit of any who may not have had opportunity for accomplishing the preparatory work elsewhere, requiring that all candidates for admission to the collegiate department shall sustain an examination in the studies of the academic course whether pursued in its own or in other institutions.

The academic course of the Columbia Institution occupies the two years immediately succeeding its primary course, and presupposes a thorough acquaintance with its studies.

The studies pursued are as follows:

ACADEMIC DEPARTMENT

First Year:	Second Year:
Analytical Grammar	Analytical Grammar
Higher Arithmetic	Algebra
Physical Geography	Natural Philosophy
History	History
Latin	Latin

It is believed that students who have completed this course of study will be prepared to pursue with advantage the studies of the collegiate department which will, for the present, occupy two additional years termed respectively the junior and senior years of the collegiate department, and the satisfactory completion of which will entitle its graduates to degrees in science. The studies pursued will be as follows:

COLLEGIATE DEPARTMENT

Junior Year:	Senior Year:
Geometry	History of English Language and
Latin	Literature
Rhetoric	Latin
Chemistry	Astronomy
Mental Science	Geology
	Political Science
	Moral Science

Facilities will also be afforded for the pursuit of art and the modern languages as optional studies in addition to those of the regular course and, in exceptional cases, in partial substitution thereof.

It will be seen, by comparing the two courses, that the critical and scientific study of the English language—under the various forms of sentence structure, style, analysis, and historical inquiry—forms an important part of both; that some one of the various branches of physical science is also constantly receiving attention; that Latin, as affording important assistance in the study of the English grammar and etymology, is pursued during each year; and that the invaluable discipline of mathematics is sought at every stage. In addition to these constant studies, as much attention will be given to moral and political science and related studies as the present abridged collegiate course will allow, which will be sufficient, it is hoped, to acquaint the student with the leading principles of each.

The expanded course embracing two additional years, which will be added as soon as called for, will afford opportunity for a more extended pursuit of these and other studies and will entitle the advanced graduate to a degree in art. Moreover, any students who, having completed the present collegiate course of two years, may desire to extend their studies over the additional two years before any formal expansion has been deemed expedient can do so as resident graduates and become equally entitled, upon passing a satisfactory examination on the entire course, to the highest degree.

To my great surprise when the board next met, Mr. Kendall did not call up his regulations, and he never again alluded to them to me in any way.

In the meantime, being clothed with power by the board, in a vote passed two or three years before, to arrange the course of study in the institution, I signed an official paper which I showed to Professor Storrs and then locked up in a drawer, in which the course we had agreed on was prescribed in detail.

I never made this document public but simply carried our work forward from year to year, and it was not until 1869, five years after the college was opened, that we had a class ready to graduate. Mr. Kendall's scheme would have graduated this class in 1867 with the bachelor's degree in the arts when it had only completed the equivalent of the sophomore year.

From time to time Mr. Kendall accepted my reports of the progress of the college, never raising a question as to the course of study. In my last interview with him in November 1869, a short time before his death,

I was strongly impelled to ask him how he came to change his mind on this important matter, but on this occasion he took such pains to assure me of his complete confidence that I would manage the institution wisely, I felt it to be best not to raise anything that might prove unpleasant to my dying friend.

With the single exception of this difference of view, all my intercourse with Mr. Kendall, covering a period of upwards of twelve years, was of the most harmonious sort. I cherish a deeply tender memory of Mr. Kendall as a truly great and noble-hearted man. The vigor of his mind was remarkable for any period of his life—doubly so for a man who, when I first knew him, had already reached the limit of three score and ten years. An illustration of this will be given later on.

Before dropping this subject, it seems only right that I should insert Mr. Kendall's remarks before the board in opposition to my plan for the course of study to be pursued in the college.

It is true, as he says, that I had spoken in the spring of 1864 of the organization and admission of a freshman class in September following. But Mr. Kendall ignores the fact which I had communicated to the board, that since making the announcement on which he lays so much stress, it had become plainly evident that the material for the organization of a true freshman class was not to be available and that it would be impossible for us to fulfill our promise in regard to such as class. Consequently, the inconsistency with which he so earnestly charged me was not real. I had been forced by the development of events I could not control to revise the plans I had formed and published earlier.

It will be interesting to note, as showing the interest Mr. Kendall took in the institution, to say that the remarks which follow were fully written out in his own hand, and that owing to shaking palsy, from which he had suffered for several years, he wrote with a great difficulty, always steadying his right hand with his left.

RESOLUTIONS AND REGULATIONS OFFERED BY MR. KENDALL:

Resolved, That the president be required to hand to the secretary a list of the books embracing the course of studies for the freshman class of our college department as prescribed by the committee to whom that duty was assigned by a resolution of the board adopted on the 7th day of June last, and the secretary is hereby directed to copy the said list into the records of this institution.

Resolved, That the president be requested to prepare and report for the consideration of the board, at their next regular monthly meeting a course of studies for the sophomore, junior, and senior years of our collegiate department, specifying in general terms, the time proposed to be devoted to each branch of study during each of the four years of the college course.

PROPOSED REGULATIONS:

1. The Annual Report of the Board of Directors to the Secretary of the Interior shall contain no proposition or statement touching on any change in the organization of the institution, the terms of admission, its discipline, general management and course of studies therein, or asking or suggesting any recommendation or action of that Department or of Congress, which shall not, prior to the adoption of said report, have been submitted in due form to the Board of Directors and approved by them and their approval duly recorded.

2. It shall be the duty of the president to prepare and submit to the Board of Directors at their regular monthly meeting in the month of September of each year a project of their Annual Report to be disclosed of by them as they may think proper.

3. All deaf-mutes, who have passed through the ordinary seven years course of study in any of the institutions for instruction of the deaf and dumb in the United States and shall be found on examination by the president and professors, to be satisfactorily proficient in the studies they have pursued therein, shall be entitled to enter the freshman class of our collegiate department, and it shall be competent for the president to admit into the higher classes such deaf-mutes as, upon like examination, shall be found qualified to enter any of said classes.

MR. KENDALL'S REMARKS IN THE BOARD MEETING:

The first objection I have to the project now presented by our president is that it is misplaced and untimely.

The proper place for alterations of our regulations or additions thereto is on the records of the institution by resolutions adopted by a regular vote of the stockholders or Board of Directors. The paper now before us purports to be a report of the Board of Directors to the Secretary of the Interior, giving a history of the institution for the last year, and setting forth, so far as deemed expedient, its purposes and wants. But the particular passage under consideration purports to inform the Secretary that the board has done what it has not done and may never do. It will not be pretended that the mere statement in a report not based on any proceeding on record can give it the force of lawful regulation. In the two meetings which have been held to consider it, only three directors were present. Suppose two of them had adopted it, and when, at a subsequent full meeting of the board, it should be brought up for regular action, the six other members should vote against it, which would constitute the law of the institution, the will of the two or the will of the six? The only legitimate mode by which the president could have effected his object was to introduce his project into the board in the shape of resolutions, and when they were adopted, it would have been legitimate to inform the Secretary what had been done.

This project is as much out of time as out of place. It was never heard of or, it is believed, suggested to any member of the board until the time arrived at which their report ought to be made to the Secretary of the Interior, and then it was prepared for adoption at two successive meetings by a board of three members. Had it been presented in regular form, there was not time, before the report ought to go to the Interior Department, to get a full board and give the subject due consideration. Not only is this project out of place and out of time, but were it now brought before us in regular form, present action upon it is expressly prohibited by our organic law. It must be considered as an alteration of or addition to our by-laws or regulations, and the 14th article of our constitution reads as follows, viz.: No alterations of the by-laws and regulations, or additions thereto, by the Board of Directors, shall be valid unless proposed in writing at a regular monthly meeting preceeding that at which they shall be adopted.

Our constitution, having been adopted in our Act of Incorporation, all its provisions became operative until altered in the way prescribed therein, as binding upon us as if directly and in terms enacted by Congress. It is a wise provision, intended to prevent hasty and ill-considered changes like that now proposed. If we have, in some instances, not thought of it in our legislation, it is no reason why we should violate it when we think of it.

I might stop here, for I am sure the board will not report to the Secretary of the Interior that they have done that which, in fact, they have not done, nor violate a plain law with their eyes open. Nevertheless this may be as suitable a time as any hereafter to examine the merits of the project. In the discussions upon this subject our president has insisted that although we have *inaugurated* a college, we have not *organized* it and the whole question of organization is now open. On this point I take issue with him and appeal to the record.

There are many things in nature and art composed of various parts which are sufficiently described by their names. When a horse is mentioned, nobody thinks it necessary to state that he is an animal having four legs. So of other animals, of chairs, and other utensils whose several parts are essential to the perfection of a being or a thing. Of the same character is the word *college*. When used without some qualifying word, it means an institution where general literature and science are taught in four classes, freshman, sophomore, junior and senior, just as certainly as the word *horse* means an animal with four legs. Whenever the meaning is otherwise, it is designated by the use of an additional word, such as medical college, law college, commercial college, etc. So far as I know, there is not a college for general instruction in the United States which has not its four-year course of study in four distinct classes. It is very true that some institutions have departments in which subjects are taught which were not embraced in the regular college courses of studies and diplomas granted, differing from the general diploma. Thus Dartmouth College accepted a donation of fifty thousand dollars on condition that they should teach engineering to others than their regular students in a term (if I rightly remember) of two years. Of like character are the law and medical departments of our colleges. They do not constitute parts of the college proper but are mere appendages which may be lopped off without marring the symmetry of the structure. The institution for teaching general literature and science in courses of four years duration, constituting a college in the established sense of the term, would still remain intact.

I shall now show from the record that we have first organized, then inaugurated, and have now in operation such a college and that no other idea has been entertained by us, by the public, or by our president until very recently.

At a meeting of the Board of Directors on the 7th of May 1864, the superintendent, after presenting the act of Congress authorizing us to confer degrees, informed the board that the progress already made by the most advanced pupils now in the institution called for the establishment, at the beginning of our next academic year, of the collegiate department, proposed in the Fifth Annual Report.

Whenupon, on motion of Dr. Sunderland, it was *Resolved*, That a committee of three be appointed, to consider what measures are necessary to the establishment of a collegiate department under the provisions of the act of Congress just read, and to recommend to the board such actions as may be deemed desirable to perfect the organization of the institution in its enlarged sphere of usefulness. On motion of Mr. Edes it was *voted* that the committee consist of Mr. Kendall, Dr. Sunderland, and Mr. Gallaudet, the superintendent.

On motion of Dr. Sunderland it was *Resolved*, That the closing exercises of the present academic year shall be held in some convenient audience room in the city of Washington, and that they shall be of a nature suited to the inauguration of the collegiate department about to be organized in this institution. It was also, *Resolved*, That the superintendent be and he is hereby authorized to make such arrangements as may be necessary to carry into effect the forgoing resolution. On motion of Mr. Edes, it was *Resolved*, That the superintendent be and he is hereby authorized to prepare or cause to be prepared suitable forms for such diplomas and certificates as may be necessary in the conferring of degrees, or the honorable dismissal of pupils leaving the academic department of the institution.

It will be perceived that the superintendent then thought some of our pupils were sufficiently advanced to enter the collegiate department; though he now thinks they were not fitted and ought to spend two years more study in a preparatory department.

At a meeting of the board on the 24th of May, Mr. Gallaudet, in pursuance of instructions, reported the form of a diploma and also the form of a seal for the college, which were adopted.

In pursuance of the first resolution adopted on the 7th, Dr. Sunderland from the committee, reported the following resolutions which were adopted, viz.:

Resolved, That the superintendent be and he is hereby authorized to employ additional instructors of the deaf and dumb at a salary not exceeding eighteen hundred dollars per annum.

The superintendent is authorized to increase the salary of the third instructor of the deaf and dumb from five hundred to six hundred dollars per annum; and to employ when occasion requires an additional instructor of the deaf and dumb at a salary not exceeding three hundred and fifty dollars per annum with board.

Resolved, That all instructors employed in the collegiate department shall be learned professors.

Resolved, That the honorary degree of master of arts be conferred upon John Carlin of New York City at the close of the present academic year.

At the meeting of the board on the 7th of June, the following resolution was adopted: *Resolved*, That a committee of two members of the board be appointed to confer with the superintendent and fix upon a course of studies to be pursued in the collegiate department of this institution.

This committee met and adopted a course of study for the freshman year; but not being sufficiently advised to fix on the course for the higher classes, and there being no immediate necessity for action, the subject was postponed. No report has been made, and none was required by the resolution; but the action taken was left in the possession of the superintendent, now president, who has doubtless been governed by it.

Now, if our college was not *organized* by these official and recorded acts, I do not understand the proper meaning of the term.

It had a president and directors.

It had an official head.

It had the form of a diploma.

Provisions were made for all needful professors.

It had a course of studies for the freshman year and a committee authorized to prescribe courses for the three other years.

Having thus organized our college, we proceeded on the 28th day of June last to inaugurate it and announce that it was ready to receive pupils. I venture to say that no man who took part in the ceremonies of that day and no person who witnessed them had any other idea than that we were inaugurating a college of the ordinary form with four classes and a course of study running through four years. That our president so understood it, is not left to inference.

At a meeting of the Board of Directors held on the 14th of July last, the president was authorized "to publish in pamphlet form 500 copies of the proceedings of the inauguration of the collegiate department." In pursuance of this authority, he did publish those proceedings prefaced by an address "to the public" prepared by himself. This address contains the following passages:

To The Public

The officers of the Columbia Institution for the Instruction of the Deaf and Dumb and the Blind have had in mind, from the foundation of the institution, the organization of a school where deaf and dumb persons, or those whose hearing is so deficient as to render their education impossible in ordinary institutions of learning, may have an opportunity of securing that high degree of mental culture and those academic honors, afforded hitherto only by colleges and universities designed for the benefit of those who hear and speak.

This purpose, which it is believed will meet the approbation of the philanthropic and patriotic everywhere throughout the land, is about being realized.

Congress heretofore liberal in its action has, during the session just closed, conferred full collegiate powers on the institution, and in view of the enlarged sphere of usefulness upon which it is now entering, has made provision for the salaries of the needed professors, and has granted about thirty thousand dollars to "continue the work for the accommodation of the students and inmates in the institution."

On the 28th of June last, on the occasion of the first graduation of a class in the academic department, the college was publicly inaugurated; and Edward M. Gallaudet, A.M., who had been superintendent of the institution from the date of its opening, was installed as president.

The addresses delivered on that occasion are published herewith.

In the College for the Deaf and Dumb it is proposed to pursue a course of study adapted to the peculiar wants of persons bereft of hearing. The branches taught will be sufficiently advanced to warrant the conferring of degrees in science at the close of the course, which will continue through four years. Degrees of higher grades will be conferred as soon as the attainments of our students call for their bestowal.

The first freshman class will commence its studies on the 8th day of September next, under the tuition of Professor Richard S. Storrs, A.M., for ten years an instructor in the American Asylum for the Deaf and Dumb at Hartford, Connecticut.

For detailed information, as to terms of admission, inquiry should be made of the president of the institution.

Washington, D.C.

July, 1864

Here it is announced, that the course of study would "*continue through four years*" and that "*the first freshman class will commence its studies on the 8th day of September next*" (last) and this annunciation, it is presumed, has been sent to many, if not all, the deaf and dumb institutions of the country.

In accordance with that annunciation, a freshman class did commence its studies under Professor Storrs, and several persons from the northern high schools have entered the junior class.

After all this, after we have organized a college and announced that it was ready to receive pupils, after it has received them and been in operation about two months, with what plausibility can it be said that the whole question of organization is now open? But if it were an open question, which it is not, I should be decidedly opposed to the proposed project for the following reasons, viz.:

First, it would expose our president and this board to just charges of ignorance, fickleness and incompetency. It would be an admission that the declaration of our superintendent to the board on the 7th of May last, that "the progress already made by the most advanced pupils, now in the institution, called for the establishment at the beginning of the next academic year of the collegiate department"—a declaration which gave immediate rise to proceedings for that purpose—was not only unfounded, but that it actually required two years more study to fit them for entry into a department deserving the name of college!

It would imply that the board, having acted upon the inaccurate representation of their superintendent, established the collegiate department, had barely put it in operation, when, upon sudden representation of the president that they had acted on incorrect information derived from himself, they hastened to undo what they had done and falsify their annunciations to the public. For one I am not willing to admit that our superintendent was in error in his representations of the 7th of May last or that the board have done anything ignorantly or inadvisedly which now ought to be altered or rescinded.

Secondly, no possible good, but much probable mischief, may arise from the proposed change. The wanting link in the chain of education, which our president has just discovered, is more fanciful than real. It is true that in the North there are common schools, academics, and colleges. But it is not necessary to study in an academy to get into college. When a young man applies for admission, he is not examined as to what school he has attended or by what tutor he has been taught. If he is found to be adept in the requisite studies, he is admitted though he may never have attended any school at all. I have myself taught, in a common school, Latin and Greek to young men fitting for college. My own fitting was partly at my father's fireside. Academics are not, in fact, established as a link in education, terminating in the college. More than half of their pupils are females who never go to college. Of the males, it is believed that less than half aspire to a collegiate education. The fitting of young men for colleges is not the main object of the academy, but an incident. They go there for preparation because the common schools, from their intermittent character and the general want of qualifications in their teachers, do not afford them the means. But were they continuous and furnished with competent teachers, we should see the young men of the country stepping from the common schools into the colleges without the least idea of the necessity of passing through an academy.

Our institution may be linked to a *continuous common school* with teachers on hand or procurable not only competent to fit its pupils for college, but to carry them through. Without adopting the name *college*, we could have done all in the way of education which we have proposed to do under the name. But the name *college*, authorized to confer degrees by the highest power in the country, had something attractive in it, and we have availed ourselves of it in the hope of extending the influence and increasing the importance and usefulness of our institution.

But, argues our president, we have made a mistake in proposing to admit students at a grade of preparation below that of the other colleges of the country and have thereby exposed ourselves to the sneers of the envious and the clamorous. If there be any mistake, it is much to be regretted that our president and no one else ever thought of the difficulty during the years this measure was in contemplation, and especially before it was announced that it had been consummated. And what is the remedy the president proposes for the alleged mistake? The obvious one would be to raise the rule of preparation for those hereafter to be admitted, and let the four-year course stand as has been announced. Instead of that, he proposes to abolish the freshman and sophomore classes, thrusting our freshmen back into a preparatory school and thus establishing a college of two years. Yet, he proposes to pursue the same studies as if the whole four years were covered by the name *college*, reminding one of a certain poem written by an eminent man more celebrated as a stateman than a poet, in which he said:

"And if we can not alter things;
By G—d we'll change their names, Sir."

Shall we avoid sneers by such an expedient as that? On the contrary, by thus attempting to avoid them on the one hand shall we not bring them upon us with tenfold force on the other? Observe, the president does not propose to increase the scale of attainments necessary to entitle our students to *graduate* and *receive a diploma*. This project is limited to increasing the scale necessary to entitle them to enter our college. Now, if they are not fit to enter college without two years more of study *out of college*, how can they be fitted to graduate without two years more of study *in college*? Will we be more exposed to sneers by admitting them *half-fitted* than by graduating them *half-educated*? And what will our diplomas be worth if given under a virtual admission of that sort? May not their holders, when showing them, be taunted with the exclamation: "*Oh, that comes from the half-college, inaugurated at Washington, with so much ceremony sometime ago—a half-horse concern.*" If we have made a mistake, let us not make a worse one in the measures taken to correct it.

But I do not concede that any mistake on that score has been committed. On the contrary, I believe the present organization of our college the best, adapted to meet the wants and wishes of the deaf and dumb community and to promote the interests of our institution, that can be devised.

There are in the United States twenty-four institutions for the instruction of that class of our fellow citizens. Two only have high schools. Our system, as adopted and announced, informs the pupils of twenty-two of those institutions, who may graduate or have graduated in good standing, that they are at liberty, at once, to enter our college and, after four years of faithful study, shall be entitled to a diploma. It holds out to those who leave the other two institutions in good standing, without going through their high schools, the same privileges, and [it holds out] to graduates of those schools the privilege of entering our junior class and, after two years' faithful study, also receiving a diploma. Could anything be devised, better calculated to bring accessions of students from all those institutions? And would it tend to encourage them to come for us now to withdraw our annunciation and say to them, "You may come, but we have changed our minds, and not considering you fitted to enter our college, you must be content to spend two years in a preparatory department"? You might urge that the same course of studies would be pursued and the same honors be bestowed as originally intended, and they might pertinently reply, "Why then change names and place us even nominally in a less honorable position than you promised us?" The effect could not be otherwise than disastrous to our material interests, lessening the respect in which our institution is now held throughout the country, especially by the deaf and dumb, and essentially restricting its usefulness.

As to the grade or qualifications for entering college, each college has its own, and probably no two have precisely the same, though they are all more or less adapted to the general state of education in the country. As that improves, no doubt the scale of preparation is advanced. I have not the proofs at hand, but I have no doubt the requisites for entering Harvard and Yale and Dartmouth are much higher now than they were fifty or eighty years ago. Our requisitions are now adapted in the best possible manner to the present state of the deaf and dumb education in the country. Should that be essentially advanced by the general establishment of high schools or otherwise, it will doubtless become advisable to raise, in a corresponding degree, the grade of qualifications to enter our college. But let us not defeat the principle object in establishing a college by requiring qualifications to enter now nowhere existing except among the graduates of the high schools in New York and Connecticut.

That in the establishment of a college in any shape we should awaken the jealousy of ambitious men connected with other institutions, enhanced by envy of the rapid advancement of our young president, I never had a doubt; and fear that our vital interests might be endangered by its finding expression through Congress led me to distrust the policy of moving in the matter at so early a period of our existence as an institution. But the step has been taken, and the best way to meet sneers and cavils is to take no notice of them but to go forward with prudent, steady, and firm steps in the path we have marked out for ourselves; so shall we deprive ridicule of the food it feeds upon, disarm jealousy, and shame envy into silence.

Having prepared the foregoing expositions, I felt so sure our president would, on presentation of the legal points, at least postpone the subjects, that I urged him to do so in a friendly letter. But he persists, though he admits that our difference is "on a mere question of technicalities" and urges me to yield the point, though I consider it one involving consistency, our self-respect, and our material interests. Why then should not he give up his "technicalities"?

Let us review this whole subject of a college. I had looked at it as a thing in the distance. We were though too young as an institution to assume prominence, even in name, over the old institutions of the country. But our ambitious superintendent, without consulting the Board of Directors as I think was his duty, went to Congress and got an act passed authorizing our institution to confer degrees. This we could have done without assuming the name *college*. But he deemed it all important that we should establish a college, collect here the graduates of the other institutions, and give them a more finished education. But it was necessary to show that there were persons here or elsewhere fitted to enter our college—else why establish it at all? Accordingly, on the 7th of May our superintendent stated to the board that the progress already made by the most advanced pupils now in the institution "called for—*yes, called for*— the establishment, at the beginning of the next academic year, of the collegiate department," etc.

Was this declaration true or false? The president now virtually assures us that it was false; that none of our pupils had, in fact, made any such progress; that it required two years more of study before a collegiate department would be called for, so far as they are concerned. Yet, on the faith of this falsehood was our college built; now he tells us that, in fact, there is nobody anywhere fit to enter the freshman or sophomore classes, and very few fit to enter the junior class, and they only at a grade of preparation which ought to enable them only to be freshmen. The remedy for so terrible a mistake would seem to be to abolish a college so prematurely established and wait until it is really "called for."

In July last, sometime after the inauguration of our college, the president, in the "Address to the Public" prepared by him, announced that "the first freshman class will commence its studies on the 8th day of September next." Now how supremely ridiculous was this announcement if there was nobody in our institution or in the country qualified to enter a freshman class! And what does our president ask of us now but an admission that it was *supremely ridiculous*. Yet, who was its author? Our president himself. He asks us now to decide that he deceived us into the establishment of a college when there was really no call for it in May last, and mocked the public with an announcement that we had a college ready to receive pupils into the freshman class in September last. There is no escaping these conclusions on the ground now occupied by the president.

He deceived us in May into the establishment of a college and deceived the public in July by a delusive announcement. Was this premeditated deceit or honest error? I admit that our president thinks it honest error; but the very fact that he had committed so grave an error after years of experience and reflection ought to warn us that his present opinions may be more fallacious than those of May and July last and admonish him to press them with less pertinacity on older heads not influenced by envious sneers or elated by recent promotion. My own disposition as well as that of the board has been, and is, to allow the president to have his own way in carrying on the business of the institution always within the limits of law and regulations; but when, on questions of organization and regulation, he leads the board one way today and attempts to drive them another way tomorrow, we cannot but conclude that his opinions are not always a safe guide.

When in argument I alluded to the fact that we actually had a freshman class under the instruction of Professor Storrs, the president denied that we had any such recognized class. If not, he has taken the liberty to disregard the arrangements of the board, as announced by himself, to abolish one of the college classes and in effect deprive Professor Storrs of the title conferred upon him by the board; for it is only those employed in the collegiate department that are entitled to be called professors. But I insist that we have, in law and in fact, a freshman class and that the president had no right to abolish it without the authority of this board.

The present may be as good a time as any to consider whether this board shall continue to be a *bona fide* Board of Directors or a body to be called together for no other purpose than ratifying the unauthorized acts of the president in a report to the Secretary of the Interior.

The total derangement of our collegiate arrangements, to meet the new light which seems to have burst on his mind during his late trip to the North, is not the only assumption of power disclosed in this report.

The cabinet shop, deemed I believe by most if not all of us a most important branch of the institution, has been discontinued by the sole order of the president, and the reason given for it in the original draft of the report was the want of suitable accommodations for it. Not at the meeting of the board, but in a conversation the next day, I suggested that this reason would sound strange to those who knew the government had lately bought for us a number of houses, some of which may readily be converted into convenient shops; that the only good reason which could be given, if such was the fact, was that the institution was unable to sustain it at present high prices; and that this fact furnished a valid reason for asking Congress to increase their annual allowance for each pupil from $150 to $200 and thus enable us to continue that branch of instruction. The president promised that he would alter the report accordingly.

Dr. Sunderland and myself were appointed a committee in conjunction with the superintendent, now president, to digest a course of studies for the entire college course and did prepare one for the freshman year. Now the president, without consulting the board or any member thereof, set forth a course of study as a part of our report to the Secretary when, in fact, no such course has been adopted and there is not time to give it due consideration. On running my eyes over it I thought some of the studies of doubtful utility to the deaf and dumb and that there was too much of others; but [I] would not so hastily form a definite opinion.

Now what I insist upon is that when our president thinks any material change ought to be made in our system or its management, or any new subject comes up not embraced in any existing regulation, he shall, before he acts, bring it before the board in a regular manner. In short, I wish him to consider himself an executive officer, whose main duty it is to execute law in accordance with the will of the board.

III

The First Years of the College
1864–1867

IT WILL BE OF INTEREST to record the names of those who were the first to enter upon the advanced course of study prepared in connection with the college.

Melville Ballard of Maine, a graduate of the high class of the American School for the Deaf at Hartford in 1860, and who had performed acceptable service as a teacher in our institution from 1860 to 1863, then voluntarily retiring, entered in September 1864 on a special course of collegiate study. He is therefore to be named as the first student in our college course and the only one for the year 1864–1865.

Charles K. W. Strong of Vermont, a graduate of the high class of the New York Institution for the Deaf and Dumb, and employed in the U.S. Treasury Department in 1864, declared his purpose of entering college on a footing similar to that of Mr. Ballard, and his name was entered upon our records. But he changed his mind and never became an actual student.

In September 1864 four pupils of our institution—Emma J. Sparks, Annie Szymanoskie, John Quinn, and Isaac Winn, all of the District of Columbia—entered upon our advanced course of study under the tuition of Professor Storrs of our college, with a view of entering on the regular collegiate course as soon as they could be prepared therefore.

James Cross, Jr., and James H. Logan, both of Pennsylvania, entered upon a similar course of study with Professor Storrs. It will be seen therefore that seven persons made up the number of those who were regarded as connected with the college as students during the first year of its existence.

Congress, in July 1864, made an appropriation of $26,000 for the purchase of about thirteen acres of ground adjacent on the two sides to

10. Melville Ballard was the first student admitted to the college program.

the lot of two acres donated by Mr. Kendall in 1857. Mr. Kendall in deeding this ground to the corporation inserted a provision that if the institution should at any time cease to occupy the property, it should revert to his heirs. Congress attached to the appropriation a proviso that this reversionary interest should be relinquished. Mr. Kendall readily complied with this requirement.

The property purchased with the $26,000 included the dwelling house originally rented of Mr. Stickney for the use of the institution and occupied for three years. This building was fitted up in the summer of 1864 for

the use of the male students of the collegiate department, and they occupied it from September 1864 on. As only one of the five young men,
occupying this building was, strictly speaking, a college student, remarks
about him were often facetiously made, by his mates as follows: "The
College has gone to the city." "The College has gone to bed." "The College
is taking a bath." "The College has a toothache today."

During the first year of the college, Professor Storrs was assisted by
Mr. Roswell Parish, a graduate of Yale College, who had been teaching
for a year in our primary department.

The friends of the college felt greatly encouraged by the action of
Congress in purchasing ground for the institution in its enlarged condition,
and it is of interest to note that this generous appropriation of $26,000
was made in what may be termed the darkest days of the Civil War. The
money was drawn from the Treasury and paid over to the owners of the
thirteen acres of land, Mr. Kendall and his son-in-law Mr. Stickney, at
a time when all communication between the Capital and the North, whether
by mail or telegraph was cut off for a few days. This was just at the time
of the Battle of Gettysburg when a Confederate raid had broken up the
lines of railroad and telegraphs between Baltimore and Philadelphia.

One of the most interested and helpful friends of the institution in
Congress at this time and for several years later, as will appear in the
narrative which is to follow, was the Honorable Thaddeus Stevens of
Pennsylvania, chairman of the Committee on Appropriations and leader
of the House.

I secured Mr. Stevens' interest by calling on him, self-introduced*,
and arranging for him to visit the institution with one or two members
of the committee. I remember that on the occasion of this visit Mr. Stevens
was much impressed by my mother, whose personality was always most
attractive in spite of her deaf muteness. Mr. Stevens observed the pupils
and their silent work in the classroom with absorbed attention, and all at
once he broke out with, "Great Heavens! How rapidly one could transact
business in the House if half the members were like these children."

In the summer of 1864 Mr. Stevens secured the passage by the House
of an increased appropriation for the current expenses of the institution,

---

*[Footnote by E. M. G.] I can say that in my many instances when I wished to gain
the aid of public men, I found it was better to introduce myself than to have a letter of
introduction.

the one of $26,000, referred to earlier, for the purchase of ground, and also $31,446 for the creation of a building intended to provide dormitory accommodations for the college and for classrooms.

The Senate struck out both their appropriations for improvements, but Mr. Stevens, by a vigorous appeal in the Committee of Conference and in the House, saved the appropriation for the purchase of the ground. And as there were buildings on this ground more than sufficient for the temporary accommodation of the college, the needs of the institution at that juncture were provided for.

The following year, mainly through Mr. Stevens' instrumentality, Congress made an appropriation of $39,445.87 for additions to the buildings, which enabled us to provide fully for the growing number of our students.

In January 1865 an event occurred in the institution which occasioned the greatest sorrow to all connected with it. This was the death of my eldest sister, Mrs. Sophia G. Hunter, who had filled the position of assistant matron for five years.

Mrs. Hunter, though suffering from impaired health during all the period of her official connection with the institution, performed her duties with such a self-forgetful and truly sympathetic spirit as to remove from the minds of her associates and those under her control all ideas that she was an invalid. She won not only the respect and esteem, but the warmest affectionate regard of every resident of the institution and was mourned at her death by us all as a beloved sister and mother.

In July 1865 another personal grief came to me which cast a great shadow over my life. This was the very sudden death of my little son born almost with the college, who, I had hoped, might grow up to follow in the profession of his father.

An act of Congress was approved February 23rd, 1865, authorizing the abolition of our department for the blind and providing for the education of the blind of the District in the Maryland Institution at Baltimore. Seven blind pupils were transferred under the provisions of this act to Baltimore in the summer of 1865. It met very hearty approval that our institution was thus relieved of its dual character.

1865–1866

During the second year of the college, it became necessary to secure means for the pecuniary assistance of most of those who sought admission to the college as students, and in the Ninth Annual Report it was urged that Congress might with propriety make provisions for the higher education of deaf-mutes from the states in the institution now sustained by it at the Federal Capital.

But without waiting for the action of Congress, I took measures to secure from private individuals, scholarships for the aid of students who were unable to pay for their board and tuition. In this effort I had the active cooperation of our Professor Storrs. Eleven scholarships yielding $150 each per annum were provided, and the interested reader will find a full account of them in our Ninth Annual Report.

In 1865 the faculty was strengthened by the addition of Rev. Lewellyn Pratt, an experienced teacher of the deaf, who assumed the professorship of natural science. I took the chair of moral and political science; Peter Baumgras, an accomplished artist of Washington, became instructor of drawing and painting.

Rev. William W. Turner, ex-principal of the Hartford School for the Deaf and an accomplished teacher of long experience, accepted our appointment as lecturer on natural history, and Hon. Jas. W. Patterson, U.S. Senator and long a professor in Dartmouth College, agreed to give lectures to our students on astronomy.

During the year ended June 30, 1866, the number of students in "the college" was twenty-five, representing the states of Maine, Connecticut, Vermont, Massachusetts, Pennsylvania, New York, Ohio, Maryland, Michigan, Illinois, Wisconsin, Iowa, Georgia, and the District of Columbia. Two young women were among the twenty-five students, and the whole were divided into classes as follows: one resident graduate, four sophomores, five freshmen, and fifteen in the preparatory class.

In the early summer of 1866, I became convinced that there was need to call in the services of some accomplished landscape architect to make a careful study of the prospective probable development of our institution and suggest plans for the laying out of the grounds and location of buildings which should secure results in harmony with good taste and the greatest utility.

Up to this time the buildings erected had, with the exception of the first which was designed by myself, been built from plans prepared by

Emil S. Freiderich, a local architect of good standing and ability. The interior arrangement of these buildings had been designed by me, and their location had been determined by Mr. Friederich and myself.

Not satisfied with the crude plan in accordance with which the buildings had, so far, been placed on the grounds, I secured, with the approval of the board, the services of my fellow townsman and friend of my early youth, Fredrick Law Olmsted, easily first among American landscape architects.

Mr. Olmsted spent some days at Kendall Green and presented plans and a report in conjunction with his partners, Calvert, Vaux, and Frederick C. Withers, which will be found in our Ninth Annual Report.*

These plans, with some modifications suggested by me, have been fully carried out, and I take pleasure in recording the fact that the present beauty and attractiveness of Kendall Green, remarked and admitted by so many residents and visitors, are largely the result of Mr. Olmsted's skill in making the best possible use of the natural advantages of the plan. Messrs. Olmsted and Vaux showed their ability also in including the three existing buildings, a group that, while it could not well be made uniform in style, has been made harmonious and is allowed to tell an interesting story of development through a series of years, which is always an interesting feature in the growth of public establishments.

In June 1866 Melville Ballard of Maine, our first college student, was graduated with the degree of bachelor of science. The exercises were conducted in the chapel of the college. The Sunday preceding I delivered a Baccalaureate Sermon, several of our directors being present, including Chief Justice Chase. His son-in-law, Senator Sprague of Rhode Island, came with him.

In 1866 several important changes took place in our faculty. Professor Storrs was compelled out of consideration for his parents, whose health was much impaired, to return to Connecticut to live near them. He very reluctantly resigned his chair in the college, which he had filled with brilliant success, and returned to teach in the school at Hartford. His place in the college was filled by Professor Samuel Porter, who had more than twenty years experience in teaching in the schools at Hartford and New York.

---

*See Appendix B.

11. The building at left under construction was designed by Emil S. Freiderich.

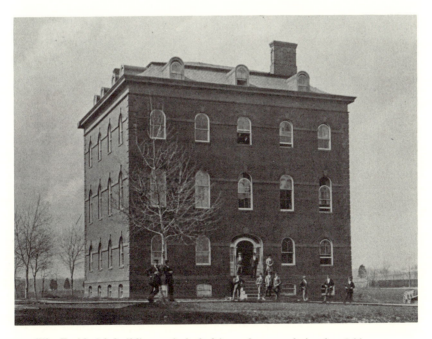

12. The Freiderich building as it looked just after completion in 1866.

A valuable addition was also made to the faculty in the person of Edward Allen Fay, who assumed the chair of history and ancient languages. Professor Fay grew up in the Michigan School for the Deaf, of which his father was long superintendent, and before coming to us [he] had several years experience teaching in the school for the deaf in New York City.

By the end of the 1865–66 school year, my mother, having entered on her sixty-ninth year and having filled the position of matron for nine years, presented her resignation of that office. Her retirement was a source of great regret to all connected with the institution, whose feelings were voiced in action taken by the Board of Directors which will be found published in our Ninth Annual Report.

In November 1866 my life was saddened by the death, after a long and distressing illness, of the wife of my early youth. Though she occupied no official position in the institution and had never taken any active part in its work, except to fill a vacancy for a very short time as a teacher of the blind, she had deservedly won the warm regard of the officers and pupils of the institution, and her untimely death was sincerely deplored by all connected with the institution.

1866–1867

The following year, again through Mr. Stevens' aid and against the opposition of Elihu B. Washburne who was second on the Appropriations Committee and often acting chairman, Congress made the handsome appropriation of $51,200 for additions to buildings and the improvement of grounds. With this money the foundations for the chapel were laid, a house for Professor Pratt was built, and work was begun on a residence for the president of the institution.

In accordance with Mr. Olmsted's suggestion, a strip of ground two hundred feet on Florida Avenue, then called Boundary Street, was purchased of Mrs. Catherine Pearson, the owner of Brentwood, for $9,000. It was in connection with this purchase that Chief Justice Chase and I had the little controversy in the board, alluded to earlier in this history.

In the early spring of 1867 I called the attention of the board to the fact that two schools for the deaf had been established, one in Massachusetts and one in New York, which were to be carried on under the oral method exclusively.

I suggested to the board that our institution ought not to lack any means that might be of help to the deaf and asked if the directors thought it would be well to send a delegate to Europe for the purpose of examining the oral and other schools in that part of the world.

The board at once authorized me to spend six months in Europe, directing me to examine carefully into all methods of teaching the deaf in use in the schools on the Continent and in Great Britain and Ireland. A full account of this, to me a most interesting and enjoyable tour, will be found in our Tenth Annual Report.*

Before going abroad in April 1867, I engaged Mr. James M. Spencer, then about to graduate from Yale College, to join our faculty in September as professor of mathematics, and he assumed his duties as agreed.

13. Faculty and students of the National Deaf-Mute College in 1867.

---

*See Appendix C for portions of this report.

On the 3rd of March 1867, very important action of Congress was approved by the President, in connection with which there are incidents of much more than ordinary interest.

A few months earlier I received a letter from Hon. Thaddeus Stevens, saying that a young constituent who had suddenly became totally deaf from sickness and having heard that there was a college for deaf-mutes sustained by the government at Washington, had applied to him to be admitted as a free student, urging that he had not the means to meet his expenses. Mr. Stevens asked if there was any reason why he could not be admitted. I at once called on Mr. Stevens and informed him that all our free scholarships were assigned and that the law did not allow us to admit students from outside the District of Columbia without charge.

Mr. Stevens at once grew much excited and said, "Do you mean to tell me that after securing all the appropriations I have from Congress in aid of the college, I can't put a poor boy in from my district?" I replied, "I am very sorry, Mr. Stevens, but the law does not permit this."

I can never forget his excited reply, which was more emphatic than elegant. "The law does not allow it? By G—d the law shall allow it."

When the Sundry Civil Appropriation Bill came up in the House a little later, the item for the support of our institution was in the following shape:

> Columbia Institution for the Deaf and Dumb.
> For the support of the institution, including $1,000 for books and illustrative apparatus, $25,000: *Provided*, That the pupils residing in the several States and Territories of the United States, applying for admission to the collegiate department of the institution, shall be received on the same terms and conditions as those prescribed by law for residents of the District of Columbia, at the discretion of the president.

In the discussion which followed Mr. Stevens' explanation of the paragraph, someone asked if the closing word *president* meant the President of the United States. At that time Andrew Johnson was President, and Mr. Stevens was one of his most bitter enemies in the House.

Mr. Stevens' reply was a most emphatic negative, and he at once moved to amend the paragraph by adding the words "of the institution." The paragraph as amended passed the House, but the Senate struck out the proviso, and in the conference committee it was restored with a limitation of the number of free students to two.

This legislation was the basis and starting point of the liberal policy since carried out by Congress in aid of the higher education of the intellectually gifted deaf youth in this country.

That this policy has often been opposed in Congress will appear later in this narration—and that it was once abandoned for a single year. It will also seem that men of standing and intelligence urged that such a policy was in direct violation of the Constitution of the United States.

My reply to this always was, substantially, that I felt justified in asking such action of Congress in view of the liberal grants of land to the states under the Agricultural Colleges Act, from the benefits of which the deaf youth of the country were shut out. To this I usually added an appeal based on the handicapped condition of the deaf.

I remember appearing on one occasion before the Appropriations Committee of the House when General B. F. Butler was a member of the committee. As the interview proceeded General Butler asked me in rather a sneering tone if I would tell the committee on what ground I would urge their appropriating money for the training of persons so deficient as the deaf and dumb were. "Why would it not be better," said the general, "if Congress wished to spend money for educational purposes, to give it to those who had all their faculties."

I replied, "I ask aid for the deaf, with confidence that it will be given, because I believe that every generous man giving help to others likes to feel that it is bestowed where it is most needed." The committee gave me all I asked for, but General Butler opposed the appropriation in the House and in the course of his speech said when a deaf-mute had received all the education that could be given him, he was at the best no more than "half a man."

This expression roused the ire of one of our students, Joseph G. Parkinson by name, who came to me to ask if I thought harm would come from his calling at General Butler's and sending in his card with the following written on it: "Half a man desires to see the Beast." Some will remember that during Butler's administration of the municipal government of New Orleans during the Civil War, the people gave him the soubriquet "Beast Butler."

PART THREE
Academics and Politics
1867–1877

IV

Europe: A New System Suggested
1867–1868

URING MY ABSENCE in Europe, the affairs of the institution were ably managed by Professor Pratt, who was made acting president. While filling this office, Professor Pratt discovered that one of the officers of the institution, whose sympathies were with the State of Maryland, was acting a most dishonorable part in a correspondence with officials of that state, the object of which was to secure the establishment of an institution for the deaf in Maryland, and the removal of the wards of that state in our institution to the new school.

Professor Pratt reported his discoveries to me while I was still abroad, and I promptly ordered the suspension from office of the disloyal incumbent. On my return, events fully justified the course that had been pursued by Professor Pratt and myself.

At the end of the 1867–68 school year, the larger part of the beneficiaries of Maryland were withdrawn, much to our regret, but not to any serious detriment of the welfare of the institution.

On the 23rd of October 1867 at a full meeting of the board, I presented my report on "the systems of deaf-mute instruction pursued in Europe."* I had completed this report in Paris, thinking it wise to do this while the memory of all I had seen and learned in my tour was fresh in my mind, and in a place where I could be free from the distractions and cares that were sure to press upon me from day to day from the moment of my resumption of my official duties at home.

I was fortunate in securing in Paris, through the kindness of our minister, the services of an Irish gentleman, a Mr. Sutton, who had lived long on the Continent and was an accomplished linguist.

---

*See Appendix D.

With Mr. Sutton's aid I was able to avail myself of the contents of many books and pamphlets I had collected in France, Italy, Germany, and elsewhere. Mr. Sutton also assisted me in the orderly arrangement of my material and was my indefatigable scribe, working night and day to hasten the completion of my work. During the month that I was engaged in the report in Paris, I resided at the Grand Hotel, occupying a room under the roof in which Mr. Sutton and I burned so much midnight oil.

The reading of my report to the directors occupied more than two hours, and I noticed that some of the younger members gave occasional signs of drowsiness, which did not surprise me, as there was much in the report that was technical and dry to the unprofessional reader. I noticed, however, that Mr. Kendall, then in his seventy-ninth year, gave the most alert attention throughout the whole reading. He made no notes and did not interrupt me with questions, but when I had finished, he sought further information on a number of points, which he brought up seriatim. I am sure every one present observed with astonishment the evidences Mr. Kendall gave of having actually taken in the report in all its details.

The board were not only ready to act favorably on the changes I proposed in our methods, providing for the instruction in speech of all pupils "until it plainly appears that success is unlikely to crown their efforts," but they were instructed to influence the schools of the country to adopt a similar policy.

The plan was considered, during the winter, of the calling at our institution of a conference of the principals of the schools of the country at which "the articulation controversy" as well as "other and more important subjects" might be considered. In March 1868 I issued "in behalf of the officers of the Columbia Institution" a circular inviting the "principals of the regular institutions of the United States to meet here (Kendall Green) on Tuesday, the 12th day of May."

It had been most unjustly asserted in certain quarters that our Conference of Principals was called with the purpose of opposing the oral teaching of the deaf and that with evil design no invitations were sent to the officers of the then newly started oral schools in Massachusetts and New York.

I have on more than one occasion made it clear that these statements had no foundation in fact, but I think it worthwhile, in the interest of the truth of history, to place the matter beyond the possibility of misapprehension. The following is the full text of the circular issued:

Washington, D.C., March, 1868

Sir: The increased interest manifested by the public during the past year in the education of the deaf and dumb, taking in certain localities the form of hostility to the system of instruction successfully practiced in this country for a half century, has led the officers of this institution to consider the present an opportune time for the assembling in conference of those best fitted by practical experience and long study to judge what measures and methods will most conduce to the welfare of the deaf and dumb of our country.

Besides the issues involved in what may be termed the articulation controversy, there are other and more important subjects which would naturally be suggested in a conference of the character referred to, the discussion of which could not fail to elicit an interchange of ideas valuable to our profession, and tending to benefit those for whose advancement all our labors are put forth.

We have, therefore, determined to invite the principals of the regular institutions of the United States to meet here on Tuesday, the 12th day of May next, to discuss on the three following days such questions as may be brought forward relating to the work of deaf-mute education. To this conference we would respectfully and cordially invite your attendance and would suggest that you prepare for presentation one or more papers on such subjects as may have received your particular attention, or which you may deem of special importance in our work.

Accommodations for all who may attend will be provided in or very near the institution. It is therefore requested that intentions to be present may be communicated as soon as convenient.

It is also suggested that those who design to submit papers announce the titles in advance.

In behalf of the officers of the Columbia Institution:

E. M. Gallaudet, President

Garbled quotations have been made from this circular with, I do not hesitate to say, an *intent* to mislead. For no intelligent and candid person can find any evidence in the circular of "hostility" to the teaching of speech to the deaf.

It *is* said "hostility" has been manifested in certain quarters against "the system of instruction successfully practiced in this country for half a century," and it is proposed to consider "the articulation controversy."

Mr. Kendall, in following my address of welcome to the conference on the day of its assembling, said, among other things, that in accordance with my suggestions the board had decided to secure the "services of a competent instructor in articulation" and that it was hoped this "could be done at the beginning of the next term."

14. The first National Conference of Principals of Institutions for the Instruction of the Deaf and Dumb (E.M.G. seated on curb, front row center).

As to the matter of our failure to include the new oral schools in our invitation, it is of record that those schools had no principals when our conference was called, which was limited to such officers and was not to include teachers or members of boards of directors.

Now, it was well known to us at the time of calling the conference that there were men interested in the "new schools" who were eager, if not bitter, partisans of the oral method to the exclusion of all others. It was from these men that the purpose had been made public to do away, if possible, with "the system of instruction successfully practiced in this country for half a century." And had any of them attended the conference, their partisan spirit would have assumed antagonism and prevented harmonious action. They were not, and never had been teachers, and it was desired that the conference should be limited not alone to members of our profession, but to actual heads of the schools.

I say frankly that there were those on the boards of management of the "new schools" whose presence in our conference I should have deeply deplored for they would have been firebrands.

As events turned out, it will appear from a reference to the proceedings of the conference that at the conclusion of the reading of a paper I had prepared with much care on "The American System of Deaf-Mute Education, Its Incidental Effects and Their Remedies," I offered to the conference the following resolutions:

Resolved, That in the opinion of this conference, it is the duty of all institutions for the education of the deaf and dumb to provide adequate means for imparting instruction in articulation and lip reading, to such of their pupils as may be able to engage with profit in exercises of this nature.

Resolved, That to attain success in this department of instruction an added force of instructors will be necessary, and this conference hereby recommends for the deaf and dumb in this country that speedy measures be taken to provide the funds needed for the prosecution of this work.

After protracted discussion these resolutions were unanimously adopted.

Several who agreed to this new policy had been in years past earnest opponents of any general teaching of speech to the deaf, and I am certain that their approval of the resolutions was secured because of the character of the conference—a purely professional body—and because no partisan spirit was shown and no appeals of that character were made.

I do not think that partisan promoters of the cause of speech teaching to the deaf in this country have been disposed to acknowledge the great service rendered to that cause by the action of the Washington Conference of Principals. In my opinion this action forwarded the cause more than any other influence that had been exerted in connection with this reform.

But this was not the only important result brought about by the conference. Steps were taken to effect the revival of the publication of the *American Annals of the Deaf* and a renewal of meetings of the Convention of American Instructors of the Deaf, both of which had been suspended on account of the Civil War.

A standing committee was appointed to accomplish both of these objects, of which I was made chairman, and my professional colleagues have seen fit to keep me in the position of chairman of the standing Executive Committee of the Convention from 1868 to the time of this writing, 1898, an honor which I most highly appreciate.

The *Annals* was placed under the editorship of Professor Pratt of our college faculty, who was succeeded two years later by Professor Fay, by whom the journal has been most successfully conducted up to the present time.*

---

*Dr. Fay was editor of the *American Annals of the Deaf* from 1870 to 1920.

Besides providing for the revival of the Convention, the conference has continued to exist and has held meetings every four years or oftener since its inception in 1868.

In connection with the publication of the proceedings of the conference an interesting incident occurred. The board had included these proceedings with our Annual Report to the Secretary of the Interior. But Judge William T. Otto, then Assistant Secretary, was not very friendly to the institution and would not have the publication recommended. So I secured a resolution of the Senate authorizing their publication. Hearing of this, Judge Otto addressed a letter to the Senate while I was away getting married, alleging that the proceedings were very voluminous and that it would cost more than $1,000 to print them. On the strength of this, the resolution to print was rescinded. On my return I had the pleasure of satisfying the Senate, with an estimate from the public printer, that the cost of printing the proceedings would be less than $200 and securing the re-passage of the original resolution.

I come now, in recording events belonging to 1868, to the story of a most remarkable opposition, which was led in Congress by Hon. Elihu B. Washburne of Illinois, against our collegiate undertaking and which had as its avowed object the complete destruction of the institution and providing for the education of the deaf of the District of Columbia in some state school.

During 1867 Mr. Stevens, being then chairman of the House Committee on Appropriations, and Mr. Washburne, second on the committee, the latter raised his voice in condemnation of what he called the unwarranted and extravagant action of Congress in supporting our college. But Mr. Stevens, though somewhat broken in health, was able with little difficulty to overcome Mr. Washburne's opposition.

I remember on one occasion hearing from the gallery a colloquy between Mr. Stevens and General Schenck, afterwards our minister to England. General Schenck started to raise a point of order against an appropriation for building purposes in our institution, that it was without the authority of existing law—which was true.

Mr. Stevens interrupted General Schenck very politely, asking if he might be allowed to say a word. And when the general had assented to this, Mr. Stevens straightened himself up, showed an approach of humor by the expression on his face and an unusual twinkle in his eye, and said in an unnaturally solemn voice, "Mr. Speaker, I only wish to express the hope that any gentleman who undertakes to open his mouth in opposition to this appropriation *may be struck dumb.*"

General Schenck's broad shoulders shook with laughter and he sat down, plainly and willingly "struck dumb."

But not so easily did Mr. Stevens overcome Mr. Washburne's opposition. Failing to accomplish anything against Mr. Stevens' championship during the session 1866–67, Mr. Washburne in the spring of 1868, having become acting chairman of the Committee on Appropriations in consequence of Mr. Stevens' increasing feebleness, determined to make a vigorous onslaught on the institution.

In the meantime a most noble and worthy successor to Mr. Stevens, as the active champion of the cause of the college in Congress, had been providentially raised up in the person of Judge Rufus P. Spalding of Cleveland, Ohio, who stood next to Mr. Washburne on the committee.

Mr. Washburne in his attacks on the institution in 1867 had directed attention to the fact that while Congress had given large sums for the purchase of grounds and other erection of buildings for the institution, the title to all this real estate was vested in a private corporation. He also argued that the control of the annual appropriations Congress was asked to make was entirely in the hands of officers of a private corporation.

As these criticisms could not be disputed by the friends of the institution, and as they were not only willing but anxious that the ground for them should be removed, a bill was framed with Judge Spalding's assistance which provided that no real estate owned by the corporation should be "aliened, sold, or conveyed except under the authority of a special act of Congress." This bill also provided for the appointment of two members of the House and one Senator as members of the Board of Directors of the institution.

Judge Spalding secured the support of a majority of the members of the Appropriations Committee for this bill, and it was reported to the House with a recommendation that it pass.

Mr. Washburne, however, secured the qualified cooperation of three members of the committee, enough to justify a minority report, and prepared for a bitter and prolonged contest. Having secured from the Treasury Department a complete statement of all the receipts and disbursements of the institution from its foundation eleven years before, he prepared a voluminous report in which he undertook to show extravagant and unnecessary expenditures.

This report he submitted to the House and had printed in advance of the discussion on the bill and caused copies to be placed on the desks of all the members on the day the discussion took place. At length, after several postponements the battle royal took place on — — — day of —.— — 1868.*

Mr. Stevens, who came now only seldom to the House, was brought in by two men in a chair and placed at the clerk's desk. He was not able to take part in the debate, but it was well known which side he favored; and the influence of his pale determined face, now and then lit up with a wan smile, and of the wave of his emaciated hand as he gave encouragement to his doughty lieutenant, Judge Spalding, was not small.

Judge Spalding moved the previous question on the bill, which gave him an hour in which to close the debate. Of this time he gave Mr. Washburne forty minutes. Mr. Washburne's speech, including some interlocutions was as follows:

Mr. STEVENS of Pennsylvania. I offer the following as a new section, to come in at the end of the bill:

> And be it further enacted, That the number of students in the collegiate department from the several States as authorized by act of March 2, 1867, shall be increased from ten to twenty-five.

Mr. WASHBURNE of Illinois. I hope that amendment will not be agreed to, and I desire to make a statement in regard to this institution.

Mr. SPALDING of Ohio. The gentleman from Illinois is opposed to the whole bill, and he has agreed with me that the previous question may be called, and then I will give him forty minutes of my time to make known his objections to the passage of the bill.

The SPEAKER. Then the question is first on the amendment of the gentleman from Pennsylvania (Mr. STEVENS).

Mr. WASHBURNE. I desire to offer another amendment after that shall be disposed of, and I hope the bill will not be closed for amendments. My amendment is a substitute for the bill, and I also desire to offer an additional section.

---

*E. M. G. never filled in the dates.

Mr. STEVENS. I appeal to the gentleman from Ohio (Mr. SPALDING) whether amendments of this sort are to be offered, and then the previous question is to be moved and debate closed in forty minutes?

Mr. SPALDING. I will hear what the amendments are.

The SPEAKER. The Chair knows nothing of any arrangement made privately by members. The bill is to be considered as in Committee of the Whole on the State of the Union and read by sections for amendments.

Mr. MULLINS of Tennessee. By what rule do we get into an hour speech by moving the previous question while considering the bill in Committee of the Whole?

The SPEAKER. For the reason that after the previous question shall be seconded and the main question ordered the consideration of the bill as in Committee of the Whole will have terminated, and the gentleman from Ohio (Mr. SPAULDING) having originally reported the bill, will be entitled to the floor for one hour to close the debate.

Mr. WASHBURNE. I would like to have the gentleman from Ohio (Mr. SPALDING) give me a portion of his time before the amendment and substitute are voted upon, because I desire the House to understand this matter.

Mr. SPALDING. Very well; I have no objections!

The SPEAKER. If there be no objection, the bill will now be considered as having been perfected in Committee of the Whole, and as being now before the House with the amendments pending.

No objections were made.

The SPEAKER. Will the gentleman from Ohio (Mr. SPALDING) take his hour now, or after the previous question shall have been seconded?

Mr. SPALDING. I will take it now, and yield forty minutes to the gentleman from Illinois (Mr. WASHBURNE).

Mr. WASHBURNE. I desire to get the attention of the House to a simple matter of business. This bill now before the House is a bill making appropriations for the service of the Columbia Institution for the Instruction of the Deaf and Dumb, and establishing additional regulations for the government of the institution. I can say that in the first instance the Committee on Appropriations were divided upon this bill, and there was a minority report of four members of the committee, the gentleman from Massachusetts (Mr. BUTLER), the gentleman from Michigan (Mr. BEAMAN), the gentleman from Maine (Mr. BLAINE), and myself.

I desire the attention of the House to the minority report in this matter that we may know what we are to vote upon, and what is this Columbia Institution for the Deaf and Dumb. It is an institution in which the Government has no interest whatever, but which has obtained from the

Government the sum of $325,000; and if we vote the appropriation here called for the total amount will be $376,860. Now, I wish to ask the Clerk to read the report of the minority of the Committee on Appropriations in order that the House may know how this money has been expended, and in order that we may know what we have been paying for the education of the deaf and dumb in the District of Columbia, while we assent to the proposition that it is but right and just that the Government should educate the deaf and dumb of the District of Columbia we deny that it has the right to educate the deaf and dumb of all the states, and to build up an immense institution here with the money of the people.

This report will show that these pupils which have been educated here have cost the Government the enormous sum of $7,200. This bill proposes to appropriate the sum of twenty-five, or thirty-five thousand dollars, when less than $7,000 will educate at the best institution in any of the States every deaf and dumb pupil we have here in the city of Washington.

The facts in relation to this whole matter are set out in this report, and I ask the Clerk to read it.

The report is as follows:

Mr. WASHBURNE. I have asked the Doorkeeper to place a copy of this report upon the table of each member. I call the attention of the gentlemen to the fourth page of this printed report, where they will see stated the amounts we have appropriated for this institution, in which, as I have already said, the Government has no interest whatever.

All this has been appropriated for the purpose of educating twenty-five pupils a year in this institution. And a little farther on in the report gentlemen will find a statement showing how this thing has grown up; how we have gone on year after year increasing these appropriations.

Yet we have no control over the institution. We put the whole of this vast amount under the control of the superintendent, who has given only one bond, which is in the sum of $3,000. Yet we appropriate thousands and tens of thousands to build up this establishment, and allow the money to be disposed of as the superintendent sees fit, without any control whatever on the part of the government.

Now, sir, I understand very well how this institution started. It was at first merely a private institution. But afterwards, those interested in it came in here and said that many benevolent individuals had made large subscriptions for the benefit of the institution; hence we were asked to make appropriations for it; and we did so. Now, sir, the aggregate of subscriptions from private sources was $16,257. How was that amount contributed? It will be seen by the statement contained in the report of the minority that the actual amount of cash subscribed was $8,557, exclusive of the money received from scholarships, which, at the rate of $150 each amounts to $2,100. To this is to be added $200 a year paid by Mr. Amos Kendall. Then there was a contribution also by Mr. Kendall of real estate valued at $10,600. The Government afterward purchased additional real estate of Mr. Kendall, paying him $26,000 and giving him credit for the full amount of contributions, including the real estate at its estimated value. The total amount of private contributions from all sources is $16,257, against $325,000 appropriated by the Government. The appropriations proposed to be made in this bill will make the aggregate $376,000, which we shall have given to a private institution in this District.

And what do we get for this amount taken from the pockets of our constituents and expended on a private corporation here in the District of Columbia? By reference to the fifth page of the report it will be seen that the number of pupils maintained and educated in this institution since 1858 has been as follows:

1858	17 pupils
1859	18 pupils
1860	20 pupils
1861	25 pupils
1862	24 pupils
1863	16 pupils
1864	24 pupils
1865	35 pupils
1866	22 pupils
1867	25 pupils
Total	226 pupils

Mr. WELKER of Ohio. Can the gentleman state how many of those pupils were actually residents of the District of Columbia?

Mr. WASHBURNE. I cannot state the exact number; but the gentleman will find on examination that the education of these pupils have cost us $7,200 apiece.

Mr. BENJAMIN of Missouri. I would like to ask the gentleman, in this connection, whether these are all indigent pupils?

Mr. WASHBURNE. They are pupils of this institution, I presume, in the accordance with the terms of the law. I know nothing to the contrary.

Mr. BENJAMIN. Is there any difference noted in the report between those who are indigent and those who are able to pay for their own support?

Mr. WASHBURNE. I think there is not. The law is very loose on that subject.

Mr. BENJAMIN. It is not to be presumed that a portion of these pupils are abundantly able to pay the expenses of their support and education?

Mr. WASHBURNE. It may be so; but I am assuming, for the purposes of the present argument, that they are all indigent; and I say there can be nothing to justify us in voting away this vast sum of money to build up a private corporation here in the District of Columbia. I say it is a private corporation. We have no control over it; we have no part in its direction. Will any gentleman on this floor say that the education of these pupils from the various parts of the country is a proper subject for these expenditures by Congress?

Mr. STEVENS. I desire to ask the gentleman a question. Are not the accounts of this institution, annually settled at the Interior Department, and have they not been ever since the institution came under the patronage of the Government?

Mr. WASHBURNE. The accounts have all to go to the Treasury Department; but there is no control there over these accounts. I have taken pains to obtain from that Department a copy of the accounts, that the House might see where the money of their constituents is going. Now, sir, here it is. I said there was no control over the superintendent, and I have the estimate here. It seems he paid $4,500 for an architect. There is a large amount for traveling expenses, for express here, for garden seed, for kitchen utensils, for furniture, for farming tools, for lounges, for carts, for rockaways, and so on. Every sort of thing is purchased by the superintendent out of the appropriations we make.

Mr. LOGAN of Oregon. Are the appropriations the only thing by which he is controlled?

Mr. WASHBURNE. If my colleague will go back, he will see that the law of 1857 has been amended by subsequent laws which are set out in the first part of the report.

Mr. LOGAN. Is there any authority other than that for any appropriation of Congress?

Mr. WASHBURNE. If my colleague will look, he will see all the statutes set out, and they will show him the full authority.

Mr. LOGAN. I have examined that. I do not know whether there is any authority other than the sums appropriated from year to year for these purposes.

Mr. WASHBURNE. Nothing but mere appropriations, and they are unlimited; and sir, it shows us how the people of the District of Columbia can come here and button hole members and get appropriations to these vast amounts for themselves. This minority report was concurred in by the distinguished gentleman from Massachusetts (Mr. BUTLER), the distinguished gentleman from Michigan (Mr. BEAMAN), not now here, and the distinguished gentleman from Maine (Mr. BLAINE). The report says:

Taking this amount from the total amount appropriated, $325,860.38, leaves $207,009.38, which the Government has invested in buildings, grounds, improvements, etc., which is about two-thirds of the whole amount, and for which it has nothing to show, and over which it has no control, the institution being, as has been shown, one of a private character. The question now is, What shall be done under the circumstances? It is evident that Congress would not be justified in making any further appropriations for this institution, unless it shall become a Government institution, with the property all transferred to the Government, and the institution to be managed and controlled by the Government. Even that is not now recommended, as it would devolve upon the Government a vastly greater expense than it would cost to educate all the deaf and dumb of the District at the very best institution in the country.

Here is a great abuse. Year after year we have been making these appropriations for putting up these buildings and saddling these great expenses upon the Government. Now, the question is, What shall we do? I propose, and I think the minority of the committee agree with me, that we shall make no further appropriation for this institution. It is our duty to take care of these deaf-mutes, but let us do it by adopting the amendment I have proposed, and make an appropriation of a sufficient sum to educate them in one of the best institutions of the country. I took the pains to ascertain the cost of educating these pupils in institutions in the States, and what do you suppose it is as compared with what we are paying here? In Pennsylvania, it is $240, in New York $223, and in Ohio $220. I say, therefore, let us appropriate the money and let these pupils be educated in some of these institutions, and instead of saddling our constituents with $50,000 a year to keep up this man's establishment, we can do all that humanity and duty require of us for less than $7,000 a year.

Now sir, I think every member upon this floor, when he comes to look upon the contributions we have made for charitable institutions in this District—and I would make all we are called on to make as human men—will agree that we should have some control of these charities. I wish, therefore, to call the attention to the amendment I have pending, and to see whether every member of the House will not agree with me that it should pass, my distinguished friend from Ohio (Mr. SPALDING), among the number. If we are to appropriate so much for the Deaf and Dumb Asylum, for the Providence Hospital, and so much for the Lying-in-Hospital in the District, then I say we should have some control over the expenditure of the money. I trust my friend will agree to my amendment which provides in the first section that the Secretary of the Interior, the Chief Justice of the Supreme Court of the District of Columbia, the Surgeon General of the Army, the Chief of the Bureau of Medical Surgery of the Navy, and the Chief Engineer of the Army, shall constitute a commission, which shall be known and designated as the "Commission of Charities for the District of Columbia."

The second section provides that the said commission shall organize immediately upon the passage of this act, and the Secretary of Interior shall be the president thereof, and he shall designate as secretary of said commission a clerk of his department who is of the fourth class, and who shall keep a record of all the proceedings and transactions of the said commission.

Now, let me ask what objection any gentleman can have to this provision of my amendment?

That the said commission shall have the full control and direction of all the appropriations made by Congress to the charitable institutions of the said District of Columbia, and of all such appropriations as may be made for the purposes of charity in the said District, and shall have the power of visitation and examination of all the institutions in the said District, to the support of which appropriations shall be made by Congress. No money shall be drawn from the appropriations made to the charitable institutions of the District or for the purposes of charity in the said District, except upon the requisition of the president of the commission made upon an order of the commission, duly entered in the journal of their proceedings, and all the accounts of the said commission shall be audited by the First Auditor of the Treasury. And it is hereby provided that the provisions of this act shall not be deemed to include the Government Hospital for the Insane in the District of Columbia.

Then I further propose by my amendment:

That no money shall be expended for the Columbia Institution for the Deaf and Dumb, for the Columbia Hospital for Women and Lying-in-Asylum, and for the Providence Hospital, until the title of the property, real and personal, of such institutions shall be transferred to the United States by conveyances, certified as being valid by the Attorney General of the United States, and conveying all the right, title, and interest of the said institutions in the property conveyed.

Now I ask gentlemen, is it right for us to go on constructing these buildings upon property which does not belong to the United States but to private parties? If we are to make large donations, is it not just and proper, nay, imperatively demanded by every consideration of public justice, that this Government should have the title to the property?

Mr. STEVENS. Allow me to ask the gentleman whether he would not be content with one half the total amount paid by Congress?

Mr. WASHBURNE. Congress is paying all this money and constructing all the buildings, and I insist that this Government should have the title. At any rate I will not consent to put up buildings on land belonging to individuals unless we shall have some control over them. Now, I propose further in my amendment:

That it shall be the duty of the said commission to make a full report to Congress, at the December session of each year, of all its transactions and of all the expenditures made under its direction, together with a statement of the condition of the charitable institutions of the District for which appropriations shall have been previously made and which shall have been expanded under its direction.

I ask my friend from Ohio (Mr. SPALDING) if he will not agree to that, so that we may have some control over these institutions. Then, if the House will pass my other amendment and appropriate enough money to educate every one of these pupils in our best asylums of the country, we shall then have cured a great abuse and accomplished a great work. I call attention to the fact that my amendment has nothing to do whatever with the amounts we have appropriated, but it provides that when appropriations are thus made, we shall have somebody to overlook and control the expenditure. Is it right that you should put $300,000 into the hands of a man here to disburse with only a bond of $3,000 a year? I trust the House will adopt both of my amendments so that we may have some control over this matter.

Now, look at what the bill before us proposes. First, an appropriation of $3,000. Then, for continuing work upon the building in accordance with plans, heretofore submitted, how much? Forty-eight thousand dollars. All for this private building. Then there is a provision:

That no part of the real or personal property shall be devoted to any other purpose than the education of the deaf and dumb, nor shall any portion of the real estate be liened, sold, or conveyed, except under the authority of a special act of Congress.

That is not what we want. If we are building upon this real estate, we want the title to the property; we want control over the institution. All the private subscriptions to that land amount to only $16,000, as I have shown, and yet we have paid out $325,000, and now we are asked to pay $51,000 more.

Mr. DELANO of Ohio. I understand there is another appropriation of $30,000 for construction and improvement.

Mr. WASHBURNE. It is only carrying out what we have commenced and what had been going on from year to year. If we pass this appropriation this year, we will have another call for a larger amount next year, and there will be no end to the demands made upon us. Hence I say here today when we have this matter before us, while we do justice to those pupils whom we are bound to educate, let us do justice to the pupils by preventing this squandering of their money in the way in which it has been done, in my judgement, heretofore.

Having given the opposition much more time than they could reasonably ask, Judge Spalding took his turn as follows:

Mr. SPEAKER. I hope the House will bear with the learned gentleman from Illinois for he means well in his course in this matter as he does in all his opposition to appropriations by Congress. But he is so morbidly constituted that he can not make any distinction between an appropriation necessary and requisite to be made and one which is improper. He does not know, he does not realize that while:

> "The primal duties shine aloft like stars;
> The charities that soothe and heal and bless
> Are scattered at the feet of man like flowers."

My friend had made it during this whole session of Congress his principal aim to destroy this appropriation bill which is intended for the benefit of the deaf and dumb, the poor mutes to the number of about a hundred assembled here in the District from all the states and territories of this great Union, and he says that we must cut it down because it is a private institution, a private corporation. Mr. Speaker, I deny that this is a private institution; I acknowledge that it had its origin in the day of small things. It had its origin in private munificence, but it could not go upon the donations of private charity for six short months. Congress was obliged at once to interpose, and it authorized these few charitable individuals in the District of Columbia to collect these poor, forsaken, stricken objects of humanity together, and attempt to make their lot more endurable. Congress agreed to pay $150 for every deaf-mute collected from the District of Columbia, and also the sons of men in the Army or Navy.

They afterward, and within the first six months, found that this provision would not answer, and they passed an act of Congress amendatory of the act of incorporation, assigning for five consecutive years $3,000 a year out of the national Treasury to pay the expense of the officers and students of the institution.

That was paid for some three years, and then it was found that this sum was not sufficient. Then it was that Congress passed another act.

And here I would say to the gentleman from Illinois that he must not complain of the founders of this institution, not of its trustees, not of its officers and agents, but the Senate and House of Representatives, and the various Presidents who have approved of these acts.

In 1862 an act was passed, and I have it here, amendatory of the first act incorporating the deaf and dumb institution and essentially making it an institution of the United States; and for the truth of this, after having read it, I would appeal to the good judgement of every man within the sound of my voice. The act is as follows:

"An act to amend an act to incorporate the Columbia Institution of the Deaf and Dumb."

Be it enacted, etc., That the sum of $4,400 per annum, payable quarterly, shall be allowed for the payment of salaries and incidental expenses of said institution, and the sum of $4,400 is hereby appropriated for the fiscal year ending June 30, 1863.

Section 2. *And be it further enacted*, That the sum of $9,000, and the same is hereby appropriated out of any moneys in the Treasury, not otherwise appropriated, for the erection, furnishing, and fitting up of two additions to the building of said association.

Section 3. *And be it enacted*, That all receipts and disbursements under this act shall be reported to the Secretary of the Interior, as required of the act of which this is an amendment.

The very first act required that report should be made annually to the Secretary of the Interior. The agent for the expenditure of the money appropriated from time to time by Congress is required to give bonds to the Secretary of the Interior.

Mr. WASHBURNE. How much?

Mr. SPALDING. I do not care. They can be given in any amount the Secretary sees fit to require. I am proud to say that there is no complaint that one-half dollar has ever been lost through the misconduct of the principal of this institution. No man dares to impute to him any want of faith or honesty. Nay, the Secretary of the Interior, in his famous report, of which my friend avails himself, says that if this be not a private institution, and if it be such an one as Congress sees fit to foster and encourage, no more faithful officers can be found in the United States of America than those who have been intrusted with the care of this institution for the deaf and dumb of the District of Columbia.

Now, further, Congress for a series of years appropriated this sum of $4,400 under this permanent law; and then found it necessary to appropriate a still larger sum. They also added to the capacity of the institution by providing that it should have the power to confer collegiate degrees; and a branch of the institution was established for the instruction of teachers for deaf and dumb institutions in other states. Now, it is of this that the gentleman mainly complains.

Mr. WASHBURNE. We want to get at the truth.

Mr. SPALDING. I hope the gentleman will not interrupt me. He has had the advantage from the very first of the session up to this time, and I have given him two thirds of my time today.

Mr. WASHBURNE. I want to ask the gentleman a question.

Mr. SPALDING. I do not want to hear the question; I do not consent to be interrupted for any purpose.

There are now in this institution more than one hundred deaf-mutes, collected from different states of the Union and there are thirty-five pupils in the collegiate department of the institution. I have seen somewhere a statement showing the different states from which they come.

And let me say here that there are young men in this collegiate department, deaf-mutes, who would put to shame the most astute and learned man found here. I would not be ashamed of them if put in competition with any man in the Senate or in the House—these poor deaf-mutes, some of whom have been instructed in this institution for only twelve months in the higher branches of philosophy and mathematics. I have seen the experiment tried, and I know it to be so. There are thirty-five of these pupils from the different states in the collegiate department of this institution as follows: from Maine, two; New Hampshire, one; Massachusetts, one; Connecticut, two; Vermont, one; New York, two; Pennsylvania, six; Maryland, two; Ohio, two; Michigan, four; Illinois, one; Wisconsin, four; Iowa, two; District of Columbia, two; and from England, one.

There are about seventy in the other branches, the primary department of the institution.

Some of these, perhaps thirty of them, are those contemplated by the first law enacted upon this subject; deaf and dumb children of the officers in the Army and Navy. In addition to those, there are deaf-mutes from Maryland who actually pay for their board in the institution. But I must be concise. The gentleman from Illinois (Mr. WASHBURNE) says the expenses of this institution amount to over seven thousand dollars each for all the boys and girls that the Government is bound to take care of in this institution. Now, will the House believe me when I tell them that in order to make out his candid argument my friend from Illinois has charged over to these deaf and dumb pupils all the expenses of the institution? He takes into account all the expenses of the land, the buildings, apparatus, and everything in connection with the institution for all time past and all time to come; he charges it all over, and divides the round sum by the number of pupils the government has to take care of.

Mr. WASHBURNE. Is not that fair?

Mr. SPALDING. Will any man say that it is fair? Suppose the gentleman charges all this over to the first five or ten pupils that entered the institution, how much would it cost them? There was laid a while ago on the table of each member a statement showing the whole amount of the appropriations to this institution. For all purposes there has been appropriated the sum of $321,824.52 during the past eleven years. Of that sum thus have been appropriated for the current expenses of the institution $104,401.50; leaving a balance expended for grounds, buildings, furniture and fixture $217,383. That property is all visible, is all tangible here. It is estimated that that very property is worth at this time at least $270,000.

Mr. WASHBURNE. Whose is it?

Mr. SPALDING. There again is a specimen of the gentleman's fairness. He came in here with the report of a minority committee. There were in fact but three members of the committee who objected to this appropriation. One of them, the gentleman from Maine (Mr. BLAINE) signs the report with the express reservation that he does not object to the appropriation provided the property be put under the control of Congress. Now, sir, this bill is specially framed for the very purpose of obviating the gentleman's objections, and he knows it. It was drawn up by a majority of the committee; and by the majority I was authorized to report it and advocate its passage as obviating those objections. The bill by its terms appropriates $3,000 which has been called for by the Secretary of the Interior as a deficiency, to pay for the increasing expense of maintaining nine or ten pupils from the different states who were admitted into the institution under the law of March 2, 1867. That amount is due as everyone admits. The institution has now one large building completed, and there is a central building which has been carried up one story and a half; but is going to decay for the want of this appropriation. By this bill, we propose to appropriate $48,000 for completing that building, so that it may furnish accommodations for the poor youth for whose benefit the institution is designed. Those are the two items of appropriations contained in the bill: $3,000 for a deficiency which, as the Secretary of Interior states, is justly due; and $48,000 for the purpose of carrying on to completion the building, the foundation of which has been laid and which has already been carried to the height of a story and a half.

The gentleman from Illinois has complained that Congress has no control over the management of this institution.

Now, sir, the directors have passed a resolution unanimously agreeing that Congress may, if it sees fit, provide for choosing three or more directors, to be members of the board, and to have a voice in the management of all the affairs of the institution. In accordance with that proposition, the second section provides:

That, in addition to the directors whose appointment has heretofore been provided for by law, there shall be three other directors appointed in the following manner: one Senator, by the President of the Senate, and two Representatives, by the Speaker of the House—these directors to hold their offices for the term of a single Congress, and to be eligible to a reappointment.

The third section meets the objection which has been raised that these donations, made by Congress may be wasted. It provides:

That no part of the real or personal property now held or hereafter to be acquired by the said institution shall be devoted to any other purpose than the education of the deaf and dumb, nor shall any part of the real estate be aliened, sold, or conveyed, except under the authority of a special act of Congress.

The board of directors have unanimously accepted these provisions, and they agree to the repeal of the provision contained in the act of incorporation providing for the payment of $150 per annum for the maintenance and tuition of each pupil admitted by order of the Secretary of the Interior. They have not taken this money for several years. They say they are not entitled to it because Congress has given them a gross sum to assist in carrying on the institution. Accordingly the fourth section makes the following provision:

That so much of the act of February 16, 1857, as allows the payment of $150 per annum for the maintenance and tuition of each pupil, admitted by order of the Secretary of the Interior, be and the same is hereby repealed.

Now, sir, I have here an exhibit showing what has been the annual expense for the pupils chargeable to the Government, and none others, during the eleven years past. The annual expenses range from $209 to $521 but the average is $294 for each pupil, for whom Congress was bound to provide. The greater part of the outlay upon which the gentleman from Illinois has dwelt so long and loudly is for the purchase of the land, the erection of buildings necessary for the accommodation of the pupils, the introduction of water, gas, and other necessary expenses.

Now, sir, although Congress has by its uniform action since 1857 recognized this institution as eminently worthy of the fostering care of the General Government and has contributed most bountifully to its support, the objection suggests itself that perhaps under a strict construction of the Constitution we ought not to appropriate money for such a purpose. But I ask where throughout our wide empire will you find any objects of charity which have been so little cared for by the Government of the United States as these stricken people, the deaf and dumb of our country.

We have provided for the insane. We have erected an institution for that purpose across the river where some three or four hundred lunatics are cared for. No one says anything against these appropriations. The gentleman says that the states will take care of these matters for themselves. To the honor of the different states, they have provided for them in a most handsome manner, and provided for them in a different spirit from that manifested upon this floor today.

Be it remembered, however, that no one state has enough deaf-mutes of its own to erect a college to educate teachers for them. It is expected that this should be done by the Federal Government, by an appropriation from the Federal Congress. Here, now, by a small outlay we can bless thousands and the nation never feel any loss. Our constituents will not feel it.

It is easy to talk about taking tax from the tax-payers and about the poor man's [p]light; taking the tax off petroleum and thereby enriching a few capitalists; but when you come to the great want of educating these deaf-mutes, every difficulty is raised. Shall we close the doors of this charitable, humane, hospitable institution, and turn these mutes out upon the world? Shall we deny them bread? Shall we deny them food for their intellects, which they crave more than bread for the body? I hope not.

I do not desire to detain the House in this warm weather. I did not want to speak. I ought not to have been required to speak in this behalf. I am only one member of the committee. It is true that I belong to the majority of the committee which recommends the passage of this bill; and I do honestly recommend its passage with all the force and earnestness I can muster. If this House sees fit to vote it down, the responsibility rests with them, not with me.

An amendment was introduced by my friend from Pennsylvania (Mr. STEVENS) to increase the number of college pupils from ten to twenty-five. This is called for by a great number of the states, and the pupils are ready to enter. The president of the institution says [the increase] will cost $6,000.

The following letter is from one of those pupils:

Aurora, Ill., May 5, 1868

Dear Sir: I wish to apply for admission to the collegiate department of the institution under your charge. I am twenty-two years of age, and have been totally deaf since my twelfth year. I was at the Hartford School a short time, leaving there in 1862. Since then I have been in various printing offices in this state, in all capacities—boy of all work, compositor, foreman, and editor; and during the closing years of the Civil War was a correspondent of the Chicago Tribune.

I can lay no claim to "scholarship" as the term is usually received, have no acquaintance with any foreign language, except such phrases as a general and too desultory reader gathers.

I regret that I was not sooner aware of the advantages which you have placed within reach of myself and fellow unfortunates, because, at my age, I do not think it will be profitable for me to undertake either the study of the dead languages or the four-year course. As to the former (Latin first) I would be willing to accept your better judgement, and make all the preparations I can in my leisure moments between now and the opening day. I should much prefer to take up German rather than Latin, as I can turn the former to practical use; also algebra the first year, object drawing and such other studies as will be most apt to perfect me as a writer.

Being entirely dependent on my own exertions for support, I ask the aid granted by Congress in such cases. In case you decide to admit me, an early reply to that effect would greatly oblige me, for the reason mentioned above in speaking of studies.

Mr. John B. Hotchkiss was acquainted with me at Hartford, and I think, will be pleased to answer questions you may see fit to ask concerning me.

Yours most respectfully
Amos G. Draper

Mr. E. M. Gallaudet

Mr. Spalding's amendment was finally passed—ayes 60, noes 50. Mr. Washburne's amendment was lost on a yea and nay vote—63 to 68.

Some days later, on the 23rd of July 1868, the bill came before the House again, returned from the Senate with amendments. It was brought up by Judge Spalding as follows:

Mr. SPALDING of Ohio. I arise to submit a report from the Committee on Appropriations on the Senate amendments to House Bill No. 541 making appropriations for the services of the Columbia Institution for the Instruction for the Deaf and Dumb, and establishing additional regulations for the government of the institution.

Mr. WASHBURNE of Illinois. Let the amendments of the Senate be reported. The gentleman has promised to give me twenty minutes.

The Clerk read as follows:

Columbia Institution for the Deaf and Dumb.

For the support of the institution, including $1,000 for books and illustrative apparatus, $25,000. For the proper inclosure improvement and enlargement of the grounds of the institution, in accordance with plans heretofore submitted to Congress, $5,600.

Mr. WASHBURNE. As a member of the Committee on Appropriations, upon which you, Mr. Speaker, placed me, it became my duty to the House and to the country to examine into the matters connected with the institution for the deaf and dumb. In my report which was concurred in by three other members of the committee, making the minority four against five, I showed that we had appropriated $325,000 to this private corporation; and that this vast sum has been expended without any control or direction of the United States. What I maintained was that when we make appropriations for charities in the District—and I will not be behind any man in making such appropriations in proper amounts for deserving objects and under adequate restrictions—it is our duty to see that the expenditure of these appropriations is under proper control and direction of the government which appropriates them.

I showed that the party connected with this institution, who has had the disbursement of this vast sum of $325,000, has been given only one bond, which was given in 1862 for $3,000; that we have no control of that disbursement and have no proper knowledge of how it was made. I ask, gentlemen, whether this is the manner in which to vote away the money of our constituents to an institution of this kind? I acknowledge that it is our duty to take care of every deaf and dumb person belonging to the District of Columbia, unable to procure an education; but I am unwilling that we shall establish here a great eleemosynary institution for the benefit of all the states in the Union. We have no constitutional right to do it. I offered the other day my substitute for the bill, creating a commission to overlook and control the funds appropriated for charity here in the District. That provision would not affect the appropriations we have already made, but would establish a commission to have control and direction in regard to the expenditure of our appropriations, to exercise the power of visitation and investigation and to report to us at every session the manner in which the money has been disbursed. As matters now stand we go on making these appropriations year after year, putting the money into the hands, not of officers of the government, giving bond for their fidelity, but of the representatives of these various institutions, who use the money as they please. Look for one moment at the manner in which your money has been applied, and observe how your appropriations for this institution have grown up. In 1864 there were twenty-four pupils in this institution, and we appropriated $4,400. In 1865 there were thirty-five pupils, and we appropriated $7,500. In 1866 there were twenty-two pupils and we gave them $12,500. In 1867 there were twenty-five pupils and we appropriated $20,434. For 1868 I have no return of the number of pupils but believe it to be about the same; and in that year our appropriation jumped up to $25,000. Where does this money go? Who has control of it? Practically in this way: The superintendent of this institution takes this money and puts into his own pocket or into the hands of those whom he chooses to employ at whatever salary he may see fit.

As to the control of the Board of Directors of the institution, it amounts to nothing. Yet the House, when this bill was under consideration heretofore, refused to agree to the proposition for the appointment of a commission to superintend the expenditure of our appropriations for these purposes, to see that the money is justly and fairly used, to examine the accounts, and to report to Congress the particulars of the disbursements. And now, sir, the Senate have put this sum of $25,000 for expenses etc., for the coming year. I have submitted an amendment to reduce that amount to $12,500, an increase of $5,000 over the appropriation of the year before. I propose to give them this same amount of $12,500 for this year. It is to pay the teachers of this institution, and for the education of the twenty-two pupils whom we undertake to educate. I showed the House the other day that while it was our duty to educate these pupils, we could send them to the best institutions in the country and have them educated better than they are here, and do it for less than $7,000. I proposed an amendment, that was lost by only three votes, to the effect that if this institution was to be kept here and if we are to make still further appropriations, [they] shall not be more than I have indicated in my amendment.

Now there is another question for you to consider. Are you ready to make those appropriations for these private institutions, to build up their immense buildings, their colleges, and their out-buildings, to furnish them with everything, and at the same time to have no control over the property? I think the sum of $16,000 or $20,000 was the amount contributed by others, while Congress has appropriated $325,000.

And how much is it now proposed to pay for this institution out of people's money? In the bill we passed the other day there was $48,000 for putting up a building and $3,000 for some other purpose. The Senate propose to add to that $25,000 and $3,500 which makes nearly $80,000 that is proposed to be given to this institution when your constituents are already groaning under taxation; you propose to take it from their pockets and give it to this private institution.

After some further debating, Mr. Washburne's amendment was agreed to. The bill as amended by the House, cutting down the amount for current expense of the institution from $25,000 to $12,500 went back to the Senate. The Senate refused to concur with this amendment but put on the bill Mr. Washburne's provisions for a Commission of Charities and sent the bill back to the House, asking a Committee of Conference.

On the part of the Senate, Senators Morrill of Maine, Patterson of New Hampshire, and McDonald of Indiana were appointed, and Mr. Washburne, Judge Spalding, and Judge S. S. Marshall of Illinois on the part of the House.

As it is necessary to have the votes of two members from each House to carry a Conference Committee, our hopes were at once hung on the action of Judge Marshall. For Senators Morrill and Patterson were our friends in the Senate.

Judge Marshall was a Democrat, somewhat of the old school, so I went to him with a letter from Amos Kendall, which carried much weight. Mr. Kendall also called on him. I did my best to make him see how much of injustice was in Mr. Washburne's criticisms of the management of the institution, and although he was reticent with me, I felt a good degree of hope that he would act with Judge Spalding on the committee. The following day I learned from Judge Spalding that Judge Marshall had agreed to stand by a report that was, on the whole, very favorable to our side, but that Mr. Washburne was using every possible influence to lead him to change his position. Mr. Washburne had succeeded in keeping our current expense appropriation down to $12,500, but Judge Spalding had secured everything else including Mr. Stevens' amendment, providing for an increase of our collegiate U.S. beneficiaries from ten to twenty-five, and keeping out of the bill Mr. Washburne's absurd scheme constituting the Secretary of the Interior, the Chief Justice of the Supreme Court of the District of Columbia, the Surgeon General of the Army, the Chief of the Bureau of Medical Surgery of the Navy, and the Commissioner of Public Buildings and Grounds [as] a "Commission of Charities."

Coming into the gallery of the House the next day, Saturday July 25, when I expected the Conference report would be handed in by Judge Spalding, I presently observed him come into the House with a document in his hand, followed by Judge Marshall and Mr. Washburne. They all went to Judge Spalding's desk, where he put his name to the document. A colloquy then followed between the three men, and I could see that Mr. Washburne was appealing most earnestly to Judge Marshall not to sign the report.

Knowing that it was entirely possible he might yield to Mr. Washburne's entreaties at the last moment, it will be readily believed that my heart was in my mouth. As the consultation proceeded my constant prayer was: "Good Lord, give us Judge Marshall." And my relief and joy can be easily imagined when I saw Judge Marshall sit down, take pen in hand, and write his name below Judge Spalding's. The expression of Mr. Washburne's face as he rushed to his seat was one to be remembered. Shortly after, Judge Spalding presented the Conference Report to the House, and it was adopted without further debate. And so the long agony of months, during which the future existence of the college hung in the balance, was over.

The strain on my mind and heart and nerves had been terrible, for the matter was never out of my thoughts and I had been racking my brains every day and nearly every hour thinking what I could do to advance our cause, and then doing what I had thought of.

Early in the progress of the controversy, I made several efforts to induce Mr. Washburne to visit the college. I saw Mrs. Washburne and enlisted her sympathy, but she could not move him. Dr. Sunderland of our board saw him and urged him to visit the college. But Mr. Washburne told Dr. Sunderland that was just what he did not wish to do, for he knew if he came within the influence of the college and its work, he would be converted.

After Judge Spalding's triumph, Mr. Washburne spoke of me with bitterness to him, declaring that he would yet "get even with that d—d little Frenchman."

At the time of which I am now writing, the session of Congress was within two days of its close and had fixed Monday July 27th as the day of adjournment. On Sunday the 26th something impelled me to go to the Capitol and look after the enrollment of our bill. I went to the enrollment room and, on inquiring, was informed by the Chief Clerk that he had just detected and caused to be corrected a radical mistake in the enrollment of our bill. The *report of the Conference Committee had been reversed*, the important sections for the advantage of the institution had been omitted, and Mr. Washburne's provisions for the Commission of Charities had been inserted.

The Chief Clerk gave me the sheets of parchment on which the provisions were inscribed, and they lie before me as I write (October 26, 1898), showing the plans left at the foot of the signatures of the Speaker of the House and the President pro tempore of the Senate.

Had not this error (or crime can it have been?) been discovered just when it was, in a few hours Mr. Washburne's scheme for the destruction of our college would have been the law of the land.

Mr. Washburne's success at one point, the cutting down by one half of our current expense fund, did not give Judge Spalding or our other friends any concern, for they said that the provision increasing the number of our college beneficiaries from ten to twenty-five compelled the large appropriation and that it could easily be secured as a deficiency at the next Congress. How near this plan came to failure will appear in the narrative of the events for the year 1869.

As soon as Congress had adjourned I sought much needed rest, going to the pleasant home in Vermont of my earliest assistant in the institution, Mr. James Denison, already spoken of in this history. There I passed several restful, happy weeks, the culminating event of which was an engagement of marriage between myself and Mr. Denison's sister Susan, to whom I was married on the 22nd of December 1868.

The coming of my bride to Washington was attended with a change in the domestic arrangement of the institution, for at that time I gave up living in the buildings of the institution, which I had done for nearly twelve years, and set up my family altar in a commodious residence which had been erected on the location designated in Mr. Olmsted's plan for the "President's House."

In March 1868 my brother <u>William L. Gallaudet</u> was appointed to the office of family supervisor, this position having been created by the board in view of my expected removal to a residence outside the buildings of the institution. In June of that year Miss Sarah A. Bliss, who had succeeded to the position of matron the year before, retired on account of impaired health, and her place was taken by Miss Anna A. Pratt, a sister of our Professor Pratt.

William Lewis GALLAUDET, Brother of EMG
father of
Henry NELSON GALLAUDET
FATHER of
RALPH LAING GALLAUDET
FATHER of
ALICE F. GALLAUDET FROHWEIN DANSEI
(1st HUSBAND) (2ND HUSBAN
MOTHER of
PETER R. FROHWEIN
PAULA A. FROHWEIN GIESA
NANCY H. FROHWEIN SCHOONOVER

PETER'S CHILDREN
KRISTINA (BIOLOGICAL)
MELISSA (Step)
JONATHAN (Step)

NANCY'S CHILDREN
JEFFEREY MARK SCHOONOVER
DAVID CHRISTOPHER SCHOONOVER

Paula - no children

V

Opponents and Supporters
1868–1871

THIS YEAR WITNESSED the retirement, to the great regret of all connected with the institution, of Professor Pratt, who had served the
college ably for four years. He resigned his professorship with us to accept
one in Knox College, Illinois, whose president was his brother-in-law.
The vacancy thus created in the faculty was supplied by the appointment
to the tutorship of Mr. John B. Hotchkiss, who graduated from our college
in June 1869.

The year then ended was one of great prosperity in all the departments
of the institution, especially in the college, the number of students in that
department having increased to thirty-six and the buildings of the institution well advanced through liberal appropriations by Congress.

The notable public event was the graduation of our first regular class
from a full collegiate course of four years study. The commencement
exercises were held in the Congregational Church at eleven o'clock, a.m.,
Wednesday June 26. A full account of these exercises, as also the alumni
dinner which followed at the Kirkwood House, will be found in our
Twelfth Annual Report.

The most interested and interesting personage present was Hon. Amos
Kendall. Venerable and somewhat enfeebled by age, and yet full of life
and vivacity, he regarded the event as one of the great occasions of his
life. His address to the graduating class was eloquent and pathetic.

At the dinner I heard William W. Corcoran the great banker say, "I
would rather have the satisfaction Mr. Kendall may justly take at the
development of this institution, which owes so much to him, than to be
the hero of Waterloo."

15. The college's first graduating class in 1869: (left to right) James H. Logan, Joseph G. Parkinson, and John B. Hotchkiss.

The graduation of the first bachelors of arts in a college for the deaf-mutes, from what could justly be claimed to be a regular collegiate course of study, excited unusual interest in the educational world.

Among those present at the commencement exercises was Mr. Sidney Andrews, a correspondent of the *Boston Advertiser*, who wrote an appreciative and intelligent account of the work of the college which was published in the *Advertiser*.

Among the guests at the alumni dinner was Professor Henry of the Smithsonian Institution, who urged the propriety of the Federal Government's full support of the college. The reader will remember that Professor Henry sustained President Gallaudet five years before in his plan for the organization of the college, in opposition to the scheme of Mr. Kendall. The latter made no allusion to the fact that President Gallaudet's plan had been fully carried out.

During the short session of Congress of 1868–69, Mr. Washburne resumed his opposition to our college, and this time his tactics were much more wary than before.

By means of which there are no records available, he secured the concurrence of the Committee on Appropriations to a paragraph which appropriated $15,000 for the care and education of the deaf and dumb of the District of Columbia in some state institution, under the direction of the Secretary of the Interior. No appropriations whatever were made in the Sundry Civil Appropriation Bill or in any other bill reported to the House for the Columbia Institution for the Deaf and Dumb. It was Mr. Washburne's intention and hope to actually break down our institution by this legislation.

Judge Spalding, who had been appointed, under the act of July 27, 1868, a director of the institution, secured in the House a modification of Mr. Washburne's paragraph so that the Secretary of the Interior, if he saw fit, might expend the $15,000 allowed for the deaf and dumb of the District for their care and education in the Columbia Institution. How important this modification was, will soon appear.

Judge Spalding felt that it was not best to resume an open controversy in the House over the institution. Senator Patterson had been appointed a director of the institution and was thus in a position, so Judge Spalding thought, to secure without difficulty all needed amendments to the bill in the Senate, which he [Spalding] thought he could successfully sustain in the Conference Committee, of which he was sure to be a member.

The Senate Committee was very late in its consideration of the Sundry Civil Bill, and as the end of the session was near it was rushed through rapidly. Senator Patterson had agreed to secure the substitution for Mr. Washburne's paragraph of (1) a deficiency of $17,500 to make up for the cut of last year's appropriation to $12,000, and (2) an appropriation of $30,000 for the year ending June 30, 1870. Senator Patterson was deeply interested in our college. He was one of the speakers at its inauguration in 1864—was himself, as is well-known, a college professor—and I have never for a moment doubted the loyalty of his friendship for the institution. But the fact remains, to illustrate how men will sometimes forget things in which they have an earnest interest, that in the rush of business he forgot even to ask the committee to make the desired changes in our behalf.

My dismay can easily be imagined when I found, on inquiry on the evening of March 3rd, that Mr. Washburne's paragraph remained in the

Sundry Civil Bill as it was reported back to the Senate at a night session when the passage of the bill was expected in a few hours. Senator Patterson, in giving me the information over which he was greatly chagrined and mortified, said he felt sure that the chairman of the committee, Senator Morrill of Maine, could easily have the whole matter put right in the Senate. He advised me to see Senator Morrill at once and said he would do everything he could to aid him.

Now Senator Morrill had for several years shown himself a very warm friend of the college, and as my personal acquaintance with him had been quite intimate, I had no doubt of his cooperation. I sent in my card to him, and he soon came out, looking haggard and nervous from the strain under which men in his position are always placed during the closing hours of a session of Congress.

I explained the situation to him [Senator Morrill] in as few words as possible and asked that he would do what Senator Patterson had suggested but did not mention his [Patterson's] name. Senator Morrill said at once, "It is too late to do anything; the bill is too near its final passage; the rules of the Senate will not allow anything to be done in the way you propose." I urged that a friend in the Senate had told me that if Senator Morrill would ask what we wanted, as chairman of the Appropriation Committee, it would undoubtedly go through.

This angered Senator Morrill extremely and he burst out with severity, "I think I know the rules of the Senate as well as any one, and I tell you it can't be done. It is too late." And he hurried away into the Senate.

My feelings were wrought up to that extent that I went away with tears in my eyes. I sought a corner of the corridor in which I might get myself together and offer a prayer for Divine guidance.

I think I am right in saying that many, if not most, men would have felt it to be useless to try anything further at the session of Congress then in progress. *But my spirit would not give up.*

In a few minutes I went into the room of the Secretary of the Senate, asked for a sheet of paper, and wrote a note to Senator Morrill, expressing regret if I had showed too great persistence and saying that in view of the serious misfortune impending over the institution, I hoped he would take advantage of any possible suspension of the rules of the Senate to secure the replacement of Mr. Washburne's paragraph by those needed for the proper support of the institution.

I then informed Senator Patterson and Judge Spalding of what had taken place. They were disposed to think the chance was small of the success of my scheme. I went into the Senate Gallery to await results, the hour being about ten.

About half past eleven I saw Judge Spalding enter the Senate Chamber and have a short conversation with Senator Patterson. He then retired to one of the sofas.

The hands of the clock were nearly at the midnight hour when the clerk completed the reading of the Sundry Civil Bill, and it was about to be put on its passage when Senator Morrill arose—half of the Senators being asleep—and addressed the Chair in a voice I could scarely hear.

The following record is from the *Congressional Globe*.

Mr. MORRILL of Maine. I have another amendment, which I ask the unanimous consent of the Senate after making the statement, to present. (This was the deficiency of $17,500.) I will state the facts. This is what purports to be a deficiency strictly for the support of beneficiaries whom by law we are bound to support at that institution; and it is not provided for in any of the bills that I have noticed. I hope I shall have the unanimous consent of the Senate to offer it.

The amendment was agreed to.

Mr. MORRILL. I have another amendment which I desire to offer.

(This was the $30,000 for current expenses.)

I desire to say only a word in regard to this institution for the deaf and dumb. The government has uniformly appropriated this sum of money for the support of this institution since I have been in the Senate; and this is the first time there has been a failure to do so. This appropriation should more properly have been on the legislative and executive appropriation bill, but it is not there. It was referred to the Committee on Appropriations informally but was not passed upon by the committee. I submit it, therefore, to the judgement of the Senate whether they will make the usual appropriation for the next year.

The amendment was agreed to.

Judge Spalding was on his feet, a wide-awake listener, as soon as Senator Morrill began to speak of our institution. Now it is the custom in the Senate for Senators often to make no reply when the presiding officer calls for a vote. When the question was put on the adoption of

Senator Morrill's first amendment, I was surprised—and especially so because of the general atmosphere of sleepiness that was prevailing—to hear a loud "aye." But I soon realized that the voice was that of Judge Spalding who, in the intensity of his interest, had forgotten he was not in the House.

The amendments for our institution were the last added to the Sundry Civil Appropriation Bill, and a few minutes later it was passed by the Senate. This was midnight, March 3rd. This great bill went at once to the Conference Committee, who had to be up all the rest of the night so that the bill could be reported to both houses by eleven o'clock the following morning, for it had to have the signature of the President before the final adjournment of Congress which was at noon, March 4th.

I need not say that I footed it home to Kendall Green that night in a grateful, happy frame of mind.

As Judge Spalding predicted, he was able to hold the Senate amendments in the Conference Committee, so the interests of the college were once more saved at a most critical period.

But the story of Mr. Washburne's last campaign against our institution is not yet complete. For that occurred, which illustrates how it sometimes happens that "God causes the wrath of man to praise Him."

In the rushing through of the Sundry Civil Bill, no one, not even Mr. Washburne himself, thought of the paragraph for $15,000, which *he* expected would be all the legislation in regard to the deaf and dumb in the Sundry Civil Bill. *So it remained in the bill, and became law.* And the Secretary of the Interior caused the amount to be carried to the credit of our institution without ever raising a question, so far as I know.

It happened one day that I learned at the department that we had credit for $45,000, where I expected only $30,000. It was given to me to be discretely silent.

Now it was true at that time owing to the great fluctuation in prices, incident to the monetary disturbances growing out of the Civil War, that deficiencies, not large in any one year, had accumulated until we were in arrears in meeting the current obligations of the institution to the amount of nearly $9,000. My purpose of asking Congress to provide these deficiencies had been pushed aside by Mr. Washburne's persistent antagonism. And lo! Here, by Mr. Washburne's own act, coupled with his carelessness at the end of the session, the means were at hand to meet our deficiencies.

Whether I did wrong to use this $15,000 as I did, I leave others to determine. But after giving the whole subject the most careful thought, with prayer for Divine guidance, I determined to say nothing of this unexpected windfall to anyone, not even to members of our board, lest they should think I ought not to draw the money.

At the proper time I drew the money, applied it as far as necessary to the payment of the debts of the institution, and reported a balance at the end of the year of $4,895.83—as appears in our Thirteenth [Annual] Report.

I have always been convinced that an overruling Providence intended that this great good should come as a little compensation for all the worry and work attending our prolonged struggle with Mr. Washburne. And I need not say that the action of President Grant, in sending Mr. Washburne to that glorious city to which all good Americans like to go, met with the hearty approval of the friends of our college.*

Before closing the records of events of the year 1868–69, I wish to record a pleasing incident of Mr. Kendall.

In January 1869, three days were indicated on the cards announcing my marriage when my wife and I would be "at home" to meet our friends.

On the first of the three days I remembered that my wife awaited the coming of her new friends, who would be strangers to her, with much trepidation as was natural to a young lady reared in the quiet of a New England village. We were standing in our parlor, I reassuring her as far as I could, when the front doorbell rang with the first caller.

Presently Mr. Kendall entered, his face beaming with cordial smiles. He was the first to welcome my bride to her circle of Washington friends, and his fatherly, affectionate manner put my wife at once at her ease. The fact that *he* should have been the first to cross our threshold with words of welcome has always been a precious memory to my wife and me.

One other event ought perhaps to be recorded here. In July 1869 I took Mrs. Gallaudet to Europe for our wedding journey, leaving all thought of appropriations, Congress, school, college, etc., far behind. I was grateful to have this means of regaining my strength of nerve and body, which, as the sequel will show, I very much needed for the work of the three years that were to follow.

---

*On March 17, 1869, President Grant appointed Washburne as minister to France, a position he held until the autumn of 1877.

1869–1870

The year 1869–70 opened auspiciously for school and college. Buildings progressed, numbers increased, and all was encouraging when it became evident early in October that our beloved and honored friend, Amos Kendall, the founder of the institution and one of its wisest and most faithful supporters, was nearing the end of his earthly pilgrimage.

Two meetings of the board were held in the autumn of 1869, neither of which Mr. Kendall was able to attend. The last meeting at which he was present was held on June 21st. It was at this meeting the degree of bachelor of arts was first voted by the board to the three members of the class about to graduate—Messrs. J. Barton Hotchkiss of Connecticut, James H. Logan of Pennsylvania, and Joseph G. Parkinson of New Hampshire.

Mr. Kendall's last official act as a director was to vote in favor of conferring the honorary degree of master of arts on James Denison of our primary department, Richard Elliott, headmaster of the London Institute for the Deaf and Dumb, and J. Scott Hutton, principal of the School for the Deaf and Dumb at Halifax, Nova Scotia.

The close of October found Mr. Kendall confined to the house and much of the time to his bed. No especial malady seemed to be upon him, but a general failure of the powers of his body became evident. His mind remained clear, and his spirits showed no depression at the prospect of being soon called to leave the earth.

Early in November I visited my old friend and was admitted to his chamber. I shall never forget the saintly, almost angelic, appearance he presented as he lay, white haired, with a face like marble, propped up by pillows. His clear blue eyes shone with the luster of young manhood; his smile as he greeted me was full of sweetness.

We chatted on a variety of subjects, and then naturally he began to speak of the institution. He expressed the greatest satisfaction that he had been permitted to live to see the establishment of the college assured and spoke of the struggle I had had to go through with, expressing the hope that nothing so severe in the future would come to me.

He was kind enough to say that he had entire confidence that the future of the institution was safe so long as I remained at the head of it. At this point in our conversation I was strongly moved to ask him to tell me how it came about that he never brought up for action the regulations he presented to the board in December 1864, but feeling that such an inquiry might disturb him, I concluded to say nothing. So I have remained in entire ignorance to this day (October 1898) how Mr. Kendall was led to abandon the position he took so earnestly before the board against my plans for the organization of the college and to allow me to carry them out to the fullest detail.

Mr. Kendall bade me an affectionate good-bye and I went out from his presence heavy hearted, feeling that I had heard for the last time on earth the voice of one who had been as a father to me, and I did not see him again alive.

My memory of Amos Kendall is one of peculiar tenderness. That he should give me the confidence he had when I came to Washington a youth of twenty was a great surprise. The internal management of the institution could not have been committed more absolutely to me than it was. I was invited to be present at every meeting of the board, was always made secretary pro tempore when Mr. Stickney was absent, and was treated in all respects as though I were a member of the board until, at Mr. Kendall's suggestion, I was elected to the presidency in 1864.

No difference of opinion ever arose between Mr. Kendall and myself except the one already alluded to and one in regard to the wording of the college diplomas.

Following the example of the oldest American colleges I proposed that our diplomas be in Latin, and the board at a meeting from which Mr. Kendall was absent approved my suggestion. Hearing of this action, Mr. Kendall called a special meeting of the board and presented a long and carefully prepared argument in favor of the use of the English language in our diplomas. Having taken pains in the meantime to acquaint myself with the practice of a number of colleges in this matter, and having found that English was used quite as much as Latin, I made no opposition to Mr. Kendall's proposal, and it was adopted by the board. One member of the board was very earnest on the other side and warned the directors that he might bring up the subject in the future and ask for different action. This, however, he never did. Mr. Kendall's lengthy argument on this subject can be found in the records of the board of June 1864.

Mr. Kendall was in favor of that system of management in a public institution which is sometimes called the "one man power system." To my surprise he had authority given me to employ and discharge all of my assistants and subordinates without any action of the board. This seemed to me to give more power than I wished to have. But on two occasions I found it extremely fortunate to have such power in my hands.

The cases alluded to involved matters of a delicate nature, in which immediate action was desirable and in regard to which it was best that as few persons as possible should know of the causes of the dismissals. I remember that in the most serious case, the party concerned demanded that he should be heard by the board and asked if it were possible that I had the power to dismiss without consulting the board. On being informed that I had, his bluster ceased, and in a few hours his resignation was in my hands accepted.

Following Hon. E. B. Washburne's retirement from Congress and from the chairmanshhip of the Committee on Appropriations, two events concerning the same man occurred of the greatest importance and advantage to the college.

Hon. Henry L. Dawes of Massachusetts was appointed chairman of the Committee on Appropriations and was at the time named by the Speaker as one of the members of the Board of Directors.

Mr. Washburne, as I was informed by Mr. Dawes himself, wrote his successor from Paris a long letter full of suggestions as to the business of the Appropriations Committee, and among these was a strong appeal to Mr. Dawes to "wipe the deaf-mute college out of existence." But the heart of the Massachusetts statesman was too philanthropic and the head too level to accept the narrow and prejudiced policy of the Illinois politician.

Far from this, having given me an opportunity to explain fully the need for a college for the deaf in our country and its possibilities for doing good, Mr. Dawes became its warm friend and earnest supporter in Congress. At the first session of Congress after assuming the management of appropriations in the House, he secured for the institution, in addition to an appropriation for current expenses, $10,000 larger than ever before, an appropriation of over $100,000 for the completion of the main central building.

During the early part of 1870, the executors of the estate of Mr. Kendall offered for sale, in small parcels, eighty-one acres of ground adjoining the premises of the institution on the north and east. This suggested to me the desirability of the purchase of the entire tract for the institution, to accomplish the double purpose of securing grounds of ample size for all time, and to protect our then existing domain of about nineteen acres from the incoming of undesirable neighbors.

The scheme was viewed by some whom I consulted as a very bold one for we had no considerable sum of money in our treasury, and our recent demands on Congress for buildings had been heavy. But my friend President Samson of Columbian University was strongly in favor of the purchase. Hon. Jacob D. Cox gave me similar advice.

I well remember a bright sunny morning in February 1870 when I brought General Cox to Kendall Green and took him to a point at the edge of the woods from which he had a commanding view of nearly the whole estate. He became enthusiastic at once for the purchase and said I must not hesitate, but trust to providence for the means to pay for the property.

General Cox's warm support of my own wish decided me to do all I could to bring about the acquisition of the whole of Kendall Green, and I brought the matter to the attention of the board as soon as possible. It is only deserved praise of our directors to say that they were not slow in deciding to adopt a liberal policy. With only $5,000 in hand they voted to buy Kendall Green for $85,000.

The negotiations were concluded towards the end of March, and it was agreed that the property should be transferred on the first day of April, on which date it would be necessary for me to sign, as president, notes for $80,000 with mortgage to secure the same. But the morning of that day found me anxiously awaiting the birth of a child, and before afternoon my son Denison came into the world. So the date of all the papers in connection with the transfer had to be changed, which was very easily done, from the first to the second.

1870–1871

The autumn of 1870 brought us a new departure in the addition to our corps of instructors, a professor of articulation in the person of Rev. J. W. Chickering of New Hampshire. He taught both in college and in school and did much to arouse an interest in the acquisition of speech by our students and pupils.

During the last months of 1870, the completion of our main central building was effected, and on the 29th of January it was dedicated with appropriate ceremonies which were presided over by President Grant in his office as Patron of the institution.

A full account of these experiences will be found in our Fourteenth Annual Report. I remember that Senator Buckingham of Connecticut, who was present, asked me at the close of the proceedings why a certain good looking young man recited the thirty-fifth chapter of Isaiah—which he did orally. I replied that he was one of our students. The Senator was amazed, it never having occurred to him that the young man might be deaf. "Why," said he, "few Episcopal clergymen could have read that chapter as well as your young student gave it!"

In August 1870 the management of the institution met with a heavy loss in the death of Hon. Benjamin B. French, who had been a member of the board for several years. My sense of personal affliction was great for the relations of our two families had become very intimate, and Major French's character and disposition were so admirable and lovable as to bind to him closely all whom he favored with his friendship. His interest in the college was most lively, and he gave to it not only his time at the council board but his money to aid poor students.

In December 1870 another of our directors passed away, Mr. David A. Hall, an original member of the board and one who had shown a most lively interest in the development of the college, giving of his money as well as of his time. The personal relations between his family and mine were, as in the case of Major French, of the most cordial sort. His death was a real personal loss.

In the winter of 1870–71 I made an effort to secure about $20,000 from Congress to help us pay for Kendall Green, and I succeeded in getting the amount put in the Sundry Civil Bill in the Senate and in getting its approval by the Committee of Conference.

Then greatly to my surprise, Mr. Dawes, who was chairman of the House Committee on Appropriations and still a member of our board, had the bill recalled from the Senate and the item stricken out. I have never been able to explain why he did this, for I had consulted him as a director in regard to the purchase of Kendall Green and understood him to be favorable to the scheme. His attitude was a great disappointment to me, and early in 1871 I decided to make an effort to raise some money by private subscription. I enlisted President Grant's interest and obtained a letter from him commending the college to his friends. With this I went to Philadelphia, taking Mr. Draper, then a junior in college, with me. President Grant's letter secured me cheerful subscriptions of $250 from Hon. A. E. Bone and A. J. Drexel and a like amount from several others.

Mr. Jas. L. Claghorn, whom I had traveled with in Europe in 1867, gave a dinner for me at the Union League Club at which Joseph Harrison and other prominent men were present. Mr. Draper made an excellent impression at this dinner, and I rolled up the subscription list pretty rapidly. One day, however, I had many refusals and started out the next morning a good deal discouraged. My first call was Mr. Clement Biddle who received me rather coldly. I stated my cause as well as I could, and he turned to his checkbook with a pretty severe look on his face. "How much did you say you wanted?" he called out over his shoulder. Mustering up all my courage I replied, "I am trying to get ten subscriptions of $250 each, but of course I cannot dictate the amount." "Hm," was his reply as he scratched away in his checkbook. My surprise may be imagined when he handed me a check for $250, with a grim smile on a very old and wrinkled face. I thanked him most warmly and said his generosity was a great encouragement for I had had many refusals the day before.

He responded with a most genial smile and a good-bye pressure of his hand saying, "Keep on young man. Do not be discouraged; they won't *all* say no."

I secured a good sum in Philadelphia and later went to Hartford and Boston, having Mr. Hill, also a junior in college, with me some of the time, and in these three places I raised nearly $10,000 with which we were able to pay our maturing obligations on the Kendall Green purchase.

In the winter of 1870–71 I had occasion to confer with Hon. Jas. G. Blaine, then Speaker of the House, in regard to the appointment of our two directors from the House. The first appointment of such directors was made in 1868 by Speaker Colfax who named two Republicans, Hon. H. L. Dawes of Massachusetts and Hon. N. Boyden of North Carolina. Following this precedent Mr. Blaine's first appointment in 1869 was of Mr. Dawes and Hon. William H. Kelsey of New York, the latter being of the same party as Mr. Dawes.

It will be remembered that at this period the number of Democratic members of the House was very small. But it seemed to me undesirable that the policy of appointing both our House directors from one party should continue. So in my talk with Mr. Blaine I brought out this idea and suggested that as Mr. Kelsey was to be no longer in the House, his place be filled by a Democrat. Mr. Blaine winked one eye at me and looked quite amused. "Why," said he, "you are looking ahead, aren't you? But you are right," he added at once, "and I will do it." Within a few days he reappointed Mr. Dawes and named Hon. James Brooks of New York as the other director. All succeeding Speakers, Democrats and Republicans without exception, have given us directors from the two great parties, so avoiding all occasion for a charge of partisan management in the institution.

VI

Erection of the College Buildings
1871–1877

IN THE AUTUMN OF 1871 we submitted, with our ordinary estimates to Congress, one of $70,000 to enable the institution to pay off its obligations on account of the purchase of Kendall Green.

The situation with reference to this important matter gave me great anxiety. I did not feel encouraged to think that large sum could be raised by private subscription, and although General Garfield, a warm friend of the college was now chairman of the Committee on Appropriations, Mr. Dawes was known to be opposed to getting Congress to pay for Kendall Green. I consulted with General Garfield and found him friendly to the measure but disposed to have me get the appropriation put on in the Senate, promising to do what he could to save it in Conference Committee.

Senator Edmunds of Vermont, who was on the Senate Appropriations Committee at this time, had become quite warmly interested in the college, partly through his and Mrs. Edmunds' friendship for my wife (who was from Vermont) and partly because one of his boyish playmates, with whom he had come to communicate freely by means of the manual alphabet, was a deaf son of the late Senator Phelps of Vermont. So good was Senator Edmunds' command of this [the manual alphabet] that on one occasion when asked to address our students, he surprised us all by spelling on his fingers with ease and clearness.

Senator Edmunds promised to do his best to get his committee to put the $70,000 in the Sundry Civil Bill when it came before them and showed great interest in the measure.

Now I ought to state, at this point, that during the early part of 1872 my health gave way in quite an alarming manner. The pressure and strain of fighting Mr. Washburne, planning and superintending the erection of buildings, and the burden of the Kendall Green purchase, added to the heavy executive duties of my position and my work as a professor, were proving too much for the physical and nervous endurance of a young man of from thirty to thirty-five years. A great sense of fatigue came upon me. I would waken nearly every morning at about three o'clock, and my brain would start actively at work on the duties that were before me.

My good Dr. Lincoln examined quite carefully into my condition and said that while he thought he could keep me at work until the end of our term in June, I must then have a prolonged season of rest—a year at least—or face the speedy coming of death or softening of the brain. An examination of my urine disclosed the fact that I was losing what was absolutely necessary for the proper nourishment of my brain and nerve tissues. So the doctor gave me phosphorous and other strong tonics, and I struggled on, sometimes hardly knowing what I did from day to day.

The Board of Directors, always most considerate of my welfare, promptly voted me a year's leave of absence, with my salary continued, and $1,500 additional to help meet the expenses of my family and myself in Europe, whither the doctor advised me to go.

It was in the condition of nervous prostration just described that I had to make an almost dying effort to secure the means of saving Kendall Green from going back to Mr. Kendall's heirs.

Relying greatly on Senator Edmunds' promise to get the $70,000 through the Senate, it will be understood that I was greatly disturbed to receive, on the morning of the very day early in June that Senator Edmunds expected to bring our matter before his committee, a note by a mounted messenger from Mrs. Edmunds, saying her husband was too ill to leave his bed and advising me to go to the committee room and do the best I could with this assurance of his interest in the measure. I confess my heart sank within me, but I lost no time in reaching the Senate committee room.

I was fortunate at that time in knowing quite well Senator Cole of California, chairman of the committee, and Senators Conkling, Windom, and Sprague, prominent members of the committee. I had also a very good friend in Mr. Pickard, the clerk of the committee, a quiet but very clear-headed man from Maine who had been clerk for many years.

When I reached the committee room soon after nine o'clock, Mr. Pickard was alone. I stated the situation to him, and he disheartened me greatly at first by saying that there would be no formal meeting of the committee that day and the bill was practically completed and would be reported to the Senate in the afternoon.

I made it clear to Mr. Pickard how much interested Senator Edmunds was in the measure, showing him Mrs. Edmunds' note, and added that General Garfield had promised his support if the Senate put the amount in the bill.

After a little quiet thinking, Mr. Pickard said in a slow drawl, "Waal, I'll put the item in, and they can strike it out if they wanter." So I left the committee room with no very sanguine hope of success. Later in the forenoon I saw Mr. Cole, the chairman, and found him disposed to let the item stay.

The session was so near its close that all were very busy, and I was not able to see either Conkling, Windom, or Sprague.

In the afternoon when I knew the bill had been just reported to the Senate, I went to Mr. Pickard for news. With quite a grin on his face his prompt first words were, "Waal! It staid. It was this way," he added. "Conkling looked over the bill, and when he came to your item he said, 'Is this for Gallaudet?' 'Yes,' said I, 'and Edmunds wants it'. 'Hm,' said Conkling. And it was the same way with Windom and Sprague, and so it staid in. I guess you will get it."

Senator Edmunds recovered in time to give his countenance and support to the measure when it was reached in the Senate, and it passed without opposition.

Having the promise of General Garfield's favor in the House, he being chairman of the Appropriations Committee, I flattered myself I had little more to do when I was staggered by Garfield's declaration that in order to carry the committee for the $70,000, he must have the clear and definite approval of our directors from the House, Messrs. Dawes and Brooks.

The reader will remember that Mr. Dawes had taken ground against this appropriation and will understand that I felt more than a little disturbed at this turn of affairs.

After much reflection I wrote to Mr. Dawes, showing him how it was in his power to secure the $70,000 for us or prevent our getting it and appealing for his support. This letter I placed in the hands of his daughter, Miss Anna, who was a very good friend of both Mrs. Gallaudet and myself, and who I felt very sure often exerted great influence with her father. I told her I depended on her bringing her father around from his position of opposition. She did not disappoint me, for within a day or two I learned from General Garfield that Messrs. Dawes and Brooks had given their approval to the measure and that the committee had agreed to it. A few days later the Sundry Civil [Bill] with the $70,000 in passed the House, and my anxiety was at an end.

I closed up the business of the term with a thankful heart, drew the $70,000 from the treasury, paid off the mortgage on Kendall Green, and put all my private affairs in such shape as would make a settlement of my estate easy if I never returned home. I sailed early in July for Europe, accompanied by my wife and family, two nieces, a nephew, a maid-servant for the little boys, and Mr. Draper, who had just graduated from our college.

During my year abroad a kind providence brought back to me a full measure of health and strength. I did some valuable studying in international law, making a complete translation of Calvo's Treatise on the subject, two volumes, octavo, into English from the French.

I think that, perhaps, an incident connected with my restoration to health may not be out of place in this narrative.

After a little sojourn in London, I took my family via Brussels, Cologne, and the Rhine to Switzerland, locating at Geneva in a pension near the lake.

I made a short tour with Mr. Draper through the Italian Lakes, to Munich, Ulm, and finally to Paris, from which place I was called back to Geneva by the very serious illness of our baby boy Edson, then only sixteen months old. Through the kindness of providence and the skill of an English physician, the child recovered from his attack of double pneumonia. As soon as he could be moved, we located in a charming old chateau five miles out of Geneva, owned by a family named Du Rouray, an old Geneva family whose impaired fortune made it necessary for them to turn their home into a pension.

We found here a lovely and salubrious home from which I could take walks, drives, and oar exercise on the lake. We came to this place early in September, and I began to feel a degree of improvement in my health as the weeks went on, but November found me still conscious of lassitude and a lack of vitality that was far from natural. One day, I think about the 20th of November, I was walking out from Geneva and had reached a point where the road leaves the lake shore and mounts a hill to enter the village of Vezenaz. Suddenly something seemed to give way in my body, I could not tell where, and a definite nervous thrill passed through my whole nervous system. I felt at once like running, dancing, and singing.

I hurried to the chateau at a rapid pace, found my wife, and asked her to take note of the date. "For," said I, "from this day I am well." And in the days immediately following I was conscious of an abounding health and vigor which made me feel like a youth of twenty. This state of health continued all through the remaining months of my stay in Europe so that, as I have already remarked, I came home in September 1873, completely restored to my most vigorous state.

1872–1873

During the period of my absence in Europe the affairs of the institution progressed successfully under the acting presidency of Professor Fay. He was cordially and effectively sustained by all the subordinate officers, and only once did an emergency arise where Professor Fay asked me in a letter to cable my advice on a certain point.

I remember that I received his letter just as I was starting for Geneva on a Sabbath morning to attend church, and I sent the cablegram on arriving in Geneva. Later I learned from Professor Fay that he received the dispatch just as he was starting for church from Kendall Green.

During this year the number of students increased, and the college grew in favor everywhere.

1873–1874

During this year several events of interest occurred that are worthy of record. When I was in Europe in 1869, I made a second visit to Doncaster to see my valued friend Dr. Charles Baker, the headmaster of the school for the deaf in that place. Dr. Baker had a rare and valuable library of works relating to the education of the deaf, comprising over six hundred volumes which he had collected during his forty years spent as an educator of the deaf. I was greatly interested in these books and ventured to ask him if he had decided what disposition should be made of them after his death.

"Why," said he, "I should like nothing better than that they should go to America and become a part of the library of the college."

Turning to Mrs. Baker who was present, I said, "I hope this wish of your husband's will not be forgotten."

In the summer of 1874 I heard of Dr. Baker's death and wrote at once to Mrs. Baker to inquire about the disposition of the books. Before my letter could reach her, she had written me that her husband, not long before his death, had spoken of the books and authorized her to offer them to the college for £250. I received Mrs. Baker's letter when I was at Saratoga and, without waiting to consult our directors, wrote her at once, closing with her terms.

It was well that I did, for I learned not long after that the officers of the British Museum were greatly chagrined to have the collection go out of England and would have gladly paid a higher price for it than £250.

Our board promptly approved my action, and we thus secured books of great rarity, the opportunity to purchase which would probably never have occurred again.

Another event of interest occurring in this year was the giving up of the old college custom of having the annual public exercises of the college at the end of the academic year, when the weather was almost certain to be hot, and professors and students were sure to be nearly worn out by the work of the year and the inevitable examinations at its close.

In place of the time honored commencement, so-called, I conceived the idea of having the anniversary in May when the weather was cool and everybody was fresh. I proposed to call the occasion Presentation Day, borrowing this term from our former use at Yale University for the occasion now called Class Day, when a ceremony takes place of "presenting" the members of the graduating class as candidates for degrees.

We made the exercises of the day the same as those of the old Commencement Day except that in place of conferring degrees on the members of the senior class, we "presented" them as candidates for degrees to be conferred a few weeks later on the completion, successfully, of their final examinations. The custom this inaugurated, I can say at this writing (August 1899), has proved most satisfactory for twenty-five years.

In the winter of 1873–74 a plan for the completion of our college building was matured by me and put into proper shape by Mr. Frederick C. Withers of New York to harmonize with our chapel building.* The design of the exterior called for considerable ornamental stone work.

---

*Withers designed the following buildings: the President's House (1867), three houses for professors—Faculty Row houses 2, 3, and 4 (1867 and 1874), Chapel Hall (1870), College Hall (1875), the Gymnasium—Ole Jim (1880), and the Kendall School building (1885).

A meeting of our board was called to consider this plan, and it was held in the room of the Senate Committee on the Judiciary of which Senator Edmunds was chairman, he having a short time before succeeded Senator Patterson as a member of our board. Now Senator Edmunds, while very friendly to the college, was well-known to be in favor of economical expenditures of public money, and I was not without fear that he would object to some of the ornamentations in Mr. Wither's plan, which were, it may justly be said, by no means extravagant.

At the meeting of the board, Senator Edmunds, Mr. Dawes, and Judge Niblack, the Congressional directors, were present with several of the local members. After I had explained the plan, questions were asked by several, and presently Senator Edmunds put his finger on the stone or-namentations one after the other and asked, "How much would the cost of the building be diminished if all this fancy work were omitted and the building made of plain brick?"

My heart came into my mouth as I replied, "About $10,000." Just at that moment a rap on the door was heard, and a Senate page stepped in with a message to Mr. Edmunds that he was wanted for an important caucus in an adjoining room. He rose smiling and, addressing the whole board said, "Well gentlemen, you will have to excuse me. I will stand by any decision you reach," and left the room.

The echo of his footsteps in the corridor had not died away when Judge Niblack, whose liberality to all educational and scientific enterprises of the Government was well-known, turned to the Chair and said, "Mr. President, I move that the plans now before us be adopted."

"Is the motion seconded?" said I. Someone called for the question, and in a moment the plans were approved by a unanimous vote.

Judge Niblack said to me with a laugh after the meeting was over, "I thought it best to lose no time; there was no telling when Edmunds might come back."

In connection with this incident I will record another which may have happened the following year but which had to do with the college building. By this time the Democrats had control of the House, and Judge W. S. Holman of Indiana, the well-known objector to appropriations, was chair-man of the committee.

I felt it to be of the first importance to secure his favor for the con-struction of our college building, and though many told me my only way was to fight him, I decided to seek his active aid. Calling at this lodgings one evening with the plans of the building, I found him ready to hear me, and the result was I secured his support and our estimates went through without a lisp of opposition.

16. Front view of the campus with the college building under construction at left. Rose Cottage had been demolished to make way for Chapel Hall (at center).

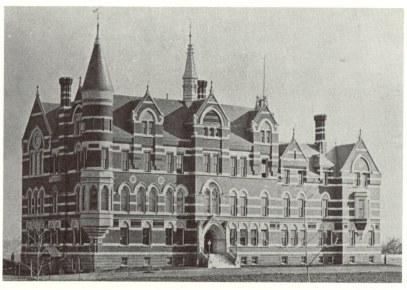

17. The college building just after its completion in 1877.

18. *E.M.G. standing at front of the campus across Florida Avenue, ca. 1876. (left to right) Gate House, College Hall, Chapel Hall, and old Fowler Hall.*

19. *View of Washington, D.C., from the campus in the late 1870s.*

1874–1875

This year presents few matters of especial interest to be recorded. In our annual report for this period, mention is made of the fact that the examination papers of certain of our students had been submitted to Professor Henry of the Smithsonian Institution and that he had commented very favorably on them. I mention this as giving evidence of the fact that our students were doing real scholarly work.

The erection of the college building was pressed steadily forward during this year, Congress giving us funds for this a little slowly, but with a very friendly spirit. Men of both the great parties have always appeared to befriend the college.

1875–1876

On the occasion of Presentation Day 1876, two distinguished friends of the college were presented, Professor Henry of the Smithsonian Institution and President Gilman of Johns Hopkins University.

I had placed in the hands of both these gentlemen, some days earlier, specimens of the examination papers of a number of our students. Their testimony as to the excellence of these papers is so decided that it seems worthwhile to give quotations from their speeches, even though they were published in our annual report for this year.

Professor Henry referred as follows to the work of our students which had come under his eye:

In 1864 a plan was submitted to me for examination, by the president of this institution, of a graduated course, terminating in a collegiate curriculum. In my report upon the proposition I warmly recommend its adoption, as a means of increasing the enjoyment and extending the sphere of usefulness of the class intended to be benefited. I am now happy to say that the experiment has been successful. The scientific examination papers of last year were submitted to me for report as to their character; while they involved the solution of questions in mathematics, physics, chemistry, geology, etc., requiring accurate knowledge and profound thought, *the answers were such as to do honor to the undergraduates of any college in this country.*

The deaf and dumb are not inferior to any other class in mental activity and power, and from the want of the sense of hearing are capable, perhaps, of more undisturbed attention and of sustained effort for the accomplishment of high mental achievement. They are specially well adapted to various scientific investigations, and may become successful laborers in the line of astronomy, heat, light, electricity, magnetism; in the great domain of chemistry and natural history; in short, in every branch of human thought, with the exception of that which relates to sound; and even in the theoretical part of this they may make advances beyond our present knowledge by deductions from the mathematical expressions which indicate the relation of sonorous waves to the forces which produce them. Why should they not, therefore, be educated to the full extent of their mental and physical capacity? The extension of their studies will certainly add to their pleasure, and prepare them as co-laborers for extending the bounds of human thought. The plan proposed of giving a collegiate course in this institution has been, as I have said, eminently successful; it has been commended in foreign journals, and while the graduates have, in several instances, been employed in scientific calculations, one has received, on account of his attainments, an honorary degree from Dartmouth College.*

For more fully carrying out the plan, however, additional means are required; a larger number of professors should be employed, and the implements of instruction should be increased. Visible illustrations of physical principles and phenomena should be amply supplied. The impressions made upon the mind through the eye are the most definite and lasting; and as this instrument of sense is the one principally employed by the deaf-mutes, it is in a state of abnormal activity, and should therefore be furnished with all the appliances best calculated to render it most effective in the acquisition of knowledge.

The whole number of deaf-mutes in the country may be estimated at 25,000, and for the education of these a large number of teachers will be required. The college, with its extended curriculum, will be the most prominent establishment for furnishing laborers in this line.

Moreover, a considerable portion of the deaf and dumb are the offspring of wealthy parents, and the prospect of furnishing to these a higher course of mental culture will increase the number of pupils of this institution in proportion as its character is developed and the results of its instruction are made known. What parent would not purchase at any price the advantage to his child of an extended field of pleasure and of usefulness in a life of devotion to scientific investigations? What pleasure could a

---

*Joseph G. Parkinson, class of 1869 and a native of New Hampshire, received this degree in 1873. He later became a patent lawyer in Chicago, Illinois.

deaf-mute not receive from the practical use of the microscope, could a taste for investigations by means of that instrument be induced through his connection with this institution, and how greatly would that pleasure be enhanced were he able to add to the sum of human knowledge by original observations! There is pleasure in the acquisition of knowledge. There is also pleasure in being able to communicate to others the knowledge we have acquired; but the pleasure of *originating knowledge* is incomparably greater than either of these, and there is nothing in the physical constitution of the deaf and dumb which would preclude them from participation in this higher enjoyment. In order to do this, however, the instruction should not be limited to scientific facts and principles, but should include scientific manipulation.

To foster and develop this institution is an object worthy of the General Government. If properly sustained, it will do honor to our nation, and to those who conceived and assisted in developing its plan; and it will serve as an illustration of the benevolence of the age in which we live. That it may continue to prosper and bring forth fruit commensurate with the object of its foundation is my most earnest prayer.

President Gilman said in the course of his speech:

I congratulate you, ladies and gentleman, on what we have this day observed in respect to the education of deaf-mutes, but I have had other and exceptional opportunities to know something of the progress of these students. Some days ago the examination papers in various branches of knowledge were submitted to me and, without pretending to have read them thoroughly or to be competent to judge them all, I can repeat with emphasis the commendation from Professor Henry, to which you have just listened, and echo his remark, that *these papers would have been creditable to the students of any college in the land.*

Knowing something of the difficulties encountered by skillful teachers in training the minds of those who have the use of all their senses, I wonder at the success of those who teach only by appeals to the eye, while the portal of the ear, on which so many ordinary teachers exclusively rely, remains closed to their instructions.

I admire, moreover, the spirit which animates the education here imparted. These young men are not treated as unfortunates, to be the lifelong objects of pity and charity, but as those who are providentially fettered by peculiar difficulties, or deprived of advantages which most persons possess. Their happiness may be the greater because of the very obstacles they overcome; their vision from the mountain-top may be clearer and more enjoyable than the prospect of those who plod along the valleys.

This is the first deaf-mute college in the world, but it is not the first time deaf-mutes have been admitted to college. I remember a passage in Stanley's *Lectures on Canterbury*, where he describes Queen's College at Oxford in the days of the famous Black Prince, and tells us that while the Master and twelve Fellows in the college-hall dined daily together, in commemoration of Christ and his apostles, the deaf and dumb and the blind were admitted to the door to receive their dole of cast-off morsels. How different this scene; how changed the times; how beneficent the progress! In the early days of our faith, when they saw the dumb to speak, "they glorified the God of Israel." Can we do less today?

So as we part, my friends, let us rejoice, as patriots, that here, first in all Christendom, a college for deaf-mutes has been begun where scholastic work is performed worthy of any college; let us rejoice, as teachers, at the demonstration that by the eye, knowledge may be acquired as sound and as comprehensive as that which is ordinarily gained by eye and ear together; let us rejoice, as philanthropists, that those classes of our fellowmen who were once treated as miserables and inaccessible unfortunates, scarcely above the dumb animals, are now erect as men among their fellowmen; let us rejoice, as Christians, that the example of the Great Teacher has, in some degree, been imitated, who obliterated the barriers between the deaf man and his fellow-men and caused the dumb to speak.

On the 2nd of June, 1876, the institution was honored by a visit from Dom Pedro, the learned and scholarly Emperor of Brazil. He showed the greatest interest in the work of the college, sat down by one of the students in a classroom and put his arm around him, questioning him on his studies. As his visit came to an end, the Emperor planted an ivy vine at an angle in the terrace wall, receiving it from the hand of my mother.

Referring to this interview, Profesor Draper in his sketch of my mother's life writes as follows:

Each of them advanced in years, each still retained much of the precious dew of youth. Each seemed to enter at once with kindred spirit into the emotions of the other. They were both of imposing but kindly presence, and most courteous manners. It was like a meeting between sovereigns. Wherever in his travels the Emperor shall hear of her death, it will surely be with regret proportioned to the interest which his demeanor then betrayed.*

---

*Professor Draper's biographical sketch of Sophia Fowler Gallaudet can be found in the *American Annals of the Deaf*, 22:3, July 1877.

On June 28, 1876, the closing day of the school and college year, all the students and pupils with some of the teachers started, under my charge, for a visit to the Centennial Exhibition then in progress in Philadelphia. A special car took us to Baltimore by the Baltimore and Ohio Railroad, landing us at the wharf of the Shriver Line, one of whose steamers we took for Philadelphia. Our party numbered one hundred, and having taken our mid-day meal in Washington before starting, we carried great baskets of provisions for our supper and breakfast on the boat.

We had a lovely sail up Chesapeake Bay and into the canal before bed time, a bright moon enabling us to see much of the country traversed by the canal. There were berths enough on the steamer for the ladies and the girls, but many of the boys had to stretch themselves out on the deck.

We reached Philadelphia early the next morning, and after breakfast and sending the baggage to a hotel near the Exhibition grounds where I had engaged rooms, we went by street car directly to the Exhibition.

I was surprised to see how readily the children, as well as the older ones, came to every rendezvous that I made for them. During the forenoon we were much scattered, but at twelve o'clock all appeared at the Southern Restaurant where we were to lunch.

Then at evening all were at a certain place, agreed upon, so that we could go to our hotel together. There we dined and slept and breakfasted, and then started in for our second day at the Exhibition. The close of that day was the time set for our separation, and excepting the District pupils and a few from Delaware and Maryland who went south with me, the company started for their homes all over the country. It was an experience long to be remembered, and I am sure our young people were grateful for the liberality of our directors who authorized the trip. The expense incurred was $750.

1876–1877

In our annual report of October 1876, an appeal is made to the governments of the respective states in our Union to make provision for the support of beneficiary students in the college.

It is of interest in the history of the college to record the fact that, from time to time, members of our board have given expression to the view that it was unconstitutional for the Federal Government to provide for the free education of students from the states. This opinion was brought forward rather urgently by Judge Niblack of Indiana in 1876, and later on by Mr. Tucker of Virginia when he became a member of the board. Hon. Frank Hiscock of New York, when chairman of the Committee on Appropriations, took this ground but said finally after a visit to the institution, "If this were before me as a new measure, I should feel bound, on principle, to oppose it; but since the institution has the sanction of many enactments of Congress, I suppose there is nothing left for me to do but to vote for the means to run it."

Mr. Tucker was in the habit of expressing his views at nearly every meeting of the board at which he was present and then, feeling he had cleared his conscience, would give in his adhesion to what the board decided to ask of Congress.

The appeal in our report for 1876, previously alluded to, was the outcome of a discussion started by Judge Niblack, and it was followed up by a carefully prepared communication sent, with documents, to the governors of the states with the request that legislative action be had. These communications were not even acknowledged, except in two or three instances, and I have never heard that action was ever proposed in any state.

My own position in regard to this measure was (1) that it was wholly impracticable unless someone were sent to each state legislature to push the scheme through by personal endeavor. This, of course, would require many years work for one person or the efforts of many agents. (2) I always held that it was entirely equitable for the U.S. Government to provide for the higher education of the deaf of the states since they were debarred by their infirmity from participation in the benefits of the great agricultural college grants which Congress had made to all the states. This argument I used many times with the members of Congress, and I never found any able to answer it.

This year was one of quiet prosperity in the institution generally. My main labor was the superintendence of the erection of the college building, funds for the completion of which had been provided by Congress without controversy or question. The architectural beauty of the building was secured by the retention of all the stone ornamentation originally suggested by Mr. Withers, the cutting off of which I feared when Senator Edmunds asked his disturbing question when the plans were before the board for the first time.

PART FOUR

Systems, Methods, Controversy
1877–1887

VII
Congressional Politics and Milan
1877–1880

1877–1878

THE OPENING OF THIS YEAR was marked by an event, the outcome of which proved of great service and assistance to me.

When I ceased living in the institution in December 1868, the domestic management of the institution was placed in the hands of my brother William L. Gallaudet, whose office was that of family supervisor. My brother's health gave way at the end of the third year, and he was compelled to resign his office.* It was not easy to find a man to fill this position, and for several years the domestic management was practically in the hands of the matron, assisted by some one of the male instructors. This arrangement devolved much labor and care upon me that I would gladly have been relieved of.

It was therefore very gratifying to me to secure, in the autumn of 1877, the service of Mr. John B. Wight, a native of Washington, a young man who proved to be remarkably well-fitted for the position which had remained vacant for six years. He had been in the hardware establishment of W. H. Campbell & Sons for several years, which gave him a good knowledge of business, and he had been for a few years superintendent of the Sabbath School of the Reverend Dr. Sunderland's church.

How well Mr. Wight succeeded in his position at Kendall Green, I shall have pleasure in recording when I reach the date of his retirement which was in 1890. I will say here, however, that Mr. Wight's presence at my right hand was a great comfort and relief from the start. He was quick to understand my methods of management and cheerful and untiring in his efforts to aid me.

---

*William L. Gallaudet eventually died in 1887.

An event of sad interest to all connected with the institution occurred in May 1877. This was the very sudden death of my dear mother who was then making me a visit. Her devoted labors as matron during the first nine years of the institution were gratefully remembered by many connected with it at the time of her death, and her frequent visits to my house in the closing years of her life had afforded opportunity for the forming and continuance of relations of friendship between her and all the officers and students of the institution.

Her life was bright and beautiful to its very end. No period of physical or mental weakness came to her. She was in full vigor, though in her 80th year, on the day when the fatal stroke of apoplexy came, and she ceased to breathe within twenty-four hours after she was stricken.

The beauty and strength of her character and the benign influence of her life have been recorded elsewhere, and I need say nothing further here than that her death, as is the death of every good mother to her children, [was] an irreparable loss to me.

The 16th of February 1878 was the twenty-first anniversary of the incorporation of the institution by Congress. As the college building had been completed and occupied but a short time before, that day was deemed a fitting occasion for a congratulatory celebration.

President and Mrs. Hayes were present—also Vice President Wheeler, who had previously been a member of our board; also Mr. Withers, the architect, and his wife—with members of our board and invited guests, who will be found mentioned in our Twenty-First Annual Report.

It was on this occasion, not the only visit of President Hayes to Kendall Green, that he kissed my son Herbert, then seventeen months old. Mrs. Hayes also performed a graceful act in the college that those present remember. While inspecting the rooms of the building, the party came to Mr. Draper's apartment. He had laid wood and kindling in his fireplace, in which no fire had ever burned, and requested Mrs. Hayes to apply a match to the shavings. With a gracious smile she stooped down, and presently the fire light of the new hearth was illuminating the room.

It was on this occasion that Mr. Dawes made public acknowledgement of the change of heart he experienced in 1872 as to the purchase of the Kendall Green. But he did not give his daughter the credit that was due her for bringing that about.

At the Presentation Day exercises of the year, General Garfield made an earnest and eloquent speech declaring his continued interest in the college and his gratification that he had been able to help forward its interest in Congress.

1878–1879

The year was one of quiet undisturbed prosperity throughout the institution.

An incident of special interest was a visit at Presentation time of President Porter of Yale University, a brother of our Professor Porter. President Porter delivered an able and interesting address at our anniversary exercises. The address was published in our Twenty-Second Annual Report.

Introducing the speaker I called attention to the fact that Yale University had furnished an unusually large number of teachers of the deaf from among her graduates, beginning in 1805 with my father, the founder of the first permanent school for the deaf in the country.

Among the estimates submitted this year was one for the erection and fitting up of a gymnasium in which the physical development of our students might be cultivated.

1879–1880

A diploma and medal were received this year from the Paris Exposition of 1878, awarded to the college for its advanced work in educating the deaf.

In Congress a debate was had on a proposal to charge over half of the expenses of the institution to the District Treasury. The effort failed, as it deserved to, and I think it worthwhile to insert the debate in this history as illustrating the frequent ignorance of many members of Congress when they make bold to legislate on matters to which they have given little study.

General Hawley's friendliness to the institution and his ability in debate are conspicuous.

Under Sundry Civil Appropriation Bill, the Clerk read as follows:

For erection and fitting up of gymnasium for the use of students and pupils $5,000 and for the improvement and enclosure of the grounds of the institution $2,500; in all $7,500: *Provided*, That hereafter one-half of the expenses of the institution shall be paid out of the revenues of the District of Columbia.

Mr. HUNTON of Virginia. Mr. Chairman, I raise the point of order on the proviso contained in this paragraph. It changes existing law, and it does not, on its face, retrench expenditures.

Mr. BLOUNT of Georgia. On the question of order raised by the gentleman from Virginia I have only to say this: that the persons in this institution from the District of Columbia have been paid for now out of the general fund and appropriation for the whole country, and this proviso which the gentleman from Virginia desires to have stricken out, is simply to relieve the United States of one-half of the expenses. The Chair will notice, of course, that the laws as they now stand require an expenditure on the part of the government, a portion of which will be saved by the proviso, and consequently to that extent it does retrench expenditures upon its face.

The CHAIRMAN. The Chair is ready to decide the question of order.

Mr. HUNTON. Before deciding that point I desire to say a word in reply to the gentleman from Georgia. According to existing law this institution is wholly a Federal institution and up to this moment has been supported by the Federal treasury, and therefore to put upon the District of Columbia one-half of the expenses of the institution is a clear change in existing law. It does not retrench expenses because on its face there is no diminution of the expenditures for the support of the institution. In regard to the persons put into this institution by the District of Columbia, the statement of the gentleman from Georgia is undoubtedly true; but there are persons in this institution from every state in the Union as well as from the District of Columbia, and why the District should not participate in the benefits to be derived from it to the same extent that the states participate in a Federal institution, I am at loss to understand.

MR. BLOUNT. I desire to have read in this connection sections 4864-65-66 of the Statutes at Large.

The CHAIRMAN. The Chair thinks it unnecessary to take up time in the discussion of this question and is ready to decide the point of order at once. The Chair thinks that although upon its face it appears to be a new legislation, it evidently retrenches expenditures. And does it in this, that one-half of the expenditures that have heretofore been paid by the Federal Government are now to be paid out of the revenues of the District of Columbia, and therefore it does retrench expenditures to that extent. The Chair therefore holds that the point of order is not good.

Mr. HUNTON. Then I move to strike out the proviso.

The CHAIRMAN. The Clerk will read the pending proposition. The Clerk read as follows: Strike out all after the word "dollars" in line 986 as follows: "*Provided*, That hereafter one-half of the expenses of this institution shall be paid out of the revenues of the District of Columbia."

Mr. HUNTON. As I said awhile ago, this is a Federal institution, and never, until now, has one cent been appropriated to the support of the inmates of that institution by the District Government. There are one hundred and eighteen persons in that institution, and of those one hundred and eighteen persons, twenty-three are from the District. And yet the gentleman from Georgia has reported a provision here putting upon the District Government the support of one-half of all inmates of that institution. I have before me the report of the president of the institution from which I get this fact: that there are one hundred and eighteen students and only twenty-three from the District of Columbia. I desire, Mr. Chairman, to call the attention of the committee to the provision in the organic act providing a permanent form of government for the District of Columbia, by which the District is charged with one-half the cost of maintaining the various institutions belonging to the District and the Federal Government with the other half. Any gentleman who will pay attention to the reading of the clause of that act will find that this institution is not one of those which the District has to support: "The said commissioners shall submit to the Secretary of the Treasury for the fiscal year ending June 30, 1879, and annually thereafter, for his examination and approval, a statement showing in detail the cost maintaining all public institutions of charity, reformatories, and prisons, belonging to or controlled wholly or in part by the United States or District of Columbia." This institution is controlled altogether by the Federal Government, and under the organic act the District Government is not liable to pay one cent of the expenses. It is a national institution for the purpose of receiving these inmates from all the states and territories in the Union. It receives inmates from every state and territory just as much as it does from the District of Columbia; and I trust, Mr. Chairman, no part of the maintenance of the institution will be placed upon the District of Columbia.

Mr. BLOUNT. My friend from Virginia certainly misunderstands the nature of this institution. The law expressly declares that all persons of a teachable age, and in indigent circumstances, properly belonging to the District of Columbia, shall be sent there by order of the Secretary of the Interior. It is an institution primarily for the District. There is a provision allowing that forty persons outside the District may come to the institution, but the number of each shall not exceed forty, and the government does not pay for them. They are compelled to pay their own way. The only persons who are educated free of charge here are the deaf and dumb persons belonging to the District. I cannot see why this District should not pay for educating its own deaf-mutes, when deaf mutes from everywhere else, except forty, are excluded from the institution.

Mr. HUNTON. Where does the gentleman get all that?

Mr. BLOUNT. In sections 4864-65-66 of the Revised Statutes.

Mr. HAWLEY of Connecticut. I had hoped that this excellent institution had passed through its fiery trial. It has been established something like twenty-three years, has been through debate after debate, and hammered and hammered, but has prospered in spite of it all. Now in the first place this is not a mere primary and preparatory or even academical school like the others of our deaf and dumb asylums in the various states, the original one having been established in my own state of Connecticut. These asylums take the deaf and dumb children unable to make anything but natural signs and teach them, putting them through a common school and perhaps an academical course. But the government has built up in this District what you call a university for deaf and dumb scholars, and the instructors in that institution take those who graduate from our State institutions and furnish them a college course here.

Mr. BLOUNT. Who pays for them?

Mr. HAWLEY. The United States, very largely.

Mr. BLOUNT. Not at all.

Mr. WASHBURNE of Minnesota. Who then pays for them?

Mr. HAWLEY. The gentleman from Minnesota very properly asks who does pay for them, and I repeat his question.

Mr. BLOUNT. They pay their own way. The statute expressly provides that the Federal Government shall not pay for them.

Mr. WASHBURNE. As a matter of fact I know personally that is not the case.

Mr. BLOUNT. I refer the gentleman to the law.

Mr. HAWLEY. I am speaking as to what is the fact. I do not know what the precise terms of the statutes are and could not give its exact construction without stopping to look at it. But I know that this deaf and dumb institution has worked its way through Congress until it is now a Government, I might almost say, a Congressional institution. Here among the names of the trustees and directors the names of Thomas F. Bayard, Senator from Delaware; J. T. Harris, member of Congress from Virginia; William Clafin, Representative from Massachusetts; H. L. Dawes, Senator from Massachusetts; William E. Niblack, who was in Congress formerly as a representative from Indiana. I have named five out of the eight directors of the institution. Not a single member of the District Government is one of the directors. And I affirm, proceeding upon the assertion of a former commissioner of the District of Columbia, that no pupil has ever gone by order of the District commissioners.

The Government of the United States has established this institution and opened its doors, and it says to the children of the District that they may come there as primary scholars, and once in a while when a pupil shows himself to be fit and more then ordinarily intellectual, he goes up and is admitted to the collegiate course.

It is a national deaf-mute university with a primary department to which scholars may come from the District as well as other parts of the United States, and we have paid its expenses for a series of years. There was a severe discussion of the whole theory upon which it was maintained, and it was then established according to provisions of law which the Appropriations Committee has since followed in making appropriations for it until this bill came in. I say there is no justice in putting this upon the people of the District of Columbia. If at this late day, after having practiced to the contrary for years, you are to take a slate and pencil and figure out how many pupils in this institution are from the District of Columbia, when you do not do that in regard to the states of the Union, then all I have to say is that you have put two or three times too much in this bill. I affirm that scarcely one-fourth of the pupils in this institution come from the District of Columbia. And those are in the primary and least expensive departments while the pupils at large represent at least from twenty-five to twenty-seven states of the Union, and the graduates represent thirty-one states. Without asking the District whether it wished for this institution or not, without giving it any share in its control, you have made it a purely national institution. Now, do not let us try to saddle on the District of Columbia the expenses of an institution you have built up for the benefit of the whole country.

Mr. BLOUNT. I move to strike out the last word for the purpose of having read by the Clerk section 4865 of the Revised Statutes.

The Clerk read as follows:

Deaf-mutes not exceeding forty in number residing in the several states and territories, applying for admission to the collegiate department of the Columbia Institution for the Deaf and Dumb, shall be received on the same terms and conditions as those prescribed by law for residents of the District of Columbia, at the discretion of the president of the institution; but no student coming from either of the states shall be supported by the United States during any portion of the time he remains therein.

Mr. BLOUNT. That statute provides simply for forty pupils from the different states, and the government refuses to pay any of the charges.

Mr. HAWLEY. The government pays for the buildings and the salaries of the professors. The cost of the board and clothing of the pupils is another matter.

Mr. BLOUNT. What the government pays is simply a donation to charity.

Mr. HUNTON. This proviso says:

Mr. BLOUNT. Is my time out?

The CHAIRMAN. The Chair thought the gentleman had concluded his remarks.

Mr. BLOUNT. No, sir. I want to add further that [if] it is found by the reports that there are in that institution persons not entitled to be there by law, then that is so much the stronger reason why we should protect ourselves from that abuse. It certainly is right and proper that the District should pay half of the expense proper. There are a great many things for which the General Government pay one-half or more of the expense and does not receive one-tenth of the benefit. It does not become this District to take issue upon a matter of mathematical calculation as to the mere number of persons admitted to this institution.

Mr. HUNTON. The language of the proviso is as follows: *Provided*, "That hereafter one-half of the expense of this institution shall be paid out of the revenues of the District of Columbia." As I read that proviso, if it shall be adopted, hereafter the District of Columbia will have to pay one-half of these additional buildings, one-half the cost of fitting up the gymnasium, one-half the cost of repairs, and all upon property owned by the Federal Government. Now can any gentleman say that that is a correct principle?

Moreover in reply to what the gentleman from Georgia (Mr. BLOUNT) said when last up. I will say that if it would be right for the District of Columbia to pay any portion of the expenses of this institution, it is utterly unjust that it should pay one-half of the expenses because, according to the report of the president of the institution, out of one hundred and eighteen students, twenty-three only are from the District of Columbia.

Mr. BLOUNT. Then discharge the illegal number.

Mr. HUNTON. I state upon the authority of the report of the president of the institution that of the one hundred and eighteen students there but twenty-three are from the District of Columbia.

Mr. BLOUNT. Then I say discharge the illegal number.

Mr. HUNTON. And yet the gentleman would have the District pay one-half the expenses of that institution; not only the expenses of the students who are there, but one-half of the expenses of the repairs and one-half of the cost of the necessary buildings for the accommodation of the students. That would be wholly unjust and wrong and unjust to the District, and I hope this proviso will be stricken out.

Mr. HAWLEY. I withdraw my formal amendment.

Mr. NEAL of Ohio. I renew the amendment. In addition to what the gentleman from Virginia (Mr. HUNTON), the Chairman of the Committee on the District, has stated, I wish to state for the consideration of the Committee of the Whole that a large portion of the improvements made in the District of Columbia have been made by special assessments upon the property here. There has been assessed upon the property of the United States in proportion to the property of individuals the sum of over $1,000,000, which is now due the authorities of the District by the Government of the United States, and not one dollar of which has been appropriated by any bill yet presented to the Committee on Appropriations. This burden has been imposed upon the people of this District, a burden of taxation which I venture to say no other people in the United States have been compelled to submit to. The property of the United States has been benefited by these improvements to the same extent that all other property has been benefited; and yet the government has not paid one cent of the special assessments made upon its property. It would be equitable that the Government of the United States continue to bear this expense, in view of these circumstances, even if the statement was correct that all pupils educated in this institution belong to the District of Columbia. But that is not correct. Every gentleman who knows anything about these deaf and dumb institutions knows that the actual expenses of supporting a student in any of them, aside from the expenses of repairs, the salaries of the professors, etc., is from $150 to $200 a year at the most. Therefore, the expense of the District of Columbia for supporting and educating these deaf and dumb scholars, instead of being nearly $2,000 a year for each pupil as would be the case if this proviso should be retained in the bill, would not be over $200 a year if the proviso be struck out. I trust that the motion of the gentleman from Virginia will prevail and that this modicum of justice will be meted out to the tax-burdened people of the District of Columbia.

The pro forma amendment being withdrawn, the question was taken on the amendment of Mr. Hunton, which was agreed to, there being— ayes 58, noes 27.

During the summer of 1880 I visited Europe, under the authority of our board, for the purpose of attending the International Congress of Instructors of the Deaf held at Milan, Italy. I had the pleasure of the company on this journey of my brother-in-law, Mr. James Denison, who was my earliest colleague in the institution.

Some account of the Milan Congress appears in our Twenty-Third Annual Report, and I need not speak of it at length here. I wish, however, to say that, by promoters of the oral method of instructing the deaf to the exclusion of the manual, the action of the Milan Congress in approving this policy has been unjustly taken as of the greatest possible weight in deciding upon the real merits of respective methods.

The Milan Congress was a partisan body, a majority of its voting members being from the Italian Schools. Out of 164 members only 21 came from countries outside of Italy and France. The Congress was, therefore, not really international in its character nor was its composition representative. It is not improper to say that its pronunciamento in favor of the oral method was the expression of little more than local opinion in Italy and France.

VIII
Federal Support Questioned
1880–1881

THE GYMNASIUM WAS FINISHED this year, and the regular physical training of our students was begun. Attendance upon this was made compulsory upon all, and the results were highly satisfactory.

The discussion in the House begun last year on the proposition to put one-half the expense of carrying on the institution on the District of Columbia was renewed this year when the appropriations for the institution came up and was as follows:

Sundry Civil Appropriations Bill. The Clerk read as follows:
Columbia Institution for the Deaf and Dumb: Current expenses; Columbia Institution for the Deaf and Dumb: For support of the institution, including salaries and incidental expenses, and $500 for books and illustrative apparatus, and $2,500 for general repairs, $53,000.

Mr. SAMFORD of Alabama. I make the point of order on that paragraph that it is not in the line of retrenchment. At the same time, I will say that if the paragraph could be amended so as to make it in accordance with existing law, I would not insist on the point of order. It changes existing law in this respect: it is one of the institutions of the District which the law requires to be estimated for by the commissioners, the District of Columbia being required to pay one-half of the expenses, while this provides that the Government of the United States shall pay the whole of it.

Mr. BLOUNT of Georgia. If the gentleman will read a little further, he will find that there is a provision which is intended to be applicable to both sections; a proviso that hereafter one-half of the expense of this institution shall be paid out of the revenues of the District of Columbia.

Mr. SAMFORD. I saw that proviso to the next paragraph; but even if it refers to the paragraph under consideration, it does not meet the objection I have made because it merely provides that hereafter one-half of the expenses of the institution shall be paid out of the revenues of the

20. *The gymnasium (Ole Jim) in 1880.*

District of Columbia. Now, what are the revenues of the District of Columbia? They are made up of one-half which the Government of the United States pays and the one-half which is paid by the District.

Mr. BLOUNT. Let me suggest to my friend from Alabama that there is not a great deal of difference between himself and the committee. If my friend would amend by saying one-half of this sum shall be paid out of the treasury of the District of Columbia and one-half of the treasury of the United States, and hereafter the expenses shall be paid in that way, I would have no objection to that amendment.

Mr. SAMFORD. I have an amendment here which I think will meet the point. I sent it to the desk.

The Clerk read as follows: Add to the end of the paragraph the following: *Provided*, That the said sum shall be credited as a payment on the one-half of the amount to be paid by the United States for the current expenses of the District of Columbia.

Mr. HUNTON of Virginia. I desire to say on the point of order raised by the gentleman from Alabama that it is an entire mistake to suppose that this is an institution of the District of Columbia. I have taken pains to look up the law originating this institution, and it is by all intents and purposes an institution of the Federal Government, incorporated by act of Congress, the report of the directors of the institution made to the Secretary of the Interior, and no sort of concern in its government or management is allowed to the District of Columbia. It is true that the Secretary of the Interior in the law which I have before me—I will read that law for the information of the committee: "That whenever the Secretary of the Interior shall be satisfied by evidence produced by the president of the institution hereby incorporated, that any deaf and dumb or blind person of suitable age belonging to the District of Columbia is in indigent circumstances and cannot command means to procure an education, it shall be his duty to authorize such persons to enter said institution, and to pay for his maintenance and tuition therein at the rate of $150 per annum." It will be seen by reference to this law that the deaf and dumb and the blind actually belonging to the District of Columbia cannot enter this institution without the authority of an act of Congress and action taken by the Secretary of the Interior under the law. I will state further that never in history of legislation has one dollar of the expense of maintaining this institution been charged upon the District of Columbia. It is true that at the last session of Congress a proviso was inserted by the Committee on Appropriations in this very Sundry Civil Appropriations Bill charging one-half of the expenses of this institution to the District of Columbia, and by a vote of more than two to one of this House that proviso was stricken out because it was a Federal institution to be supported by Federal contributions and nothing else. If my friend from Alabama (Mr. SAMFORD) is right, let us see the effect of what he desires to have done. This bill appropriates $63,742 for the buildings and the maintaining and support of this institution. According to the proviso at the end of another paragraph and according to the views of the gentleman from Alabama, one-half of that amount would be chargeable to the District of Columbia. That is, the District of Columbia would be forced to pay $36,871 for the maintenance and instruction of twenty-seven pupils in that institution, or at the rate of nearly $1,500 a year for each pupil. The law says that the District of Columbia shall not be charged more than $150 for each pupil. According to the views of the gentleman from Alabama, the District of Columbia must pay one-half of the expenses of the buildings and one-half of the repairs. Yet while the District is paying for the building and the repairs of buildings, when erected and repaired, those buildings belong to the Federal Government. There is no justice in it, no law in it. The law now makes this a Federal institution to be supported and appropriated for out of the Federal treasury.

Mr. SAMFORD. What law?

Mr. HUNTON. The law organizing this institution. And when the next paragraph is reached, I will move, as I did last year, to strike out the proviso which puts one-half of the expense of this institution on the District.

Mr. BLOUNT. I might as well say here what I desire in relation to this Deaf and Dumb institution. I ask the attention of the committee to the law regulating it. I am surprised—no, not surprised either—but I cannot conceive how my friend from Virginia (Mr. HUNTON) can permit such errors as he has urged to have effect upon his mind in this matter. What is this deaf and dumb institution? If the buildings do belong to the Government—the Government bought the land though I believe a portion of the land was given to the Government—the Government pays the expenses for improvement and repairs, the Government pays all the expenses of the institution, and who are the beneficiaries? Do they include any human being outside the District? There two classes of persons, and two alone, who can obtain admission into this institution. I ask the committee to listen while I read the law: "Whenever the Secretary of the Interior is satisfied, by evidence produced by the president of the Columbia Institution for the Instruction of the Deaf and Dumb, that any deaf and dumb person of a teachable age, properly belonging to the District of Columbia, is in indigent circumstances and cannot command means to secure an education, it shall be his duty to authorize such persons to enter the institution." That is one class. Now, another class: "Deaf-mutes not exceeding forty in number, residing in the several states and territories applying for admission to the collegiate department of the Columbia Institution for the Instruction of the the Deaf and Dumb, shall be received on the same terms and conditions as those prescribed by law for the residents of the District of Columbia, at the discretion of the president of the institution: but no student coming from either of the States shall be supported by the United States during any portion of the time he remains therein." If he comes from any other section of the country, the expense does not come out of the District and does not come out of the General Government but must be paid for by the friends of the student. And only forty of such students can be admitted. The institution is therefore essentially an institution for the District of Columbia and for the people of this District. And when we have gone beyond what is our just proportion of the expense and have paid all the expense of maintaining this institution, my friend from Virginia (Mr. HUNTON) says that we ought to go further. He says, "You have already given us the buildings; now because you have been liberal in that particular, you ought to go on and pay every dollar for the support of this institution." I conceive that when this committee comes to understand the proposition, it will not hesitate to say that the people of the District ought to pay one-half of the expense of this institution. The gentleman says the law does not authorize that. If it does not authorize it now, it is competent for us to enact such legislation and insert it here, reducing expenditures on the part of the Government. I trust that this will no longer continue. (Here the hammer fell.)

Mr. HAWLEY of Connecticut. If any gentleman will consult the *Congressional Globe* and the *Record* for the last fifteen years, he will wonder that this discussion annually arises. After long and careful investigation, after a long debate, the character and policy of this national institution were established. And among the present directors of the institution under its charter are Senators Bayard and Dawes, Representatives Harris and Clafin, Judge Niblack, formerly a member of the House, and others. It is a national institution of that sort here many years ago which gave up its property and rights and merged itself into this national school. Now, the law provides, of course, that forty pupils from outside of the District, residing in the various states and territories, may be admitted on the same charitable terms as pupils within the District. But there is nothing forbidding any number of pupils coming here from any part of the country. Let me explain how the necessity for this school arises. A great many States have large and admirably conducted institutions for the primary instruction of the deaf and dumb. They carry a pupil up to the standard of a common school education, possibly something more than that. But many of the deaf and dumb are persons who deserve and will repay a much higher education. But what state or private association can provide a college for five or ten such persons in a state? When you take the United States at large, you can collect in a national institution such of this unfortunate class as ought to have a collegiate or university education. This national institution supplies that want. Its character and policy have been stated time and again. There are twenty-seven pupils from the District of Columbia, only four of whom are in the collegiate department. The others are mere primary scholars, such as we find in all of our local schools. Now, if you saddle the expense of half of these upon the District of Columbia, you make the expense to the District for these twenty-seven pupils, twenty-three of whom are in the primary department, $2,333 each for the year. Nothing could be more unjust. The pupils from outside number more than forty. Forty of them have all the privileges of the local pupils as to allowances; but all these from outside provide for their own clothing, pay for their own books, stationery and incidental expenses; they are all required to provide for themselves during the summer vacation, which continues during the months of July, August, and September; all of them meet their own traveling expenses incurred in going to and from their homes at vacation, some of them coming from distant places. The Revised Statutes are not to be construed as forbidding the directors to render assistance to needy and worthy deaf-mutes by an abatement or remission of the ordinary charges of tuition. That has been the practice in all cases properly recommended to them, so far as the means at their own disposal will allow; and they are required to do it by the first part of section 4865 of the Revised Statutes.

Now it has been said that some pupils have been admitted contrary to law. I am authorized by the highly respectable and responsible gentlemen connected with the management of this institution (some of whom I have known from boyhood) to deny this. They would court investigation upon any intimation that they have deviated a hair's breadth from the law.

During the past year the president of that institution has received requests from twenty-two members of Congress for the admission of bright young pupils from their respective States, persons who had already received a primary education and desired to be admitted to this collegiate institution and enjoy the usual advantages offered to indigent pupils— some remission of the tuition charges, I suppose, or something of that kind. All ordinary pupils pay the expenditures to which I have made references.

I say that the amendment ought not to be adopted and that the proviso in the bill, beginning in the one thousand and forty-fourth line, ought to be struck out because its adoption would be a radical departure from what has been the policy of the Government for many years past and would impose a grossly unjust burden upon the District.

Mr. SAMFORD. Mr. Chairman, I am not familiar with previous legislation upon this subject, but it might be a sufficient answer to the gentleman from Connecticut (Mr. HAWLEY) to say that the organic law now in force, passed only two years ago, with reference to this District makes a radical departure necessary. That organic law, among other things, for the first time in our history imposed upon the General Government one-half the expenses of this District and requires the commissioners of the District to estimate the cost of maintaining all public institutions of charity, reformatories, and prisons belonging to or controlled in whole or in part by the United States or the District of Columbia. These estimates are to be revised by the Secretary of the Treasury and afterwards transmitted by the commissioners to Congress and then the law provides that "to the extent to which Congress shall approve of said estimates Congress shall appropriate the amount of fifty percent thereof." The remaining fifty percent is to be levied and assessed upon the taxable property of the District. Now, Mr. Chairman, I do not understand by what authority my friend from Virginia says this is a United States Government institution. I find by referring to the act incorporating the institution that it is entirely a private institution, that the United States has not the right and does not pretend to take charge of it in any shape or form. Why then shall the government support it? No deaf and dumb child from any of the states has any right to enter that institution without paying his way and cannot under any circumstances be a charge upon the Government of the United States.

Mr. NEAL of Ohio. What does he pay?

Mr. SAMFORD. I say he does not come unless he does pay his own expenses for tuition.

Mr. NEAL. How much?

Mr. SAMFORD. I do not know.

Mr. NEAL. About one hundred and fifty dollars.

Mr. SAMFORD. If I am to understand my friend from Ohio (Mr. NEAL) as proposing to make this appropriation because the amount which pupils outside of the District of Columbia are required to pay by the rules of the institution is not sufficient, then I say the law on the statute book forbids such a law, and that too, in direct and emphatic terms. The act says that no student coming from any state shall be supported by the United States during any portion of the time he remains in the institution. If, therefore, it is intended by this appropriation to supplement what the gentleman may conceive to be too small a charge for the care and tuition of pupils by an appropriation from the public Treasury, I say such a proposition violates that provision of the law. Mr. Chairman, at the instance of the gentleman from Georgia, I do not intend to insist upon the point of order, though I think under a point of order it would go out; but I know its stay out would be only temporary. I am willing this measure should stand or fall upon its merits, and I will leave it to the House to decide on my amendment. I say this is an institution providing alone for the benefit of the District of Columbia, providing for the deaf and dumb children of the District of Columbia alone and exclusively, giving no benefit to any other portion of the country. And while these little children have my hearty and cordial sympathy in their misfortune, still it does seem to me that the District of Columbia ought to pay for a part of its expense at least. The Government of the United States, under the organic law, for which I am not responsible and which I think is wrong, pays for one-half the expense in this District. I ask the gentleman on what ground of equity, much less of law, he would contend that the Government of the United States ought to pay for the whole of this. It has not been estimated for by the estimates of the District commissioners. It comes here in the bill. It should be in the bill for the District of Columbia, but it has not been provided for in that bill and therefore the necessity of my amendment that this should be credited to the one-half of the expenses of the District government which is paid by the Government of the United States.

Mr. HUNTON. I will say a word on that point of order.

Mr. SAMFORD. I withdraw the point of order, but I ask for a vote on my amendment. It does seem to me that there ought to be some end to this everlasting drain upon the United States Treasury. This city is getting millions of dollars annually from this government, making itself a grand imperial city at the expense of the whole people of the country—$900,000 is appropriated for paving streets alone. But I have long since found that it is easier to get this House to vote in, than to vote out of a bill, an amendment appropriating money. I do not understand why, but it is true.

The CHAIRMAN. The amendment of the gentleman from Alabama will be read.

The Clerk read as follows: At the end of line 1038 insert the following: "*Provided*, That said sum shall be credited to the payment of one-half of the amount to be paid by the United States for the current expenses of the District of Columbia."

Mr. HUNTON. It is true that this is a private institution in one sense of the word, as the gentleman from Alabama has said. It began with a body of incorporators who were incorporated by Congress to carry on an institution for the education of the deaf and dumb. And it was located in the District of Columbia. I take it for granted that every corporation that is thus domiciled in the District of Columbia is not necessarily an institution belonging to the District Government. In that sense, therefore, it is a private institution. It is also true, for one cause or another which it is not necessary in this discussion for me to inquire into, that the Government of the United States has undertaken to appropriate year by year large sums of money for the support, at least in part, of this private corporation.

Mr. SAMFORD. It is not controlled in part by the Government?

Mr. HUNTON. Not in any particular.

Mr. SAMFORD. Does not the Secretary of the Interior give permits?

Mr. HUNTON. I misunderstood the gentleman. Did you say by the District?

Mr. SAMFORD. No, sir, but by the government in part.

Mr. HUNTON. Yes, it is.

Mr. SAMFORD. Then I ask under the organic law whether—

Mr. HUNTON. The gentleman must excuse me as I have only five minutes. Now, the Government of the United States in incorporating this institution provided the terms under which the deaf and dumb should be admitted to it. It had the right to so provide. When this was placed under the agency of the Secretary, Congress thought proper, as a matter of generosity to this afflicted class of the community, to pay most of the expenses of the institution. But I will say to my friend from Alabama, as well as to my friend from Georgia, never until last session was it ever supposed this institution came within that provision of the law providing for the sharing of the expenses of the District government between the United States and the District of Columbia.

The gentleman from Alabama read an extract from the organic law of this District, and he no doubt read it accurately, in reference to the institutions in the District which were to be supported by the District of Columbia and the government conjointly. If my friend will look to the construction of the language, and he is a lawyer, he will be satisfied that this institution never was intended to come within its meaning. He cannot put any such construction upon that statute. I wish to call attention to the language, because I am sure if that organic act does not number this institution within its terms, my friend from Alabama will not insist further on his amendment. I can assure him that if he will sit down quietly and read that act and apply the law governing this institution, he will conclude that it does not come within forty miles of this provision. What does that organic act say? That the said commissioners shall submit to the Secretary of the Treasury for the fiscal year ending June 30, 1879, and annually thereafter for his examination and approval a statement showing in detail— I will here skip a portion and come to that which is pertinent to the subject under consideration—showing in detail the cost of continuing the public institutions of charity, reformatories, and prisons belonging to or controlled by, wholly or in part, the District of Columbia. Now there is no man on the floor of this House who will undertake to say that this institution at the date of this act or at any period of its existence belonged wholly or in part or was controlled wholly or in part by the District of Columbia. There can be no pretense of that sort. There is nothing in the original act of incorporation or acts amendatory thereto which gives the control or ownership wholly or in part to the District of Columbia; and if I am right and I know I am, I sincerely believe the gentleman will agree with me that this amendment is not proper or just. (Here the hammer fell.)

Mr. HAWLEY. I move to strike out the last word.

Mr. NEAL. Mr. Chairman.

Mr. HAWLEY. I yield to my friend from Ohio on the committee. I did not observe that he was about to address the committee.

Mr. NEAL. Mr. Chairman, if the committee clearly understood the question, I doubt very much whether there would be half a dozen members on this floor on either side of the House who would be willing to place themselves on record as sustaining the motion made by the gentleman from Alabama. It has already been said by my colleague on the Committee on the District of Columbia, the gentleman from Virginia (Mr. HUNTON), that this is not in any sense of the word a District institution, and he has read from the organic law in support of that statement. Now I want to call attention for a while to some facts and figures bearing upon this point which will show, I undertake to say, clearly and unequivocally to the mind of any gentleman upon this floor the gross injustice that will be perpetrated upon the people of the District if the committee agrees to adopt the amendment which the gentleman proposes.

There is a list of one hundred and twenty-eight pupils who were in that institution during last year. Mr. Chairman, of that number twenty-seven only were from the District of Columbia. Out of the one hundred and twenty-eight pupils gathered together from all the states and territories in the Union, twenty-seven only were from the District of Columbia, and of the sum that was collected for board and education, according to the report of the president to the Board of Directors of the institution, there was only $1,601 collected outside the District. In other words the states and territories of the Union sent their pupils here, one hundred in number, at a total cost to the whole country of $1,601, for their year's board and education, while the few students from the District of Columbia who were placed in that institution paid the sum of about $32,000 and for only twenty-seven persons. Is that justice? Is that what you call right?

Mr. BLOUNT. Will the gentleman allow an interruption?

Mr. NEAL. Yes, sir.

Mr. BLOUNT. I wish to ask the gentleman if there is any law fixing the amount that these persons are required to pay? And I wish to ask him that if he does not know that if they do not pay a sufficient sum, it is the fault of the administration of the institution itself?

Mr. NEAL. Mr. Chairman, I will answer the gentleman by saying that this is under the control of the Federal officials and not under the control of the District.

Mr. BLOUNT. If that is the only difficulty, let me say to my friend from Ohio it can be very easily regulated; they can fix a price that will cover the expense.

Mr. NEAL. I wish to call the attention of the committee and of Congress to the injustice that this Committee on Appropriations proposes to perpetrate upon the people of the District by saddling upon them in this appropriation bill an expense of $32,000 for the care and education of twenty-seven, or at a rate of nearly $1,200 a year for each, while the people of this whole country, from all the states and territories, pay but $1,600 for the privilege of keeping one hundred students there. Now, Mr. Chairman, I want to call the attention of the committee to another thing. In the regulations of this institution I find a regulation as follows: "The charge for pay students is $150 per annum." But the gentleman from Alabama would make this committee believe that it is right that the students of the District of Columbia ought to pay an admission of almost $1,200 a year while the students who come here from other parts of the country are allowed to come at an expense of $150 a year. And the amount collected does not even reach that.

Mr. BLOUNT. There is not a dollar paid by a student from this District.

Mr. NEAL. But the gentleman proposes that they shall pay, and he wants to make it the amount I have shown.

Mr. BLOUNT. They do not pay a dollar, not a dollar.

Mr. NEAL. You propose to levy upon the property of District of Columbia, on the citizens of the District a sufficient sum of money to make up this balance of $32,000 of the expenses of this institution, which is an average of $1,200 for each student who is sent there. Now, Mr. Chairman, I trust that no member of the committee will sustain any such proposition as that. There is such a thing as fair dealing towards this District, and I sincerely hope that it will be exhibited in this manner, and this committee will not in this way saddle upon the people of this District an expense which is so exorbitant and unjust as that.

Mr. SAMFORD. Will the gentleman yield to me for a question?

The CHAIRMAN. The gentleman's time has expired.

Mr. SAMFORD. I only want to ask a single question.

Mr. NEAL. My time is out.

Mr. SAMFORD. It is very well that it is out for the gentleman could not answer my question.

The CHAIRMAN. The question is on the motion of the gentleman from Alabama.

Mr. HAWLEY. I can strike out the last word, I suppose, by way of amendment?

The CHAIRMAN. Yes, sir.

Mr. HAWLEY. I wish to say a single word and then let the proposition go on to the committee.

Mr. HUNTON. I desire to make a parliamentary inquiry. I believe the only matter before the committee is an amendment of the gentleman from Alabama.

The CHAIRMAN. It is.

Mr. HAWLEY. I will not detain the committee a moment. I desire merely to call attention to the catalogue of the students of this institution, which shows that they come from twenty-five different States.

The question being taken on Mr. Samford's amendment, the Chair stated that in the opinion of the Chair the "noes" had it.

Mr. BLOUNT. I call for a division and ask that the amendment be read again.

The amendment was again read.

Mr. HUNTON. I hope the amendment will be voted down.

The Committee divided; and there were—ayes 43, noes 77. So (further count not being called for) the amendment was not agreed to.

The Clerk read the following: "Buildings and Grounds, Columbia Institution for the Deaf and Dumb: For the completion and fitting up of the gymnasium $8,240, for the erection of a farm barn $2,000; in all $10,240: *Provided*, That hereafter one-half of the expenses of this institution shall be paid out of the revenues of the District of Columbia."

Mr. CHAFLIN. I offer an amendment which I send to the desk.

The Clerk read as follows: In line 1043 after the word "dollars" insert, "for the building and repair of fences $4,000."

Mr. BLOUNT. The trustees of the institution say this is needed. This is a large institution having a considerable plot of ground, and in the neighborhood there is an increasing population which makes it necessary that a proper fence should be put up.

(The amendment was not agreed to.)

Mr. HUNTON. I offer the amendment which I send back to the desk.

The Clerk read as follows: "Strike out the proviso beginning in line 1044, namely, these words: "*Provided*, That hereafter one-half of the expenses of this institution shall be paid out of the revenues of the District of Columbia."

Mr. HUNTON. This question was fully discussed a while ago, and I do not care to say anything on it unless discussion is wanted on the other side.

Mr. BLOUNT. This proviso, as my friend from Virginia has said, contains substantially the same idea as the amendment we have just been discussing. I will repeat in part what I said in connection with that amendment—the section of the statutes to which I referred that two classes of persons may enter this institution. In the first place, there are the indigent deaf and dumb of the District of Columbia who are paid for at the public expense. And then forty persons from other states and territories may be educated, but their expenses, it is provided, shall be paid by their own friends. This proviso does not change the law, and I trust the House will see fit to sustain the Committee on Appropriations in incorporating it in this bill.

Mr. HAWLEY. This is substantially the proposition which has just been voted down by the House. This country has spent hundreds of thousands of dollars on its insane institutions. It has spent enormous sums for education of various kinds. The government began seventy years ago to make national appropriations for the deaf and dumb. The first school in the country was established in my own town, on my own street, and the government gave a large grant of land to support it, and it is now called the American Asylum for the Deaf and Dumb. It afterwards became a local institution but still has the benefit of the land given by the government. It is a policy seventy years old.

I hold in my hand a catalogue of the Columbia Institution in this city, and as I have said, its pupils come from twenty-five states in the Union. In every respect it is a national institution. There are still many states in the Union that send pupils to the institution in Hartford, my own town. The rights of most of the states in regard to it have been relinquished; but Maine and Massachusetts and some other states still send pupils to that institution.

The Columbia Institution is supported in continuation of the national policy adopted seventy years ago when the institution was established at Hartford, a policy of supporting a national college for deaf and dumb pupils because there were not enough deaf and dumb in any one state to support one such institution.

After some unimportant debating between Messrs. Blount, Hunton, Samford, and Neal the hammer fell. The question was taken upon the motion of Mr. Hunton to strike out the proviso; and upon a division there were—ayes 77, noes 48. *So it was stricken out.*

IX

"Teachers of All Methods United"
1881–1887

1881–1882

THE YEAR 1881 BROUGHT SORROW to the institution by the death of two members of the board, its treasurer, and its Patron, the honored President of the United States.

Notices of Hon. H. D. Cooke, George W. Riggs, Esq., and Hon. William Stickney, will be found in our Twenty-Fourth Annual Report, as also of our beloved President Garfield, who was with us and spoke on Presentation Day 1881 but a few weeks before he was stricken down. The deaths of Mr. Stickney and President Garfield were personal griefs to me, for strong ties of friendship had grown up which made me feel I could lean on and trust them.

In Congress in the summer of 1882, an attack was made on the institution, chiefly by Mr. Blackburn of Kentucky, which reminded us all of the old days of 1868 et seq. when Mr. Washburne paid his respects to us.

All efforts on my part to bring Mr. Blackburn to reason or even to see him failed. He would not hold any communication with me or receive any information in regard to the institution.

The interesting debate in the House is as follows:

DEBATE ABOUT SALARIES

Columbia Institution for the Deaf and Dumb:
For the current expenses of the Columbia Institution for the Deaf and Dumb: For support of the institution, including salaries and incidental expenses, and for books and illustrative apparatus, for general repairs and

[154]

improvements $47,000: *Provided*, That no more than $22,000 of said sum shall be expended for salaries and wages, which shall be adjusted by the Secretary of the Interior.

(After a little preliminary debate about a point of order, Mr. Randall said the following.)

Mr. RANDALL of Pennsylvania. I am acting for another in this matter. (Mr. Tucker—sick). I now move to strike out what is left of the proviso and also move to amend the amount appropriated by this paragraph by increasing it from $47,000 to $55,000. The amount appropriated last year for salaries and wages in this institution was $29,000. There are very few men in this country who are qualified for this service of educating the deaf and dumb. The consequences are that they command perhaps what might be called liberal salaries; but I do not know why the government should not pay salaries equal to those paid in like institutions throughout the country. During my service on the Committee on Appropriations I think I struck pretty thoroughly at all appropriations which I deemed to be too large. But I think I never did strike at sciences or charity. This is one of the institutions of the District which I would like to see maintained in efficiency and with thorough means for educating the deaf and dumb. I would like to attract to its professorship the first talent in the country, such as I think this institution now has. I do not think it wise for us to cut down the salaries of these professors. That is the reason I have offered this amendment.

Mr. SPRINGER of Illinois. I move to strike out the last word. I believe this is the first instance we have had brought to our attention, since this Congress assembled, of a disposition on the part of the Republican majority to retrench expenditures. If it had begun upon some other part of the government to cut down appropriations, I should have been delighted. But after this session has gone on for months, after we have piled Pelion on Ossa until our appropriations will exceed those of any other Congress, it is very unfortunate that these gentlemen should have selected the persons connected with the deaf and dumb institution as the objects of their efforts at retrenchment and reform. Perhaps they imagine that these poor deaf and dumb people cannot hear this debate, that they can deprive their teachers of their proper pay, and then go before their constituents and tell them how much they have done in the interest of economy, and these poor deaf and dumb people will never know the difference. But the country will look with alarm at the efforts of the Republican Party to retrench expenditures by beginning with this institution at Washington for the unfortunate deaf and dumb. I wish that they had begun with the Indian Bureau.

Mr. KASSON of Iowa. I beg the gentleman not to mix politics with this question. I speak as a trustee of the institution.

Mr. SPRINGER. I speak as a representative of the people.

Mr. KASSON. We do not want politics connected with the deaf and dumb institution.

Mr. SPRINGER. I am trying to get politics out of it. The Republican Party is endeavoring here to make a reputation for economy by cutting down the pay of the teachers in the deaf and dumb institution, and I am opposed to it. I hope that the amendment of the gentleman from Pennsylvania will be adopted, and that the gentleman on the other side of the chamber will find some other place than this institution upon which to begin retrenchment.

Mr. KASSON. In the absence of my colleague (Mr. Tucker), appointed by the Speaker as one of the trustees of this institution, will the Committee of the Whole pardon me for leaving the Chair to say one word on this subject? I want to thank the gentleman from Pennsylvania (Mr. RANDALL) for representing my colleague in asking simply a restoration of the amount which has heretofore been appropriated for the support of this institution. I wish to speak in all moderation to my associates on this floor; but I cannot speak without some feeling. Recently I have seen the work done by these patient, plodding, persevering men who devote their lives to this specialty of recovering the human mind and restoring human nature to intelligence and usefulness in life. No man can witness their efforts— taking the child from a condition of beastiality so far as the intellect is concerned, and by the most extraordinary perseverance and patience, bringing him not only to the condition of ordinary intelligence, but carrying him on until he is fitted for the ordinary employments of life and for the gratification of all the demands of humanity—I say no man can witness such efforts as these without having his heart stirred and his mind moved in support of an enterprise so charitable and so much in the line of the Almighty's wishes touching His creatures. I say, Mr. Chairman, and gentlemen of the House, that men who do this, men who, without the rewards accorded to instructors in the ordinary cultivation of the intellect, are obliged from morning until night to labor with persistent effort and by the slowest processes possible to the human mind to reclaim these creatures, are entitled to your respect and mine. They are not men whose pay, moderate as it is, is to be reduced. If they were receiving greater pay than that allowed at the Naval or Military Academy, there might be some reason for a reduction, though I should even then doubt its propriety for their work is much more painful and trying. But these teachers at the deaf and dumb institution receive even lower pay than that allowed at the institution I have named. I beg you gentlemen to consider this question seriously, and if possible to acquaint yourselves with this institution—to observe the work that is going on there. Support these men in their labor and give them a reasonable reward for their services, as you hope to be rewarded in the world to come. When these instructors are, by their patient toil, sending out men who would otherwise be helpless and useless to take places of intelligence and responsibility, I implore this House for heaven's sake to cherish the interests of such an institution and to treat it with fairness and justice. I hope the pending proposition of the gentleman from Pennsylvania, which is simply to keep the compensation of these instructors where it is, continuing what the gentleman's party did when he was in the Chair, will be adopted.

Mr. BLACKBURN of Kentucky addressed the Chair.

The CHAIRMAN. Debate on the pro forma amendment is exhausted.

Mr. SPRINGER. I withdraw the pro forma amendment.

Mr. BLACKBURN. I renew it. Mr. Chairman, I am not ignorant of the fact that this institution appears upon the floor of the House with exceptional advantages. It has its advocates here in the persons of its managers, who are members of the House. I do not mean to intimate (for I never deal in intimations) that these gentlemen have been improperly influenced, but I do mean to say, and I think the sentiment of the House and the country will support me in the assertion, that it is very unfortunate when any institution supported by appropriations out of the Federal treasury has on this floor from year to year, covering a period of a quarter of a century, its advocates serving here as lawmakers, as members of the Senate and the House. The gentleman from Iowa (Mr. KASSON) is one, and the gentleman from Virginia (Mr. TUCKER) is another. *Now sir, this institution is nothing but a lazar house.* It is open for the admission of pupils from every state in the Union. It is supported every dollar of it from the Federal treasury. It has one hundred and four pupils. It has fourteen professors and teachers, and their salaries range from $7,000 down to $1,500 a year.

Mr. KASSON. Does the gentleman say that all the money is derived from the treasury?

Mr. BLACKBURN. Yes, sir.

Mr. KASSON. There are students who pay.

Mr. HISCOCK of New York. How many of them?

Mr. BLACKBURN. I will answer if the gentleman will permit me. Five out of a hundred and four. There are five paying pupils. They are charged $300 a year for tuition and board and clothing, and according to the figures which the superintendent of this institution gives me, it costs this government $526.23 per capita to maintain them. The superintendent of the institution has his house; he has $4,000 a year cash; and he has all his supplies for himself, his family, his servants, all furnished him. He expends this $55,000 as he pleases, although nominally he is under the charge of the Secretary of the Interior, and the return or report he furnishes, which I hold in my hand, shows $500, for instance, in one item as his expenses on a tour to Europe and $395 for the painting of his father's or somebody else's portrait. It is all very well for the gentleman from Iowa (Mr. KASSON) to appeal to that sense of humanity which I trust belongs in a measure at least to all of us alike, but the question is whether the U.S. Government means to establish and maintain and hold, beyond the realm and boundary of common prudence in the matter of expenditures, an institution of this sort for the benefit of all the states in the Union. You have government institutions here in the city of Washington today, presided over by gentlemen as eminent in their professions as this one, and I have not a word to say against him, drawing salaries of $1,800 per annum, while his salary is at the lowest calculation $7,000 a year in the aggregate.

The CHAIRMAN. The gentleman's time has expired.

Mr. BLACKBURN. I withdraw the pro forma amendment.

Mr. RANDALL. I renew it. I regret I did not [know] in time from the gentleman from Virginia (Mr. TUCKER) for whom I am acting to enable me to inquire into the details of the expenses of this institution. There is one fact, however, I think I know, and if I am not correct, I hope the gentleman from Kentucky or some other gentlemen will correct me, and that is that the late Amos Kendall contributed this property or left it in trust to the United States on the condition that the United States would maintain such an institution as this on that ground. The United States having assumed this trust, I think we should execute it. The foundation of the institution is a very interesting one. Mr. Amos Kendall started the institution under peculiar circumstances. A man came here with some deaf and dumb pupils, and Mr. Kendall out of the largeness and generosity of his heart discovered that these deaf and dumb pupils were being exhibited for gain and at once began legal proceedings in the District of Columbia courts to obtain possession of them. Owning that property, now called Kendall Green, he devoted the latter part of his life to the care of these pupils. Realizing that he was near his end, he dedicated that property to the United States in trust for the maintenance of this institution.

Mr. BLACKBURN. Will the gentleman allow me to correct him?

Mr. RANDALL. Certainly.

Mr. BLACKBURN. I think he donated half an acre of land or maybe two acres.

Mr. KASSON. More than that.

Mr. BLACKBURN. Not as much as five.

Mr. RANDALL. In the main, then, I am correct. My only object was to answer that portion of the remarks of the gentleman from Kentucky which would seem to imply that the Government of the United States was not wise in keeping up this institution; and therefore I felt called upon to give the history, so far as I could recollect it, of the way the government came into possession of it. I think it is a trust which the Government has assumed and that it is humane to keep it up, *and for my part I will never vote to cut down or cripple it in any manner whatever.*

Mr. CANNON. I move to strike out the last word. I rise only to make a suggestion to my colleague from Illinois (Mr. SPRINGER). There is no man who has more sympathy for these people than I have; but it did strike us, when we came to look at these expenditures, that possibly somebody who could hear and speak, under the guise of supporting the deaf and dumb or of educating them, was receiving greater salaries than they deserved. This then is not a war against the deaf and dumb; it is no attempt to prevent the extension of this charity to those people who are so unfortunate; but we want to know if we could not draw a line somewhere, and whether or not there was too much of the money, which in the fullness of the breast of the people of this country they devote to such a purpose, that does not reach the persons who were intended to be the beneficiaries of it, or whether one dollar out of every two spent reached the deaf and dumb.

Now, having said that much, I have here in my hand the expenditures and I am perfectly willing to put them into the Record. This is from the official reports. Last year we appropriated $53,500 for the deaf and dumb; $29,886 or largely over one-half of which was used in the payment of salaries and wages alone, while $24,000 was used for the deaf and dumb children, less the subsistence of the professors and their families out of the $24,000 in addition to their pay.

Mr. ROBINSON. Besides their salaries?

Mr. CANNON. Yes sir, besides their salaries.

Mr. ROBINSON. I desire to ask this question in order to give the colleague of the gentleman a chance to take back what he has said.

Mr. SPRINGER. I take nothing back.

Mr. CANNON. Now, in my opinion the pay is too much, and we had better, out of this amount, devote a little more to the deaf and dumb and less to the compensation of these people who are not deaf and dumb.

Mr. RANDALL. I only want to suggest that if the salaries are too high, the board of managers can, after this debate, change them.

Mr. KASSON. Mr. Chairman, I ask the indulgence of the committee for a moment to say a word in response to the gentleman from Kentucky and the gentleman from Illinois. The whole question, it seems to me, resolves itself into this, will you, by reducing the salaries and wages, cripple the operations of the institution in one of two ways? Will you reduce the just amount of compensation of those who are there? Or on the other hand will you reduce the number of people necessary for the education of these pupils? I ask the attention of my friend from Kentucky. He says that this gentleman, the head of this institution, has been abroad as it were for some idle purpose, costing some $500, I think, or more. Let me tell the gentleman that the president of the institution was learning in that trip how to teach, by action of the throat muscles, the man made dumb by a mysterious providence to utter the human voice. The system was first introduced by the Jesuits in Belgium.

Mr. HISCOCK. When did he go abroad?

Mr. KASSON. I only recollect it was during one of the years I was abroad. I met him while engaged in that work, and he informed me what he was learning. He was also teaching Europe the great progress made by the United States in the education of the deaf and dumb, that the charity of the world might be benefited by that knowledge. There is no institution in the world of the rank of this today. It is the only one that gives a liberal education to the deaf and dumb, and it is pointed to throughout the world as of the highest rank.

Mr. SPRINGER. I beg the gentleman's pardon; the institution in Illinois for the deaf and dumb is the largest in the world.

Mr. KASSON. I am speaking, not of the largest institution, but of that which is giving the highest education in the world; its graduates ranking with the pupils that are taught in the general institutions of the country. And not only that, Mr. Chairman—

Mr. BLOUNT. Will the gentleman allow me?

Mr. KASSON. I beg the gentleman will permit me to finish my statement. Now, I say these men deserve as much as your professors at West Point and Annapolis are paid. From morning till night the work is going on of putting the human voice where the providence of the Almighty has omitted to provide it. And are you to strike down these men! Go among them if you want to know what they are doing, and hear the trials made by these pupils under the patient instructions going from morning till night, while the pupils are taught to pronounce the letter *a*, the letter *b*, and the other letters of the alphabet, and to combine two or three letters into one syllable. You have some response from the ordinary child; you have no intelligent response for months, hardly for years, from these children. Oh, strike them down if you want to; but I will vote every time for reducing my salary and yours before I will vote to take a dollar from men who are devoting themselves to Almighty God and the purposes of charity in the work of reclaiming humanity. (Applause)

Mr. BLACKBURN. I would like the gentleman from Iowa (Mr. KASSON), as he has seen fit to explain away the five-hundred-dollar item to which I alluded, which covered the expenses of a trip made by this superintendent to Europe, to go through the list if he will and explain the balance. He is, nominally, under the supervision and control of the Secretary of the Interior. Practically, he is under the supervision and control of nobody, and the $53,000 which you are asked to appropriate here, and which you are in the habit of appropriating, he does with as he pleases. I would like to know whether the gentleman from Iowa, as a member of the board of managers, audited his account of $395 for a painting of his father or himself out of the funds of the treasury.

Mr. KASSON. As one of the trustees along with the gentleman from Virginia (Mr. TUCKER), I am aware that there is a portrait of the father of the present superintendent hung in the hall as an inspiration to the students as to the proficiency they may attain.

Mr. BLACKBURN. And a costly inspiration to the Government. I wish to know if the House intends to vote $50,000 every year to the support of a purely eleemosynary institution, after the fashion of a lazar house, and does not intend to put any limitation or restriction on the expenditure of the money. I say it is a salary which with all the money commutations is worth $7,000. The institution has one hundred and four pupils and fourteen professors and teachers, more than one teacher for every ten pupils, a higher proportion than in any educational institution on this continent, and they are paid higher salaries than in any educational institution in this land.

Mr. SPRINGER. I desire to say one word on this matter. It has been said $395 of the funds appropriated by the government to support this institution has been used to procure a portrait of the father of the present superintendent. Now I want to say to the committee that the father of the present superintendent of this institution is one of the original founders of the science of sign language, one of the most distinguished teachers of the sign language in the world. It was a proper recognition of the distinguished services of the father of the superintendent of this institution that his portrait should be in this national institution. If you will go into the Interior Department you will find the portrait of every Secretary of the

Interior hung on the walls of that department. If you go into the War Department, you will find the same, and in the President's house you will find the same. I state this merely to show that there are precedents in every department of the Government for such expenditures, and the gentleman who has charge of this institution ought not to be criticized for doing what has been done in all the other departments.

(After a little more unimportant discussion the amendments were voted upon and lost, and the appropriation remained at $47,000, the salaries being cut down for that year.)

Although the action of the House and of Congress was to limit our salaries to $22,000, our board took a liberal view of the matter and decided to make up the deficit out of our general expenses fund.

1882–1883

Our Twenty-Fifth Annual Report, submitted in October 1882, contains a brief account of a visit of President Arthur and prominent officials of the government, on the occasion of the twenty-fifth anniversary of the acceptance of the charter of the institution by the Board of Directors, February 23, 1857.

The occasion was one of more than usual interest. The President having signified his willingness to be the guest of honor on the evening named, invitations were issued "to meet the President of the United States." Naturally few would decline such an invitation, so we had present more than was common of the chief public functionaries.

We received the guests in the gymnasium and gave them an exhibition of athletic exercises by the students. President Arthur showed particular interest in these and told me he was given to such things in his young days.

From the gymnasium we went to the Chapel Hall, where some of the students gave a pantomime and exhibitions of their attainments in various ways. We then took our distinguished guests to the students' dining room where a dainty supper was served by our matron, and a very pleasant social hour was passed. I do not remember an occasion in the history of the institution when a more agreeable experience was had in the entertainment of guests.

On the occasion of our Presentation [Day] exercises in May 1883, a marble bust of President Garfield was unveiled with appropriate exercises. This work of the eminent sculptor, Daniel C. French, was presented to the college by the "deaf people of the United States and a few of their friends," to keep in perpetual memory the great services rendered to the college by General Garfield while he was a member of Congress. The sum of $1,461.52 was raised by subscription in twenty-six states and the District of Columbia for the purchase of the statue and the expenses incident to its being placed permanently in the Chapel. Addresses were made by E. A. Hodgson, editor of the *Deaf-Mutes Journal*, New York, and by Robert Patterson, now principal of the Ohio Institution for the Deaf and Dumb, a graduate of the college. These will be found in our Twenty-Sixth Annual Report. But I must insert here the closing paragraph of Mr. Patterson's address in this narrative because of its beauty in expression and the loftiness of its sentiment.

Students and Alumni: We do well in thus giving a public expression of our affection and honor for Garfield; but honor, true and enduring, can come only from our inner selves. Let us emulate the tireless vigil he kept at the shrine of knowledge, which won for him the admiration and confidence of the nation; let us imitate the purity and nobility of heart which made him a blessing to the world; and let us copy the simplicity and sincerity of character which made him a king among men. Then, and then only, will we confer true honor upon his efforts in our behalf and upon our Alma Mater forever!

1883–1884

The work of the institution proceeded during this year in a satisfactory manner without incidents of unusual interest. Mention may, however, be made of the receipt by the institution of the sum of $1,391.30, the avails of a legacy left some ten years ago by Richard J. Ryon of Washington. This is the first bequest of money ever left to the institution.

In the report for this year mention is made, at some length, of a tour I made in the south and west for the purpose of interesting officers and teachers in schools for the deaf in those sections of our country in the work of the college. The tour was a successful one, and I was able to visit fifteen schools.

1884–1885

In March 1885 Hon. T. F. Bayard of Delaware, who had been the Senatorial member of our board for six years, became Secretary of State in Mr. Cleveland's cabinet. Through his instrumentality the office of the president of the Columbia Institution for the Deaf and Dumb was recognized at the White House and placed on the official list of those to be received on New Year's Day and other state occasions.

Mr. Bayard also interested President [Cleveland] to be present at our Anniversary exercises in May, and the President presided as Patron on that occasion; Secretary Bayard made a very felicitous speech.

1885–1886

During this year an important addition to our buildings was made by the erection of a laboratory with funds provided by Congress.

The subject of admitting young women to the college was presented to the board from several sources and received serious and favorable consideration, and it was finally decided to commend the matter to Congress in our annual report.

In the summer of 1886 the president of the institution, accompanied by nine of the officers and teachers of the institution and three of his own family, made a notable journey to California where the Convention of American Instructors of the Deaf met in July. Arrangements were made through Dr. Philip G. Gillett, superintendent of the Illinois Institution for the Deaf and Dumb, for travel to and from the Pacific Coast at very low rates, making it possible for a large number of teachers of the deaf and their families to enjoy a tour of very great interest at very moderate cost.

The hospitality of the Illinois Institution at Jacksonville, the Colorado Institution at Colorado Springs, and most lavish of all that of the California Institution at Berkeley, where the delegates to the convention and their friends were entertained as in a luxurious hotel for a week, made the trip one to be long remembered by all who were able to take it.

In the spring of 1886 I received an invitation through the British Minister and our Secretary of State, to appear and give testimony before a Royal Commission appointed by the Queen of the United Kingdom to inquire into the matter of the education of the deaf, the blind, and the feebleminded. I accepted the invitation and sailed on the Cunard steamer

21. Eleventh Convention of American Instructors of the Deaf and Dumb, Berkeley, California, July 1886.

Etruria on Saturday, October 9th for Liverpool. My trip was an interesting one to me in many respects, and my reception by the Commission, of which Lord Egerton was the chairman, was most flattering.

I was before the Commission for two whole days and presented, besides my verbal testimony which was taken down verbatim, a great collection of books, pamphlets, and reports, including a complete set of the *American Annals of the Deaf*.

Lord Egerton invited me to visit him at his country seat, Tatton Park, near Manchester, and I spent a delightful two days there. Other members of the Commission showed me courtesies.

A notable and interesting feature of my welcome to England, was a dinner given in my honor at the Holborn Restaurant by the headmasters of the schools for the deaf of the whole country. It was really a magnificent affair and was presided over by Hon. William Woodall, Member of Parliament and of the Royal Commission, a man who had taken great interest in promoting the education of the deaf in his country.

A large number of headmasters and some teachers were present. Some of them had travelled many miles thus to do me the honor. A beautiful testimonial address of welcome, engraved on parchment and handsomely framed, was presented to me.

Mr. Woodall in his speech alluded to the fact that when my father, early in the century, visited England with the purpose of learning the art of instructing the deaf, the schools of the country were closed against him, for which all good Englishmen were now very much ashamed. He hoped that an atonement for this lack of hospitality was now being, in a measure, made by the cordial welcome extended to the son of his father. Thus was all said in most graceful fashion.

Teachers of all methods united in this testimonial to me and altogether it was an occasion ever to be remembered.

1886–1887

The event of importance during this year was the admission of young women to the college.

In the very first years of the history of the college four young women pursued the studies of the introductory class for a time, but none of them entered a higher class, and no other young women were received until the autumn of this year, 1887. In order to provide suitable accommodations for the six young women who presented themselves at this time, I gave up the greater part of my residence, and the matron of the institution, Miss Ellen Gordon, was installed as the lady of the house.*

My family removed to Hartford, Connecticut, where two of my sons had been at school for two and three years respectively, and I was allowed by vote of the board to spend about half my time in Hartford with my family. When in Washington, my home was with the young ladies in my old house.

The admission of young women to the college was agreed to by me with a good deal of reluctance and considerable apprehension that the college education of the sexes together might lead to unsatisfactory results. I had never been warmly in favor of co-education.

The experience of the first year, while not absolutely satisfactory, was so much more so than I had expected that I felt disposed to continue the experiment, and I am compelled to say at the date of the present writing,

---

*The six women were Ella F. Black, Indiana; Anna L. Kurtz, Indiana; Alto M. Lowman, Maryland; Margaret Ellen Rudd, Nebraska; Ide L. Kinney, Pennsylvania; and Hattie A. Leffler, Pennsylvania.

November 1899, that my apprehensions have not been realized. On the whole I feel that the presence of young women in the college has had a favorable influence.

22. *First group of women students with their matron, Ellen Gordon, standing outside President Gallaudet's residence.*

23. *Agatha Tiegel (Hanson), the first woman awarded a bachelor of arts degree in 1893.*

PART FIVE

Preparing for the Future

1887–1907

X

"Unveiling of the Statue"
1887–1891

1887–1888

IN JANUARY 1888 the institution lost a valued friend from its Board of Directors through the death of William W. Corcoran, whose name will ever be cherished in Washington as a man of great benevolence and purity of life. He was a warm personal friend of Amos Kendall and an early contributor to the funds of the institution.

A meeting of the board was held at Mr. Corcoran's house but a short time before his death, at which—in spite of his great age, for he was then nearly ninety—he displayed the liveliest interest in the welfare of the institution.

On the 23rd of January of this year, 1888, a distinguished Englishman was a visitor to the college, the Right Honorable Joseph Chamberlain, M.P., who was then in Washington on a special diplomatic mission.

Senator Dawes assisted me in receiving the visitor, whose lively interest in all he saw surprised and delighted teachers and students. Mr. Chamberlain carefully examined all the departments of the institution and asked many questions which gave evidence of his remarkably acute and observant mind. As I was conducting him into the chapel where the students and pupils were assembled to bid him good-bye, his quick eye fell on a tablet in the corridor to the memory of Edward Stretch, one of our most brilliant students, who died in his senior year. On this tablet was a quotation from a letter of the young man's to a sister, written two weeks before he died, as follows: "It will take away half the bitterness of death to have been allowed to learn something."

Mr. Chamberlain asked me about this young man and read the words just quoted with great seriousness. Five minutes later, in response to a few words of greeting from one of our students, Mr. Chamberlain made one of the most eloquent finished addresses that could be imagined with young Stretch's words as his inspiration.

Two months later, almost to a day, Mr. Chamberlain was summoned before the Royal Commission to give an account of what he saw at Kendall Green. The record of his testimony shows a degree of close and accurate observation, and a clearness of understanding in regard to peculiarities of methods and processes of instruction absolutely amazing. His testimony was of the greatest value, and had, as it deserved to have, great weight with the Commission.

In the summer of 1888 death removed one with whom the connection of the institution was of a peculiar and tender nature, one with whom my intimate personal relations covered a period of more than thirty years.

When I came to Washington in 1857, Mr. Kendall had as his family physician, Alexander Yelverton Peyton Garnett, of an old Virginia family, and son-in-law of Governor Wise of Virginia. Very naturally Dr. Garnett became the attending physician of the institution. He served in this capacity for twenty months without charge. I have alluded earlier in this narrative to Dr. Garnett and have told how he left Washington at the outbreak of the Civil War.

Twenty-four years thereafter he became for the second time the attending physician of the institution, continuing in that office up to the time of his death. He was a man whom to know was to admire and love.

His bright cheerful ways in the sick room sometimes made other prescriptions unnecessary—for they were a mind-cure of wonderful efficacy. His death was a real personal affliction to me. He deserves a place among the saints of Kendall Green.

1888–1889

In 1888 a second member of the Board of Directors was removed by death. James C. McGuire, named by Act of Congress as one of the first board in 1857, had served for more than thirty years.

He was a warm personal friend of Amos Kendall and contributed handsomely to the funds of the institution during its early years. Until his health failed he was regular in his attendance upon the meetings of the board and often, even in later years, was present at such meetings at no little sacrifice of his personal comfort.

During this year I had to encounter Mr. Randall, chairman of the House Committee on Appropriations, in his effort to cut down our appropriation for current expenses, at which I was greatly surprised as Mr. Randall had previously been very friendly to the institution.

Without calling me before his committee, he cut down our annual support fund $5,000 and had the Sundry Civil Bill reported to the House. I consulted the directors, and they directed me to try and get the amount of the cut restored. I called on Mr. Randall and told him that the institution would be seriously crippled if the cut should be sustained by Congress.

He was quite unmoved, and I told him that as directed by our board I should try and get the Senate to give us what we asked for. At this he broke out on me with great vehemence saying, "If you try that, I will make you sorry for it."

I felt he was putting me in a very hard position, but I made my effort with my friends in the Senate, and they put the $5,000 back. In conference Mr. Randall fought and succeeded in cutting out $2,500. But the following session I got that amount in the deficiency bill.

24. Kendall School building, 1885.

25. The cabinet shop and laboratory building. At left is the back part of College Hall.

Under date of May 8, 1888, I find in my diary the following: "Called on Mr. Randall at his house and found him ill and fierce."

During 1888 the laboratory building was fitted up and fully occupied. This made an important addition to the facilities of the college for teaching natural science.

In the spring of this year I represented the college at a Conference of Principals of American Schools for the Deaf held at Jackson, Mississippi. On my return I visited the School for the Deaf at St. Augustine, Florida.

During the summer of 1888, I had to work hard with the commissioners to keep our water privileges free from interference, they wanting to impair the efficiency of our private pipe by allowing parties along the route to tap it. Senator Dawes went with me to the commissioners, and they yielded.

The autumn of 1888 increased the number of young women in the college to eight, and we began to regard the experiment a success. In November of this year I visited Evansville, Indiana, and delivered an address to aid a school for the deaf which had been established by Charles Kerney, a recent graduate of our college.

In December I renewed my fight with Mr. Randall for our appropriations. My diary records of an interview with him: "He seemed rather jovial and said I had come for my 'post mortem.' I suppose the poor man felt near his last summer."

1889–1890

The year 1889 opened with a hard fight with Mr. Randall. He was determined to keep our current expense appropriation down, to limit our salaries and wages absolutely to $25,000, and to allow no more students to have free admission to [the] college.

In my diary under date of January 5th I find the following: "I worked in the office much of the morning over figures from Reports of Institutions for Deaf-Mutes to show the unreasonableness of Mr. Randall's position. With God's help I will win a signal victory over him." January 8th: "I was a good while getting to sleep, for the fight with Randall weighs my mind down very heavily in spite of my good courage."

Mr. Burnes of Missouri came into the fight [against] our college and was disposed to help Mr. Randall quite earnestly. We had the promise of a visit from Mr. Burnes and others of his committee on Sunday January 13th, but they disappointed us. On the 24th Mr. Burnes died, and thus was my work a good deal simplified. On the 28th our institution was under discussion in the House. I quote from my diary: "Mr. Randall by a most vigorous use of his power as chairman of the Committee on Appropriations was able to hold his measure as to restricting salaries, but the proviso forbidding aid to poor students in college as to their board was so amended as to make the law much more favorable than it has been. The debate was long and animated and developed a feeling of marked friendliness to the institution."

My diary under date of February 2nd says: "We had eight of our directors together this forenoon, and the situation in Congress was discussed with interest and intelligence. I found all ready to cooperate in securing the largest possible aid from Congress. The keen intelligence, broad views, and hearty sympathy accorded me by the directors is most grateful and encouraging. I am most highly favored in this regard."

In my struggle against Randall I found Senators Allison, Hale, and Gorman most helpful and friendly. The struggle over these matters ended with the close of Congress in March, and I had the great satisfaction of securing a handsome increase in our appropriation for salaries and the extension of the number of our college beneficiaries from forty to sixty. But by a strange inconsistency, such as often occurs in the action of Congress, it was provided that the sixty beneficiaries authorized, "shall only have the expenses of their *instruction* in the collegiate department, *exclusive of support*, paid from appropriations made for the support of the institution." And yet in the very paragraph enacting this provision, a full amount was appropriated for the "support" of the beneficiaries we were forbidden to support.

This enactment would have worked great embarrassment to our college had there not been in our treasurer's hands a fund of about $4,000 on which we could draw in aid of the poor students which Mr. Randall's unfriendly legislation was intended to cut off.

Within a few days after the passage of Mr. Randall's proviso, I received a letter from one of his constituents and ardent supporters in Philadelphia, asking for the admission of his deaf-mute son as a free student in our college.

In the meantime our board had authorized me to draw on the $4,000 when necessary to aid such students as might be recommended by members of Congress. Mr. Randall had refused to recommend the son of his constituent, and the father had appealed to me to see Mr. Randall and secure his aid if possible.

On the 18th of March I called on Mr. Randall and was shown to his chamber where he lay in bed, evidently very feeble. I spoke to him of the application of his constituent, told him of the fund at the disposition of our board, and said that the young man in his district could have the benefit of it if he, Mr. Randall, would request it.

He pondered over the matter for some time and finally said it would be inconsistent with the ground he took in the House for him to recommend the young man and he could not do it. I then asked him if I should write to his friend in Philadelphia to that effect.

Rising suddenly on his elbow he said with great emphasis, "No, I will conduct my own correspondence with my constituents."*

---

*The young man in question was Andrew Sullivan. E. M. Gallaudet wrote the father after this meeting explaining that his son's admission was dependent on Mr. Randall's authorization.

The young man in question was kept out of college a year in consequence of Mr. Randall's refusal to recommend him and came in then on recommendation of his successor, Mr. Randall having died in the meantime.

In our annual report for 1889 a very earnest appeal was made to Congress to repeal the legislation taken at the instance of Mr. Randall.

In the summer of 1889 an event of more than ordinary interest occurred on Kendall Green. This was the unveiling and presentation to the institution of a beautiful bronze statue of Thomas Hopkins Gallaudet, founder of deaf-mute education in America. This statue, the work of the eminent sculptor Daniel Chester French, stands on the lawn in front of the chapel and represents Dr. Gallaudet teaching his first pupil, Alice Cogswell.

The expense of the statue, some $13,000, was met by subscriptions from deaf-mutes representing every state and territory of the United States.

The unveiling of the statue took place on the 28th of June in the presence of the officers and pupils of our institution and some three hundred deaf-mutes, who had come from all parts of the country, meeting in convention, as they are accustomed to do every three years. A full account of the unveiling ceremonies will be found in the Thirty-Second Annual Report of the institution.

During the year 1889 a printing office was fitted up in which certain of our students, who had some knowledge of printing, might improve themselves therein.

The year 1889 marked the completion of twenty-five years in the history of the college, and the exercises of Presentation Day were of more than usual interest. President Harrison presided. The orator of the day was Hon. James W. Patterson, State Superintendent of Schools in New Hampshire, who as then a member of the House represented Congress at the inauguration of the college in 1864. It was an especial pleasure to have this early friend of the college with us at our quarter-century celebration. Honorary degrees were conferred on several prominent educators of the deaf, the most eminent of these being my warm personal friend, Monseigneur De Haerne, member of the Parliament of Belgium and for many years director of a school for deaf-mutes in Brussels.

Our Professor Draper was commissioned by our board to present in person our diploma to Monseigneur De Haerne, attending, on his way to Brussels, an International Congress of the Deaf in Paris.

26. *New England group at the unveiling of the statue of Thomas Hopkins Gallaudet in 1889 (taken by the deaf photographer, Alexander Pach).*

27. *The first Gallaudet College alumni reunion coincided with the unveiling of the statue.*

In September 1889 I resumed the full occupancy of my home on Kendall Green, which had been given up to the young women of the college for two years, and my family returned from Hartford. The young women of the college were furnished accommodations in the east building of the institution.

1890–1891

In January 1890 Mr. John B. Wight, who had been our efficient and faithful family supervisor and disbursing agent since 1877, decided to resign his position and engage in business in Washington. His leaving was a serious disappointment to me, for besides being a most capable officer, he was an agreeable and lovable man to whom we had become strongly attached.

His place was taken by Mr. Wallace G. Fowler of Connecticut, a cousin of mine, who proved to be a worthy successor of Mr. Wight in all respects. At the time of this writing, February 1906, Mr. Fowler is filling his position most acceptably.

The committee which had charge of the erection of the Gallaudet statue turned over to our board the sum of $479.54, a balance remaining in their hands after meeting all the expense of the statue, with a view of providing for the care of the statue.

Our directors felt that the institution could well afford to keep the statue in repair and, after adding out of their private funds enough to make an even $500, decided to invest that sum as a Gallaudet Memorial Art Fund, the income of which should be appropriated to the purchase of works of art for the pleasure and instruction of our students and pupils.

A movement was started in 1890 at the suggestion of a gentleman from Cincinnati, Mr. L. S. Fechheimer who had a deaf son, for the establishment of a normal department in our institution in which young men and women, having all their faculties, might be trained to be teachers of the deaf under the two principal methods now in use. The attention of Congress was called to this project in our annual report, but nothing was done towards the establishment of the department.

The most important event of the year 1890 was the passage by Congress of legislation, approved August 30th, repealing the unfavorable action of the previous year which forbade the giving of free board to students in the college.

I took much pains to secure the friendly cooperation of Hon. Joseph
G. Cannon, then chairman of the House Committee on Appropriations,
and induced him to prepare a paragraph which should give us the right
to receive and care for sixty free students. The paragraph passed by
Congress will be found in our Thirty-Third Annual Report. I remember
that this was written by Mr. Cannon, not typewritten, and when I told
him we might need to provide for more than sixty in the near future, he
said it would be an easy matter to have the number increased. That he
opposed such an increase a few years later, as will appear later in this
record, was a great surprise and disappointment to me.

In June 1890 a young man graduated from the college, whose connection with it in view of certain incidents recorded in this history, is of
more than ordinary interest.

Cadwallader L. Washburn, above referred to, was a son of Senator
William D. Washburn of Minnesota and a nephew of Elihu B. Washburne
of Illinois, who in 1867, 1868, and 1869 did his utmost as chairman of
the Committee on Appropriations in the House to destroy our college,
declaring repeatedly in the House that there was no good reason why a
college for the deaf should be maintained.

Mr. E. B. Washburne was not living at the time of his nephew's
graduation, but he lived long enough to know that he *had* a nephew in
the college he had tried to break down.

It is worthy of note that young Washburn made a highly creditable
record as a student and that his graduation essay on "The Mind of the
Spider" attracted so much attention as to find a place in a school reader
published soon after he completed his college course.

Our Thirty-Third Annual Report has an appendix prepared by Professor Draper which gives an interesting statement of what many of our
college graduates had done in the various positions of importance they
had been able to take and fill creditably.

In the autumn of 1890 Dr. and Mrs. F. J. Campbell of London visited
Washington. Dr. Campbell who is at the head of the Royal Normal College
for the Blind which he has created and developed wonderfully, he being
a blind man, tried to interest members of our board to adopt the idea of
establishing a college for the blind as a part of our institution. I felt rather
in favor of the project but was not eager for it. None of our board, however,
could be induced to act on Dr. Campbell's suggestion.

Toward the end of 1890 I made an effort to secure the presence of President Harrison and a number of prominent members of the Senate and House at a dinner with the members of our board. The President expressed a willingness to accept and said he hoped he could attend the dinner. But his official engagements prevented him doing so.

We had a dinner all the same at which Senators Dawes and Cockrell, Representatives Cannon, McComas, Cogswell, Clements, Henderson, and Hemphill were present with Commissioner Douglas, Doctors Weiling and Fox, and Judge Niblack of our board, also Professors Fay, Gordon, and Chickering of our faculty. The dinner was at Wormley's Hotel and did much to secure the friendly cooperation of the public men present for our institution.

XI

The Graduate Program Established
1891–1898

1891–1892

IN JULY 1891 the management of the institution sustained a severe loss in the death of Dr. Robert C. Fox, who had been for ten years secretary of the Board of Directors. The relation of son-in-law to Hon. Amos Kendall gave peculiar interest to Dr. Fox's connection with the institution, and his colleagues on the board especially regretted his death for the reason that it served the last personal tie between the institution and the family of its earliest benefactor. The high regard in which Dr. Fox was held is shown by a minute of the board in our Thirty-Fourth Annual Report.

In March 1891 Congress made a special appropriation of $3,000 to provide for instructors of articulation. This grew out of an effort I made to secure the support of Congress for the establishment of a normal department, in which young men and women, having all their faculties, could be thoroughly trained to be teachers of the deaf.

This scheme for a normal department was suggested, as readers of this history will remember, by Mr. Fechheimer of Cincinnati, Ohio, a strong advocate of oral teaching. In speaking of this plan to Professor Alexander Graham Bell some months after it had been suggested, I told him I should want him to give some lectures to the normal students. He was pleased at this suggestion and seemed to approve of the idea of our normal class. I was therefore a good deal surprised to learn on January 23rd, 1891, from General Cogswell of Massachusetts, a member of the House Appropriations Committee, that Professor Bell had asked to be heard by the committee in opposition to the measure. On the 26th of January I had a long talk with Professor Bell and found his opposition to our normal class was based on what he *said* he understood was our purpose, viz.: to train *deaf* teachers of the deaf.

I told him plainly that he was entirely mistaken in this idea, that no deaf persons would be admitted to our normal class, and that all its members would be thoroughly trained in the oral method of teaching the deaf. And yet on the very next day Professor Bell appeared before the Appropriations Committee and spoke for forty-five minutes, asserting flatly that our purpose *was* to train deaf teachers of the deaf and opposing the plan mainly on that ground.

I spoke in reply for thirteen minutes, laying bare Professor Bell's disingenuousness, and had the satisfaction of learning on January 30th (quoting from my diary): "that the Committee on Appropriations had sustained us fully as against [Alexander] Graham Bell's attack. General Cogswell said they were not disposed to do anything for Bell."

But Professor Bell carried the controversy over to the Senate committee, in the meantime securing petitions from a number of the oral schools for the deaf in the country against the measure, still holding to his unwarranted assertion that our normal class was to be for the training of deaf teachers of the deaf.

With the Senate committee, Bell succeeded in getting the appropriation of $5,000 given by the House cut down to $3,000 and specifically given for the payment of articulation teachers.

Bell telegraphed to some of his friends that "the normal department was defeated." But this was far from the truth, for [with] the appropriation given by Congress we were able to organize and carry forward the normal department *exactly as we had planned.*

As I look back on this affair, writing fifteen years later, I feel justified in characterizing Professor Bell's course as a piece of most unwarrantable interference based on statements, which he plainly understood from my own lips, had no foundation in fact.

The year 1891 put another controversy on my hands which threatened the interests of the institution quite seriously. The Baltimore and Ohio Railroad Company surveyed a new route of connection for their eastern and western lines directly across our grounds, within three hundred feet of our gymnasium building, and had a bill introduced into Congress authorizing the laying of the tracks. The carrying out of this plan would have made our grounds unfit to be the location of an institution such as ours and would have depreciated the value of our property to a most destructive extent.

I naturally put forth all my strength to defeat this scheme, laboring not only with friends in Congress, but with officers of the Baltimore and Ohio Railroad, to induce them if possible to acknowledge that a connecting route just north of our grounds was not only feasible, but more desirable than the one across our grounds.

Our directors in Congress, Senators Hawley and Dawes and Representatives Hitt and Hemphill, gave me much valuable aid, and the result was that a signal triumph was won for the institution. I hope I may be pardoned for quoting from my diary a remark I find recorded there from Senator Dawes under the date of January 30, 1891: "Senator Dawes, when I told him of the surrender of the B & O Railroad, said, 'You are bigger than Congress for they can't beat a great railroad which you have done'."

We had an interesting visit from a company of Indians on February 1st. They took great satisfaction in talking with our students by signs. The natural gestures made by the Indians among themselves were found to have a close resemblance of those used by deaf-mutes.

In March of this year a social event occurred at my house which I think deserves to be recorded in this history as illustrating the value of Mrs. Gallaudet's efforts in the social life of Washington to gain the interest of prominent and influential people in our institution. This was a luncheon given in honor of Mrs. Garfield, the widow of the late President. The other guests were Mrs. President Harrison, Mrs. Blaine, Mrs. Noble, Mrs. Carter (of Hawaii), Mrs. and Miss Dawes, Mrs. Senator Chandler, Mrs. Senator Washburn, Mrs. Lander, Mrs. John Hay, Mrs. Pollok, and Mrs. Pomeroy.

Towards the end of July 1891, I sailed for Europe, taking my oldest son Denison with me. The object of my going was to deliver an address before the Congress of Deaf-Mutes of Great Britain and Ireland held in the city of Glasgow.

I made the address on the combined system of educating the deaf before a large assemblage on the evening of August 7th. My invitation to address the Congress was suggested by Mrs. Francis Maginn of Belfast who was a student in our college a few years earlier and, at the time of my visit to Glasgow, a missionary to the deaf-mutes of Belfast and vicinity. After leaving Glasgow I spent some weeks with my son travelling in England and on the Continent, getting much needed rest and relaxation after the labors of the year in Washington which had been more of a tax on my nervous energies than usual. The congenial companionship of my son . . . added greatly to the pleasure of my trip.

28. *Faculty and normal school students in 1891.*

With the opening of our college term in September, we inaugurated our normal department, the class consisting of seven students, six young men, all college graduates, and one young woman, a graduate of a high school.* I expect great benefit to the cause of the education of the deaf in our country from this (department) class for it will give a most valuable re-inforcement to the teaching force of our schools.

Before the close of 1891 the institution received a gold medal award from the Paris Exposition Universelle of 1889. This is the third time the work of the college has been so commended in foreign nations, the first medal coming from Chile in 1875 and the second from France in 1878.

Under the date of November 7th in my diary, I find a record which I think worthy of insertion in this history as showing how the students of our college came into pleasant and creditable relations with those of other institutions of learning: "Our football team, with a good many others, went to Annapolis today. The cadet's [team] won by a score of only 6 to 0. They said our team was the finest they had met this year."

---

*The normal fellows were: Charles R. Ely, B. A. Yale, 1891; George R. Hare, B. A. Amherst, 1890; Oscar Vaught, M. A. DePauw, Ind., 1890; Guy M. Wilcox, B. A. Carleton, Minn., 1891; Joseph A. Tillinghast, B. A. Davidson, N.C., 1891; and Wirt A. Scott, B. A. Univ. Miss., 1891. The normal student was Annie E. Jameson, Boston High School, 1889.

1892–1893

Early in 1892 some of the oralists in Philadelphia and New York made an effort to oblige us to have recitations in college conducted orally with some students as had been orally taught and could read the lips. Mr. Greenburger, the principal of the New York Oral School, proposed that his Board of Directors should ask Congress to increase our appropriation so that his ideas might be carried out. This scheme did not command the approval of our faculty or our board, and nothing came of it.

In the summer of 1892 I represented the institution at a Conference of Principals held in the Colorado Institution for the Deaf and Blind at Colorado Springs. My son Herbert accompanied me. I had some hope that the experience might have influence with him to lead him to become a teacher of the deaf.

Our seven normal students who graduated in June 1892 all secured good positions as instructors in various schools, so our policy in establishing the normal department was justified.

The year 1892 seems to afford little for this record so I will pass on with the remark that a run through my diary shows that it was a year of a full amount of labor and care on my part for the institution, with much personal anxiety during the autumn growing out of the fact that my sons Edson and Herbert both had typhoid fever at the old home of their mother in Royalton, Vermont.

1893–1894

In May 1893 Hon. William E. Niblack of Indiana, who had been a member of our board for nineteen years, was called from earth. His death was the source of sincere grief to all connected with the institution. No member of our board had ever manifested a more active and earnest interest in the welfare of the institution, and his influence in Congress in overcoming opposition and securing support for our college was most helpful. His memory will be cherished by all who knew him.

In the summer of 1893 memorials were presented to our board from the Conference of Principals and Superintendents of Schools for the Deaf in the United States and from the Alumni Association of the College, urging the establishment of a technical department in the college.

The proposal was considered favorably by our board, and in our Thirty-Sixth Annual Report the matter was brought to the attention of Congress.

The following year a small increase was made in the appropriation for our current expenses, and our course of study in the college was modified so as to give greater facilities for technical training than before.

An important exhibit by schools for the deaf in the United States was made at the Chicago World's Fair of 1893. The work of our institution was well shown by publications and photographs, and the entire exhibit of the schools was in the daily charge of a graduate of the college, Mr. Lester Goodman of Chicago. Mr. Goodman, who had a perfect command of speech, made constant explanations to visitors of the exhibits of the various schools and was in himself a living exhibit of the system of education pursued in the schools and in the college.

Among other interesting things in the exhibit was a plaster cast of French's statue of Thomas Hopkins Gallaudet, which stands near our college chapel.

A gold medal and diploma were awarded the college for its exhibit. A quotation from Mr. Goodman's account of the exhibit will be of interest:

The statue occupying a central position in the exhibit, the pedestal bordering on the boundary line of one of the main aisles running north and south the entire length of the building of manufactures and liberal arts, challenges the eyes of the passer-by, bids him pause, and by the mystery of poetic beauty and artistic touch, stirs something in the heart which rises to the brain and causes him to look at the whole exhibit. This statement is not hyperbole, but plain prose. I have in my possession the written words of one the most cultivated of the journalists of Chicago, who, after a long study of the statue, approached me and said, "It tells such a grand story." On my remarking that I was happy to meet a man who had the poetic insights to read between the lines, he said "As I stood there the moisture came into my eyes, and as I am a newspaper man, you may perhaps understand what power there must be to move me so."

The photographs exhibited, which filled a large folding wall case and were fine, were taken and printed by Mr. Ronald Douglas, a former student of the college.

1894–1895

The year 1894 was marked by the death of two valued officers of the institution, Dr. James C. Welling, for seven years a most useful and devoted member of our board, and Mr. Almon Bryant, for twenty-five years the master of our cabinet shop.

Dr. Welling, an accomplished and experienced educator and for many years president of Columbia University, was eminently fitted to advise in the management of our institution, and his great natural courtesy and friendliness attracted and endeared all who came in contact with him.

Mr. Bryant was a typical New England mechanic, cabinet-making being his trade but having great knowledge in other lines of handicraft and a manual dexterity that made him useful to a degree quite unusual in an ordinary mechanic. His ideas of duty were of the stern New England sort, and I could always feel sure that anything for which he was responsible would be thoroughly looked after. Several mantels in the president's house stand as specimens of Mr. Bryant's skill as a woodworker.

On Presentation Day 1894 President Welling made an announcement of recent action of the board which was of great interest to the students and alumni of the college. This was that the board had decided, in compliance with a recommendation from the faculty and an earnest petition from the alumni, to change the name of the collegiate department of the institution. The alumni and students had often during a number of years expressed their dislike of the presence of the words *deaf-mute* in the name of the college, and they felt it to be a misuse of terms to apply those words to the college which certainly was not a deaf-mute. And the alumni desired that the college should receive the name of some distinguished benefactor of their class, so they asked that it might be called Gallaudet College in honor of the founder of deaf-mute education in America whose statue adorns the campus.

After very mature consideration, the board decided to accede to the request of the alumni and the recommendation of the faculty, and Dr. Welling's announcement was of this action of the directors.

In regard to this matter I naturally had a good deal of feeling lest some might think I was anxious that the college should have *my* name. Some of my friends and members of my family thought the name Gallaudet should not be given to the college while I was its president. But I wish to record here that my wish was to have the name given with the clear understanding that it was *in no way* in honor of me, but solely to honor my father who richly deserved such an honor. And I feared that if the name were given after I was gone, there might be an effort to have me *at least* divide the honor with my father, which was what I *did not want*. So I was willing to be placed in a position where I might, perhaps, be misunderstood for the definite reason I have tried to make clear.

Whether it was well to have done it or not, the change in the name was a source of great satisfaction to the students, alumni, and friends of the college.

1895–1896

In the autumn of 1895 a building was completed and occupied, the plans for which were drawn by a graduate of our college, Mr. Olof Hanson, a successful architect living in Faribault, Minnesota. Mr. Hanson drew up complete specifications for this building and made careful estimates of its probable cost. It was to his credit and greatly to our satisfaction that the expense of constructing the building fell a few hundred dollars short of the estimates. The building is a dormitory for the boys of the Kendall School, is well adapted to its purpose, and has no little architectural beauty.

An important addition was made to the laboratory during the summer of 1895, and the east main building was much changed so as to give improved accommodation to the young ladies of the college.

29. *Laying the cornerstone of the boy's dormitory in 1894 (E.M.G. standing top row center).*

An interesting addition to our normal class was made this year in the person of a Mr. Jamini Nath Banerji, a high-caste Hindu from Calcutta. Mr. Banerji was fitting himself to conduct a school for the deaf in Calcutta which had been started in a small way before he left India. He returned to India after completing his course with us and took charge of the Calcutta school.

An interesting incident occurred on Presentation Day before Mr. Banerji's graduation. As he was a British subject, I gave Lord Pauncefote, the British Ambassador, a special invitation to be present and asked him to make an address. He accepted the invitation to attend the exercises of Presentation Day but declined to make an address saying it was his invariable rule not to make public addresses. He made a smiling allusion to one of our ambassadors to England (Mr. Bayard) who pursued a different course.

At the exercises of Presentation Day, Mr. Banerji made an interesting and eloquent address. In spite of his declination to speak, Lord Pauncefote was so moved by what Mr. Banerji had said that he rose to his place, took Mr. Banerji by the hand, and made a short but very earnest speech. This is understood to be the only public address made by Lord Pauncefote while he represented Her British Majesty's Government at Washington.

1896–1897

During the summer of 1896 an interesting meeting of alumni of the college was held at the college, the president being authorized to extend the hospitalities of Kendall Green to the alumni for three days. Twenty-two classes of the college had representatives at this meeting, several papers of interest were presented, and on the sabbath, services were conducted by alumni of the college who were regularly ordained clergymen.

At the closing dinner a valuable set of books and silver furnishings for a library table were presented by the alumni to the president of the college with expressions of sincere personal regard.

1897–1898

In the spring of 1897 immediately after Presentation Day, I left Washington, taking my son Edson with me, and sailed from New York on May

30. E. M. Gallaudet with his sons Denison, Herbert, and Edson.

8th in the North German Lloyd Steamer *Kaiser Wilhelm II*, known as the "Rolling Billy." We made the acquaintance of Captain Hogemann whom we found to be a most charming gentleman.

I had two professional objects in going to Europe at this time, one being to carry to the educational authorities of a number of European nations a "message" from our Board of Directors, giving our mature conclusions as to methods after forty years of work at Kendall Green.

The other end I had in view was to meet with educated adult deaf-mutes in a number of cities in Europe and learn from them their opinions as to the relative value of methods.

I was able to carry out this program very successfully, as will appear from a reference to the Fortieth Annual Report of our institution. I managed also to derive much pleasure as I journeyed and returned to America in August much refreshed by the trip. My enjoyment was greatly increased by the companionship of my son Edson who proved a most congenial travelling companion.

My friend General A. W. Greely wrote and published this year (1897) in the *Review of Reviews* a well-written and complimentary article in regard to the forty years work of our institution rounded out this year. It was gratifying to have the story so well told.

On the day before Christmas I received a very disquieting letter from the Secretary of the Interior informing me that Attorney General McKenna had given him an opinion, sustaining the claim of the department to exercise control over the disbursements of the institution. A copy of this opinion was forwarded in the letter.

This was a great surprise to me, for the claim of the department to control the disbursements of the institution had been forward on two occasions in previous years, once by Secretary Teller, and again by Secretary Hoke Smith. In the first instance the matter had been settled in our favor by a decision of Assistant General McCammon of the Interior Department, and in the second by an opinion, also in our favor, by Acting Attorney General Holmes Conrad.

It came to my knowledge that a man named Acker, at the head of the miscellaneous division of the Interior Department, was the mover in these efforts to get control by the Department of the Interior of the disbursements of our institution, and that he had worked secretly to secure the opinion of Attorney General McKenna without giving the least opportunity to our institution to be heard.

Very naturally I was much roused by all this, and as our directors fully agreed with me that it would be very unfortunate for the institution that its disbursements should be controlled by the Interior Department, I referred the matter to them with confidence that they would sustain me in an effort to defeat the purpose of Acker.

Very fortunately, Hon. Sereno E. Payne of New York, the leader of the House, was on our board, and he was a personal friend of the Secretary of the Interior, Hon. Cornelius N. Bliss of New York. On December 27th Senator Hawley accompanied me to the Attorney General's office, and we saw Mr. McKenna and Solicitor General Richards who had evidently written the "opinion." They were quite set in their views, yielding nothing to what we urged.

The next day I called at the Interior Department and had a pleasant talk with Assistant Secretary Ryan who was always friendly to me, having been a member of our board when he was in the House from Kansas. Judge Ryan told me that the Secretary [Bliss], who was in New York, cared nothing about controlling the institution and suggested if the board wished to maintain its control, it would be easy to get legislation from Congress that would override and set aside the Attorney General's opinion.

XII

"Success Has Attended My Efforts"
1898–1907

1898–1899

SENATORS WALTHALL AND HAWLEY, members of our board, advised me to seek the counsel of some eminent lawyer, and acting on this advice I consulted with Mr. R. Ross Perry, an old friend and one of the leading lawyers of Washington. Mr. Perry took in the situation* very quickly and thought the matter could be put into good shape without difficulty if the Secretary of the Interior would acquiesce in the course proposed.

In connection with Acker's movement came a letter inspired by him, claiming that our institution was paying unreasonably high prices for many articles consumed in the institution. This called for much labor and some worry on my part, but I was successful in showing that the charge of extravagance was entirely without foundation. On January 7th by previous appointment, Gen. John W. Foster, Hon. Sereno E. Payne, and I called on the Secretary of the Interior, Mr. Bliss, and had a very satisfactory interview with him. He assured us he would interpose no objection to our securing legislation from Congress to settle matters as our board wished.

On January 8th our board met with seven members present and took unanimous action sustaining my views as to what course should be taken in the present juncture. It was very gratifying to me to be so sustained.

Owing to a fortunate imperfection in the legislation originally had by Congress, providing for the appointment of members of our board from Congress, the way was opened for the legislation we now wanted in what seemed a natural and almost necessary manner. The law authorizing

---

*[efforts to get control of the disbursements of the institution by the Department of the Interior]

Congressional directors limited their service to a single Congress, thus leaving the board without such directors from March 4th to the first Monday in December in alternate years.

So our new legislation, which I drew up, and which Mr. Perry did not change was as follows:

> *Provided*, That directors appointed under the provisions of section 4863 of the Revised Statutes of the United States shall remain in office until the appointment and acceptance of office of their successors; and the directors of the institution shall have control of the disbursements of all moneys appropriated by Congress for the benefit of the institution, accounts for which shall be settled and adjusted at the Treasury Department as required by the provisions of section 236 of the Revised Statutes.

The securing of the passage of the foregoing important legislation was only after much labor and anxiety on my part.

I have reason to believe that Acker of the Interior Department exerted himself a good deal in opposition to the measure. Interviews with Messrs. Cannon and Sayers of the House satisfied me that they had been labored with against me. At one interview with Mr. Cannon he advised me to "agonize" with Mr. Sayers. At this time Mr. Sayers was a member of our board, and it will be easily seen that a hostile attitude on his part would be damaging to our cause.

7th, under which date I find the following record in my diary: "This stands as a red-letter day for I learned this morning from Mr. Cleaves, clerk of the Senate Committee on Appropriations that the Conference Committee had agreed to our proviso. 'Praise God from whom all blessings flow!' A heavy load of care that has burdened me for six months, *heavily*, is lifted and I am a thankful man. I have felt like singing all day long. About ten years of youth have come back to me."

1899–1900

During 1898 and 1899 I made efforts in Congress to secure an increase in the number of the free scholarships in the college, the number allowed by law, sixty, having been fully reached.

The law increasing the number of free scholarships from forty to sixty was carried through chiefly by the friendly cooperation of Hon. Joseph

31. E.M.G. camping with students, ca. 1898: (left to right) E. A. Fay, Roy J. Stewart, George Andree, Captain Davis, Walter Rosson, and E.M.G.

G. Cannon, then chairman of the Committee on Appropriations. Mr. Cannon wrote the paragraph with his own hand and said, when I remarked that the limit of sixty might be reached in a few years, that it would be easy to increase the number allowed. This law was passed August 30, 1890, and the limit of sixty was reached in 1898. In that year Mr. Cannon was again chairman of the Committee on Appropriations, and I went to him confident of securing his aid to authorize the raising of the number to one hundred.

Greatly to my surprise he declared himself opposed to any increase. I got my friends in the Senate to give the increase, but Mr. Cannon opposed the measure successfully. In 1899 I made a second attempt, with a similar result.

In 1900 it happened that five applicants for admission to the college from Iowa could not be received because of the limitations of existing law. I laid the matter before Speaker Henderson who was from Iowa and who had been a good friend of the college for many years.

I had recommendations from five members of Congress from Iowa, asking for the admission of the five young people. General Henderson was naturally *for Iowa* as well as for the college. He advised me to get the provision for one hundred put on in the Senate and said he would do all he could to carry it in the House.

The provision was agreed to by the Committee of Conference, and I was told that Mr. Cannon, making use of language more emphatic than elegant said, "With the Senate and the Speaker against me, what in ――― could I do?"

The importance of this legislation cannot be over-estimated. I regard it as equivalent to an endowment of a million and a half dollars. The law was approved June 6, 1900, and the day deserved to be regarded as one of the memorable days in the history of the institution.

On the 8th of July 1900 Professor Fay accompanying me, I sailed from New York for Geneva in the *Kaiser Wilhelm II*, the same steamer in which I crossed the Atlantic in 1897, occupying the same room, and having the pleasure of the company of the genial Captain Hogemann.

Our purpose in visiting Europe at this time was to attend and take part in an International Congress of friends and teachers of the deaf and the deaf themselves to be held at Paris in connection with the great Exposition in progress during that year (1900).

The Congress was largely attended, but there were few from America. [Alexander] Graham Bell was on hand and, speaking just before me at the opening of the Congress, said much of what I had intended to say, making it necessary for me to think *very fast* in order to be prepared to say something appropriate in French. Professor Bell had his remarks written out, but I had to speak extempore. Professor Fay and I spoke intelligibly and to the point.

Professor Fay and I both read carefully prepared papers. I had mine printed in English, German, and Italian, but read it in French.

The Congress was wholly in the hands of pure oralists, but the educated deaf who were present in large numbers were for the combined system almost to a man.

The presiding officer Dr. Lachariere, who had been the attending physician of the Paris Institution, was a bitter and unscrupulous oralist, making several most unjust rulings which treated me very unfairly. The officers of the Paris Institution felt themselves so much aggrieved by the placing of Dr. Lachariere in charge of the Congress that none of them would attend its sessions. Had I known about this state of affairs in advance, I do not think I should have taken any part in the Congress.

1900–1901

During the latter part of 1900, the Board of Charities of the District made efforts to take some control of the institution, claiming the board gave it power over our institution.

The sentiment of managers of schools for the deaf in the United States had, of late years, become so decided against regarding such schools as charities that I felt it would be a great misfortune to have our institution acknowledged as a "charity." I submitted the matter to our directors, and they agreed with me.

On the 28th of December Senator Cockrell, Mr. Dawes, and Mr. Wight accompanied me to a meeting of the Board of Charities and represented our views. The board thought them not unreasonable but held that the law required us to come under their control. It was decided to submit the matter to the Attorney General for his decision.

After some time he rendered an opinion that existing law made our institution one of charity. The board was very considerate and agreed to give us time to secure legislation of Congress that might put the situation as we wished it to be. After considerable effort and a good deal of anxiety from the fact that the House Committee on the District of Columbia declined to adopt a proviso I had prepared, I succeeded in getting the following put on our District of Columbia appropriation by the Senate Committee on Appropriations and in securing the agreement of the House:

Provided, That hereafter all deaf-mutes of teachable age, of good mental capacity, and properly belonging to the District of Columbia, shall be received and instructed in said institution, their admission thereto being subject to the approval of the superintendent of public schools of the District of Columbia. And said institution shall not be regarded nor classified as an institution of charity.

This proviso became a law March 1, 1901, and put the institution in exactly the position we had desired.

During February 1901 I had the most severe attack of illness that had come upon me during all the years of my residence in Washington, narrowly escaping pneumonia. I rallied well, however, and early in March spent a few days at Atlantic City with wonderful recuperative effect.

During the autumn of 1900 the management of the institution sustained a severe loss in the death of Hon. Wm. L. Wilson of West Virginia, who had been a director for several years.

In the summer of 1901 Rev. Byron Sunderland, D.D., the only one remaining of the original Board of Directors appointed in 1857, was called suddenly away from earth. He was present at our closing exercises June 19th and seemed then in vigorous health though he had passed the limit of four score years.

Dr. Sunderland's death was a real personal grief to me, for it served the last link that connected me with the early days when, hardly more than a boy, I took the management of the institution on my shoulders. Forty-four years had passed since the time when he gave me a cordial welcome to Washington and to the church of which he was pastor and with which I remained connected more than twenty years.

On the 3rd of September 1901 another official of our institution died, who had made a notable record and who left a fragrant memory. Professor Samuel Porter, who became a member of our college faculty in 1866 and had continued an active member until 1884 when he reached the age of 75, continued to reside in the college as an emeritus professor until a few weeks before his death.

His eminence as a scholar and his success as an instructor were great. His lovableness as a man was unusual. During the seventeen years that he went in and out as an emeritus professor, he made himself helpful to students and professors, being always ready to take up duty in an active way whenever there was need for his services. His mental faculties were clear and his physical force unabated up to a few months of his decease at the ripe age of ninety-two.

1901–1902

On Presentation Day 1901 we had an address of unusual interest from His Excellency Wu Ting Fang, the Chinese Minister. His complete command of English, his keen sense of humor, and his power of adapting himself to his environment made his speech of unusual appropriateness and merit.

On this occasion my brother, Rev. Thomas Gallaudet, D.D., Rector of St. Ann's Church for Deaf-Mutes, New York, was with us as one of our chaplains for the last time. He was present and took part in the exercises of the inauguration of the college in 1864. It was his custom to visit the college as often as once each year, and few of our public anniversaries passed in his absence. His apostolic benediction given with the voice and by signs simultaneously seemed always a real blessing from Heaven. His death which occurred in the summer of 1902 brought sincere grief to many of the residents of Kendall Green.

1902–1903

During 1902 medals and diplomas were received by the college for exhibits in the Paris Exposition of 1900, the Buffalo Exposition of 1901, and the South Carolina Inter-State and West India Exposition.

In the autumn of 1903 the institution experienced a grievous loss in the death of Mrs. Gallaudet. It is her due that mention should be made in this history of the important part she bore in the upbuilding of the college and what she did for the happiness of the officers, students, and pupils.

Her birthday parties for the pupils of the Kendall School brought great pleasure to the children. They were looked forward to with eager interest and remembered with gratitude. Mrs. Gallaudet's frequent evening receptions for officers and some of the older students were valued highly and did much for the social life of Kendall Green. Her entertainment of public men and their wives at dinners and lunches made many warm and helpful friends for the college, [this] being most helpful to her husband in his sometimes, even often, strenuous efforts to secure from Congress the support needed for the college.

Mrs. Gallaudet's Presentation Day receptions, continued during many years, were regarded as brilliant events in the social life of Washington. The performance of all these social duties involved an amount of labor that was often exhausting to Mrs. Gallaudet and which probably shortened her life.

In the autumn of 1902 Hon. Charles A. Russell, a valued member of our board from Connecticut, was called away from earth by death. He had been a faithful and interested director, having rendered valuable service in Congress.

In January 1903 Hon. Henry L. Dawes passed from earth. Ex-Senator Dawes had been a member of our board since 1869, and from the time of his joining the management of the institution, he had been a most valued and devoted friend. He succeeded Hon. E. B. Washburne as chairman of the House Committee on Appropriations and received from him, so he told the writer, a letter written in Paris where Mr. Washburne had become U.S. Minister, in which he urged Mr. Dawes to certain courses in regard to certain appropriations. Among these he earnestly enjoined the duty of cutting off all appropriations for the college for the deaf, which he had tried unsuccessfully to do.

Happily for the college, Mr. Dawes was not inclined to follow Mr. Washburne's advice. So far from this that in the first year of his chairmanship of the Committee on Appropriations, Mr. Dawes secured a special appropriation of nearly $100,000 to provide for the completion of the main central building.

During the years following, while he remained in the House and later as a Senator, Mr. Dawes proved his devotion to the interests of the institution on many occasions, and even after he left the Senate, having become a corporate director, he would travel all the way from his home in Massachusetts to attend meetings of the board.

1903–1904

During this year a good deal was done in the college to increase the facilities for technical study, especially in chemistry and assaying as well as in engineering and electricity. It has been found that our graduates, in spite of their deafness, could work successfully on these lines.

On Presentation Day 1904 an interesting incident occurred in the gift to the college, from a large number of the alumni, of a memorial to the late Professor Porter in the shape of a complete set of the *New International Encyclopedia*. Mr. Samuel G. Davidson, an instructor in the Pennsylvania Institution for the Deaf and Dumb and a graduate of our college, made the address presenting the memorial.

On the same Presentation Day the president of the college, noting the fact that the fortieth annual milestone had been reached, gave a somewhat detailed account of the history and progress of the college during the four decades of its existence.

To mark the fortieth anniversary, honorary degrees were conferred on nine graduates of the college who had attained distinction in various lines. A list of these honors will be found in the Forty-Seventh Annual Report of the institution.

Another interesting feature of this day was the presence of President Gilman of the Carnegie Institution, ex-president of Johns Hopkins University, who delivered an address. This was the third time that Dr. Gilman had spoken at our public anniversaries, and he expressed great satisfaction at the progress of the college.

1904–1905

In March 1905 the institution experienced a heavy loss in the death of Hon. Joseph R. Hawley who had been a member of our board for seventeen years, part of the time as representing the Senate of the United States and in the later years as a corporate director. Senator Hawley's interest in the institution was manifested long before he became a member of the board—in fact it was co-existent with his connection with Congress as a Representative and a Senator. His long residence in Hartford made him familiar with my father's work as the founder of the parent school for the deaf in that city, and he knew me well personally from the days of my boyhood on. The warm personal friendship that had existed between us for more than forty years made his death to be most deeply felt by me.

During this year a central heating and lighting plant was completed under the direct charge of Mr. Isaac Allison, the master of our industrial shop and an instructor of electrical engineering. This new system of heating and lighting did away with the individual boilers in seven different buildings and with the lighting by gas in the same, substituting electricity generated by the same steam power that furnishes heat.

Important legislation was enacted by Congress in regard to the education of the colored deaf-mutes of the District. From the very early days of the institution we have had colored pupils. But the number was so small for many years as to occasion no particular difficulty. We had separate sleeping rooms and separate tables for them but placed them with the white pupils in the classrooms. Within the past few years the number of the colored increased until we had fourteen. On a good many occasions we had complaints from the parents of white children and protests against the mixture of the races in our school. Some difficulties also arose, growing out of the treatment of the colored by the white. Other considerations made it seem best, on the whole, that there should be a separation. Senator Cockrell rendered very important aid in securing the necessary action of Congress authorizing the transfer of the colored deaf children of the District to the Maryland School for Colored Deaf-Mutes in Baltimore.

The transfer was successfully made in September 1905, and the new arrangement works well in all respects. The principal of the school in Baltimore is a graduate of our normal department,* and two of the teachers were graduates of our college.

During this year medals and diplomas from the St. Louis Exposition were received by the institution, the college, and by Professor Hall who was secretary of the exposition jury on the education of defectives.

A "grand prize" was conferred upon the president of the institution "for distinguished life-long work in the education of the deaf, and for the foundation and successful maintenance of the only institution for the higher education of the deaf in the world."

1905–1906

In September 1905 the president of the institution visited Germany, on the invitation of an organization of instructors of the deaf in that country, for the purpose of delivering an address at the unveiling of a monument to Moritz Hill, one of the most eminent educators of the deaf in Europe. President Gallaudet had an especial interest in accepting this invitation, for on the occasion of his first visit to Europe in 1867, he formed the acquaintance of Mr. Hill, visiting his school at Weissenfels and gaining many valuable suggestions there.

The monument to Hill stands in the grounds of the school of which he was the principal for more than forty years, and the ceremonies of

---

*This was John F. Bledsoe.

unveiling were in the open air around the monument. Dr. Gallaudet gave his address in German, and it was well received, although some of the views expressed, sustained as they were by quotations from Hill's writings, were not in harmony with the opinions of a majority of the German teachers.

On the occasion of the forty-second anniversary of the college, Presentation Day 1906, we had the honor and the great pleasure of the presence, in the Chair of the presiding officer, of the Patron of the institution, Theodore Roosevelt, President of the United States. This was the first time a Patron had been [here] on Presentation Day since the visit of President Harrison in 1889. In previous years Presidents Grant, Hayes, Garfield, Arthur, and Cleveland had honored the college with their presence, President McKinley being the only Patron who had failed to visit us since the college had had public anniversaries.

President Roosevelt showed great interest in the college and made a very felicitious address to the graduating class. The young men of the college greeted him as he alighted from his carriage with the college "yell," surprising him with the noise of the voices of those whom he expected to find *mute*.

32. President Theodore Roosevelt visiting the campus in 1906.

1906–1907

The closing year of the first half-century of the institution was not marked by any unusual event unless, indeed, almost entire absence of discipline in the history of the college may be taken as such; for it is a matter of record that only one instance occurred when the faculty was called upon to consider any infraction of the rules of the college. And this misconduct was not of a serious character.

On the occasion of the public anniversary of the college in May 1907, exercises were arranged to commemorate the completion of the first half-century of the institution. Historical addresses were made by Principal Denison of the Kendall School and by myself. Both of us could date our connection with the institution back to the year of its beginning, 1857.

We had the honor of the presence of Hon. James R. Garfield, Secretary of the Interior, who delivered an earnest and eloquent address to our students. In introducing Mr. Garfield I had great pleasure in alluding to the services rendered by his father to the college in its early days when it needed the support of influential friends in Congress. I felt justified in placing the name of James A. Garfield at the head of the list of those who gave the college important aid at critical times. Full statements of the valuable services of General Garfield to the college will be found in the Twenty-Fourth and Twenty-Six Annual Reports of the institution.

Immediately following Presentation Day, Professor Edward A. Fay, for many years vice president of our college faculty, entered upon a special leave of absence, granted him by the board, and sailed for Europe, Mrs. Fay accompanying him. Professor Fay well deserved this mark of regard for his long and faithful services.

At the closing of the term at a meeting of the board, resolutions were adopted on the motion of Justice Brewer, expressing approval of my half-century of duty as the head of the institution, for which I venture to record in this history my most sincere appreciation and thanks.

In bringing the story of the first half-century of the institution to a close, I wish to express my gratitude to that kind providence which has permitted me to be at the head of it during all these fifty years.

I am deeply conscious that I have not done as well as I ought to have done for the interests of the institution, but I hope it is not presumptuous in me to hope that my services have been of some value to the cause, to promote which the institution was established.

For whatever of success has attended my efforts, I recognize my obligations to that "providence which shapes our ends, rough hew them as we may"; then to the intelligent and ready support always accorded me by the distinguished men who have formed the Board of Directors; and last but not least to the faithful and efficient corps of officers and employees whose devoted services and cordial cooperation have given success to the working of the institution.

My prayer is that the blessing of heaven may ever attend the institution, and all who have, or may in the future have, any connection with it.

33. Edward Miner Gallaudet in 1907.

Extracts from Annual Reports

APPENDIX A

Extracted from the Seventh Annual Report of the Columbia Institution for the Deaf and Dumb and the Blind for the Year Ending June 30, 1864.

Inauguration of the College for the Deaf and Dumb, at Washington, District of Columbia, June 28, 1864.

INTRODUCTORY ADDRESS BY THE RETIRING PRESIDENT, HON. AMOS KENDALL.

LADIES AND GENTLEMEN: About eight or nine years ago, a man appeared in this city having in charge a number of deaf and dumb children whom he exhibited to the citizens, asking contributions to aid him in establishing an institution for the instruction of that class of unfortunates in the District of Columbia, including also the blind. He excited much sympathy among our citizens, and succeeded in getting up a considerable school. Professing a desire to make it permanent, he solicited a number of citizens to act as trustees, and a board was formed composed of Rev. Byron Sunderland, D. D., James C. McGuire, D. A. Hall, W. H. Edes, Judson Mitchell, and myself. But the board was barely organized when it discovered that the objects of the individual in question had not been understood, and that he was unfit to be intrusted with the management of such an institution. The question for the consideration of the board was, whether they should abandon the enterprise, or proceed under the discouraging circumstances then existing. The tender of a house and lot adjoining the city limits, previously made, was repeated, and, actuated by sympathy for these children of misfortune, the board resolved to proceed, relying for support upon the liberality of their fellow-citizens and Congress.

In the mean time rumors of the ill-treatment of the pupils in the deaf and dumb school by their teacher reached the public authorities, and at the instance of the district attorney my name was used as their next friend in a legal process to test the truth of these rumors. They were proved to be true by abundant testimony, and the court directed such of them as belonged to the District of Columbia to be restored to their parents. There were among them, however, five deaf-mutes who had been brought from the State of New York, having no parents, or none who seemed to care what became of them. These were bound to me as their guardian by the orphans' court, and formed the nucleus of our institution. And now I am most happy to present you with three of my

[209]

wards, all well advanced in moral and intellectual culture, one of them the young lady whose beautiful composition on Florence Nightingale has been read in your hearing.

In January, 1857, the board petitioned Congress for an act of incorporation, which was readily granted, with provisions for the payment out of the public Treasury of one hundred and fifty dollars per annum for the tuition and support of indigent pupils belonging to the District. At a subsequent period Congress directed the admission of deaf-mute children of persons in the military and naval service, and also provided for the payment of salaries and incidental expenses, so that the institution became very properly a public charity supported in the main by the Government. An appropriation of $9,000 was also made to enlarge a brick building which had been constructed for the use of the institution, so as better to accommodate the officers, teachers, and pupils.

Material aid has also been derived in the department of manual labor from a transfer of the funds of " Washington's Manual Labor School and Male Orphan Asylum," originally organized by the agency of P. W. Gallaudet, the grandfather of our present superintendent, but never put in operation.

Our institution was fortunate enough soon to attract the attention of the government and people of the State of Maryland, and for several years past the legislature of that State has made provision for the education therein of a number of their mute children.

The example of the State was followed by the city of Baltimore, whose councils provided for the support of ten mutes from that city. So pleased were the members of those councils, on a late visit to the institution, with the progress made by their protégés, that on their return they voted to double the number and increase the compensation for their tuition and support.

Our present superintendent, E. M. Gallaudet, was appointed on the 30th day of May, 1857. His mother, the widow of the late Thomas H. Gallaudet, was, at the same time, appointed matron. Under their charge the progress of the institution, beginning with *five* pupils, has been as follows, viz:

Number of pupils July, 1858..................................... 17
Number of pupils July, 1859..................................... 20
Number of pupils July, 1860..................................... 30
Number of pupils July, 1861..................................... 35
Number of pupils July, 1862..................................... 38
Number of pupils July, 1863..................................... 52
And now it is... 58

During all this period there has not been a death from sickness among the pupils of the institution. This remarkable fact is undoubtedly attributable in a very high degree to the excellent care bestowed upon the children by the matron and her assistants.

But it is not so much the increase of numbers or the excellent health of the pupils of which we are proud, as their advancement in knowledge and in moral training. It would be difficult to find in any of the schools of the country the same number of children brought together promiscuously who have made in the same time the same advance in reading, writing, arithmetic, and composition, whose notions of moral right are more correct, or whose conduct is more exemplary.

Having advanced thus far in an enterprise undertaken with humble means, we now propose to take another step forward.

The deaf-mutes are numerous enough in the United States to be considered a separate class in the community, having a language of their own. Most of the States have established schools for their instruction in elementary knowledge; but in most if not all the States they are too few in number to justify the establishment of colleges for their instruction in the higher branches of knowledge. One college for the whole United States would probably be adequate for all those who will wish and have the means to acquire a more finished education. And where can such an institution be more fittingly located than in the District of Columbia? Congress has furnished us a foundation broad enough to build upon, and while we do not look to them for the support of students coming from the States, we have no doubt they will secure to the enterprise every appropriate aid and encouragement.

It is a great mistake to suppose that deaf-mutes are in general inferior in capacity to children having all their senses in perfection. The inferiority is not in the want of capacity, but in the want of its development. We wish to supply that want, and that we have done it in a degree we hope we have satisfied you by this day's exhibition.

If the whole human family were destitute of the sense of hearing, they would yet be able to interchange ideas by signs. Indeed, the language of signs undoubtedly accompanied if it did not precede the language of sounds. Men are created, not with a God-given language, but with a God-given capacity to make signs and sounds, and by the use of these to form a language. No child comes into the world with a language; *that* is an *acquisition*, and the child always acquires the language of its parents, or of those by whom it is surrounded. It has ideas before it has a language in which to communicate them to others. Its only language is signs or incoherent cries. We read that Adam named the beasts and birds. But how could he give them names without first pointing them out by other means? How could a particular name be fixed upon a particular animal among so many species without some sign indicating to what animal it should thereafter be applied? Names are but sounds or combinations of sounds. If a company of uneducated deaf-mutes were, for the first time, brought into contact with an elephant, without knowing his name, they would soon devise some sign by which he should be represented among themselves. So, were it possible for a company of adults with their senses entire to be placed in a similar situation, they would probably point him out by a sign accompanied by some exclamation, and that exclamation might become the name of the animal. Thenceforward the perfect man would convey the idea of an elephant by sound, while the deaf-mute could only do it by a sign. Hence they may be considered distinct races in language or in their means of interchanging ideas.

It is our function to teach, improve, and enlarge the sign-language; make it co-extensive with the language of sound, and through its instrumentality open the minds of deaf-mutes to the wonders of creation and the secrets of science and art. This will have been effected when every material word in the written language shall have its corresponding sign communicating the same idea. Then, while the English deaf-mute will write in English, and the French deaf-mute in French, they will have among themselves a universal language of common signs, *into which may no Babel ever enter.*

To this great and good work we dedicate the future labors of this institution.

Mr. Kendall then addressed the president-elect as follows:

MY YOUNG AND ESTEEMED FRIEND:

In accordance with my own wishes, and the unanimous decision of the members of the association at their recent meeting, I now relinquish to you the presidency of this institution. It is an honor richly due to you for the services you have rendered to the institution, not only within its walls, but in Baltimore, in Annapolis, in Congress, and in the country. To you more than to any other man is it indebted for its rapid progress, and for the high position it now holds in the estimation of the community. It is, therefore, fitting that you should be clothed with all appropriate authority needful to maintain discipline within the institution, and all practicable means of influence to protect its interests without. The members of the association have, in the history of the past, abundant grounds of confidence that under your prudent and skillful management it will not only realize their highest hopes but secure to yourself a degree of gratitude and affection in the hearts of this class of unfortunates, and a reputation for disinterested usefulness, not inferior to those acquired by your honored father. And most happy shall I be if permitted to live to see this institution, under your judicious management, become one of the brightest jewels in the coronet of the republic, once more, by the mercy of God, united, peaceful, and free.

INAUGURAL ADDRESS BY THE PRESIDENT-ELECT,
EDWARD M. GALLAUDET, A. M.

MR. PRESIDENT: No language at my command can adequately express the feelings to which the remarks you have addressed to me have given rise.

While your words of commendation on the part I have been permitted to perform in the rearing of our beloved institution are precious and most cheering to me, I cannot feel that they are deserved. I have been but an instrument in the hands of Him who rules the hearts of men, and whatever of success has attended the efforts which have been put forth in behalf of the Columbia Institution is owing to His especial aid and blessing.

To Him, therefore, let us humbly ascribe the praise for our past history, and in Him let us put our trust for the future, believing that in His own good time He will perfect the work which we in His name are now met to inaugurate.

The interest you express in our institution, the hope you record for its future advancement, and the purpose you indicate of continuing to further its progress, find a ready response in my heart. As from the beginning of our enterprise, so from this time onward, I shall rely very greatly on your ripe experience, your sound, prompt judgment, and your far-seeing sagacity to sustain me in the discharge of the important duties devolved upon me. May God in His goodness spare you long to our institution and to those who look up to you with veneration and affection.

To you, Mr. President and revered friend, to you, gentlemen of the board of directors, and to you, my friends, members of the association, by whom the high honor of elevating me to the presidency of the institution has been conferred, do I return my most heartfelt thanks for the unwavering confidence and support you have given me in the past, and for this new token of your regard which has been manifested on the present occasion. I implore the source of all strength so to bear me up that I may henceforth be more faithful, more earnest, and more successful in my labors for the improvement of the deaf and dumb and the blind than I have been in the years that are past.

LADIES AND GENTLEMEN : We are now entering upon a most important period in the history of our institution. We are about making advances that may materially change its character.

We are preparing for a work, deemed to be of great importance to the deaf and dumb, that has been hitherto unattempted.

When the western pioneer, urging his adventurous way over the mountainous ridges that divide our continent, reaches, after weeks and miles of toilsome journey, the summit of some o'erlooking peak, whence he may view the land to which his aspirations lead him, it is natural that he should direct his gaze backward and encourage or warn himself with the memory of difficulties surmounted, of dangers passed, and of advances accomplished.

In like manner the true reformer, the practical inventor, he who would introduce among his fellow-men, for their advancement, new elements of civilization, calls to his assistance the experience of the past, and ere entering upon untried fields of labor, ponders well the record of efforts directed in similar channels, that he may gather inspiration both from the achievements and the failures of those who have gone before him.

It will not, therefore, be deemed inappropriate on the present occasion, having as its object the inauguration of an undertaking without precedent in the annals of institutions of learning or of benevolence, and which may in after years be looked back upon as an era in the history of the improvement of the deaf and dumb, to consider what has been done for the amelioration of the condition of the deaf and dumb in our own and other lands.

That deaf-mutes were found in the earlier ages of the world we have the most undoubted evidence. It is plain also that they existed in such numbers as to form a class in the community, for we find them mentioned in the Code of Justinian, the Mosaic Law, and still earlier, fifteen hundred years before Christ, (and this appears to be the first mention of deaf-mutes in any recorded history,) by Jehovah himself, when he remonstrates with Moses on account of his diffidence, and says : " Who maketh the dumb or deaf, or the seeing or the blind ? Have not I, the Lord ?"

The student who would attain a full knowledge of this subject must pursue his investigations over a period of three thousand years. Hence it will not be expected at this time that anything more than a *résumé* can be given of the results of researches so extended.

That the deaf and dumb in early times were a degraded and despised class of beings is evident from the injunction in Leviticus xix, 14, "Thou shalt not curse the deaf, nor put a stumbling-block before the blind." This prohibition being, doubtless, against practices which had obtained among the Israelites, and were denounced by the Almighty.

In the Justinian Code, the foundation of most of our modern European and American jurisprudence, the deaf and dumb from birth are, without exception and without regard to their degree of intelligence, condemned to a perpetual legal infancy, in this respect being considered as on a footing with the insane, and those who were incapable of managing their affairs through the affliction of permanent disease, and hence, like them, were to be placed under guardianship. Mente captis, et surdis, et mutis, et qui perpetuo morbo laborant, quia rebus suis superesse non possunt, curatores dandi sunt. (Digest, Lib. 1, tit. xxii, De Curatoribus, § 4.)*

Among the laws of the Hindoos, we find in the ordination of the Pundits, or Code of Gentoo Laws, whoever was "deaf from his mother's womb," or whoever was dumb, was classed among persons incapable of inheritance. (Halked's translations of the Gentoo laws, from the Persian and Sanscrit, London, 1776.)

We have no evidence that attempts were made among the enlightened heathen nations to instruct the deaf and dumb. This seems the more surprising from the fact that with the Romans, in the time of Nero, the pantomime of the stage (essentially our present language of signs) had been carried to such perfection that a king from the borders of the Euxine, seeing a pantomime performed at Rome, begged one of the performers of the Emperor, to be used as an interpreter with the nations in his neighborhood at home.

Pliny, speaking of the most eminent painters of Rome, mentions "Quintus Pedius, grandson of that consul, Quintus Pedius, who was named in Cæsar's will, co-heir with Augustus." "This young man, being a mute from birth, the orator Messale, of whose family he was, thought might be instructed in painting, of which also Augustus, of sacred memory, approved." And it is stated "the young man made great proficiency in the art."

And yet, though the ancient Romans had before their eyes intelligent deaf-mute youth, and were familiar with the very language of all others adapted to their use, not only were no attempts made to open their minds, but the possibility of instructing them was denied by the wisest men. Lucretius did but express the acknowledged opinion of all classes when he said:

---

* I desire to acknowledge my indebtedness for much valuable information on the early history of deaf-mute instruction to Dr. Harvey P. Peet, the respected principal of the New York Institution for the Deaf and Dumb, in whose learned and exhaustive articles on the "origin and history of the art of instructing the deaf and dumb," published in the proceedings of conventions of American instructors of the deaf and dumb, held at New York in 1850, and of Jacksonville, Illinois, in 1858, will be found a full and interesting account of the advance of deaf-mute education from the earliest times down to the present century.— E. M. G.

"To instruct the deaf no art could ever reach,
No care improve them and no wisdom teach."

So firmly fixed was this opinion of the permanent and necessary intellectual and moral inferiority of the deaf and dumb, that in the fourth century Saint Augustine, commenting on the words of the apostle, "Faith comes by hearing, and hearing by the word of God," remarks that deafness from birth makes faith impossible, since he who is born deaf can neither hear the word nor learn to read it.

So far as recorded instances of instruction of the deaf and dumb afford information on the subject, the first effort was made among the Anglo-Saxons in the seventh century by John, Bishop of Hagulstad, afterward known as Saint John, of Beverly.

The success of the bishop was esteemed at the time miraculous, as appears from the account given in the Ecclesiastical History of Bede. One youth only was taught by the bishop, and the intellectual development of the pupil must have been but slight.

A single case appears in the fifteenth century, mentioned by Rodolph Agricola, a native of Baffle, near Groningen, and a distinguished scholar of his time, but no details are given of the person, place, or mode of instruction.

It was about the year 1550 that Pedro Ponce de Leon, of a noble Spanish family, opened a school for deaf-mute children in the convent of Benedictines at Oña. His triumphs, according to the testimony of contemporary writers, were complete, and some of his pupils showed great proficiency in the study of science as well as of languages.

In the course of the seventeenth century the subject of deaf-mute instruction received considerable attention in Italy, England, and Holland, and early in the eighteenth century successful efforts were made in Germany; but it was between the years 1755 and 1760 that the first considerable movements were inaugurated in behalf of the deaf and dumb.

It is a noticeable fact that in three separate nationalities the men who now stand in history as the founders of three distinct methods of instructing the deaf and dumb should have commenced their labors almost simultaneously. These instructors were Charles Michel de l'Epee, in France; Samuel Heinicke, in Saxony; and Thomas Braidwood, in Scotland.

Time will not allow any extended notice of the achievements of these pioneers in the work of establishing permanent schools for the deaf and dumb. Each of them succeeded in securing for the class they sought to benefit a lasting hold on the sympathies of the public, and all existing institutions for the deaf and dumb trace their origin to the impulses communicated by the labors and success of these three instructors.

The method known as the "French," and having as its basis the use of pantomimic signs, was invented by de l'Epee, and improved by his pupil and successor, the Abbe Sicard.

Dr. Thomas Hopkins Gallaudet, who founded the system of deaf-mute instruction now prevalent in America, gained his knowledge of the art from the Abbe Sicard.

Dr. Gallaudet gave to the world the most convincing proof of his belief that the deaf and dumb could through education be made the social and intellectual equals of those possessed of all their faculties, by taking one of his own pupils as his wife. He, having lived to see twenty noble schools for the deaf and dumb in successful operation in this his native land, filling with joy, in the knowledge of things human and divine, thousands of immortal beings, who otherwise would have been doomed to lives of intellectual and moral darkness, has passed from earth to the bosom of that Saviour in whose name and strength he labored for the welfare of the afflicted and distressed.

She, my mother, whose ears have ever been closed to the sound of her children's voices, whose tongue could never sing a lullaby to calm their infant fears, now sits before me, an intelligent and joyous participant in the exercises of the day. Released, by the advance of years, from the cares of a family now grown to maturity, she has since the organization of the Columbia Institution devoted her life to its interests, and, in the motherly care she has exercised over the pupils, has contributed in no small degree to the success with which, in the good providence of God, its labors have been crowned. And though her days have been length-ened to well-nigh three-score years and ten, yet a full measure of strength remains, and she is pursuing her peaceful way toward the shore of the dark river, in the hope that many years of active usefulness yet remain to her, wherein she may continue to point out, to infant minds, the shin-ing way that will lead them where their unstopped ears may listèn to the joyous songs of heaven, and where their loosened tongues may join in anthems of praise to Him who doeth all things well.

In the introduction into America of the art of instructing the deaf and dumb, Dr. Gallaudet was assisted by a pupil of Sicard, a deaf-mute gentleman who had had, prior to coming to the United States in 1817, several years' experience as a teacher in the Royal Institution in Paris; and the name of Laurent Clerc will ever be held in grateful remem-brance by deaf-mutes and their friends in this his adopted country, as a pioneer and a life-long laborer in their behalf. Having spent a full half century in developing and training the minds of his fellow-mutes, Mr. Clerc is now, in the calm evening of a life prolonged beyond the allotted time of man, enjoying that rest to which his untiring and useful labors richly entitle him. Warmly alive to every movement tending to the advancement of the deaf and dumb, he has, in spite of many infirmities, journeyed from his home in New England to Washington, that he might give his personal blessing to the new department of deaf-mute educa-tion, to inaugurate which we are assembled on this occasion.

Born while the venerated de l'Epee was still alive, Mr. Clerc stands among us to-day a living monument of an age long past, a witness of events, a contemporary of men, soon to be known only in the pages of history.

Happy are we, indeed, when ushering into existence an institution which we trust may complete the system of deaf-mute instruction in the United States, in having the benediction of him who bore a hand in the establishment of that school which will ever be regarded as the Alma Mater of all American institutions for the deaf and dumb.

'The advance of the cause of deaf-mute instruction in this country gives evidence unmistakable of the humanity of our people and their willingness to respond to appeals for the unfortunate.

Institutions have been established and well endowed by legislative appropriations and private munificence in every quarter of the land, and even in a time of civil war schools for the deaf and dumb have been successfully organized in the new States of the West.

A system of instruction prevails which, in the judgment of men of learning who have examined critically the methods pursued in other countries, affords the speediest and most practical results, and the priceless benefits of education are within the reach of rich and poor alike.

Do any, regarding complacently the work already accomplished for the deaf and dumb, comparing their present happy condition with that degraded state to which public law and universal sentiment consigned them in former years, argue that no further advances should be made in the development of their minds; that enough has been done already; that no additional facilities are needed to give deaf-mutes the fullest opportunities for the mental development of which they are capable? Let such consider what progress has been made during the present century in affording means of acquiring knowledge to those possessed of all their faculties, and it will directly appear that while colleges, universities, free academies, and high schools for the hearing and speaking have been multiplied throughout the land, no institution has hitherto been opened where the deaf and dumb can pursue a collegiate course of study, and secure that mental training and that foundation of learning which may enable them to engage successfully in scientific or literary pursuits.

The last census shows that the deaf-mute population of our country numbers upward of fifteen thousand. Is it to be supposed that none of these are capable of receiving benefit from those courses of instruction which are so highly valued by their more favored fellow-citizens? But let us review the opinions of those who have made the matter of deaf-mute instruction their especial duty.

Dr. Gallaudet often before his death expressed to the speaker his belief that the time would come when a college for the deaf and dumb would be established. He considered deaf-mutes capable of attaining to a high degree of mental culture, and felt that every practicable opportunity should be afforded them for advancement.

In the year 1851 a convention of instructors of the deaf and dumb was held at Hartford, Connecticut, where the first institution was established. Among other important subjects discussed was that of a high school or college for the deaf and dumb.

An elaborate paper was read by Rev. William W. Turner, then an instructor of many years' experience in the American Asylum, and since for ten years its principal. Mr. Turner, after recounting what had been done for the deaf and dumb in the then existing institutions, says:

" The institutions for the deaf and dumb in the United States hold the same relative position as the better class of public schools in our cities. Like the latter, they teach beginners the elements of language; then, its principles and construction; afterward, arithmetic, geography, and history. But as all this must be done in five or six years, it is obvious that a thorough knowledge of these subjects cannot in most instances be acquired. In view of the difficulties to be overcome, some instructors have chosen to teach facts and science at the expense of language, while others have labored to elucidate and fix in the minds of their pupils the rules and idioms of language, without leaving sufficient time for the other branches of a common-school education. In point of fact, our pupils go from our institutions with the ability to read and write the ordinary style of letters, narratives, and conversation more or less correctly, without being able to comprehend the import of elaborate essays on elevated subjects. They understand as much of arithmetic as they will have occasion to use in their respective vocations, and they can pass a fair examination in geography and history. In short, they have laid the foundation of a good English education without having completed the superstructure. This account of the matter is not, however, strictly applicable to all. While some dull or inattentive pupils fall below the ordinary level of a class, a few gifted minds rise considerably above it. These are to be regarded as exceptions to the general rule. But notwithstanding the incompleteness of their education, a majority of them will return home to friends less perfectly educated than themselves, and will consequently be thought to know more than they really do. And as most of them become farmers or mechanics, their education may be considered sufficient for persons for their stations in life.

"The question still recurs whether their usefulness and happiness would not be promoted by a more thorough mental training, and by a more extended and complete course of study. We do not hesitate to affirm that this would be the case. The same arguments which go to show that knowledge is power, that the condition of a people is improved in proportion as the masses are educated, have their application with equal weight to the deaf and dumb. Indeed, those who can hear and speak will much better make their way through life without education than the former. The ability which uneducated persons possess of obtaining, through the ear, information communicated orally, and of imparting to others their own ideas through speech, affords them advantages which nothing but education can supply to the deaf-mute; and very much in proportion to his knowledge will be his position and influence in society."

After noticing the difficulties which would arise were the various institutions to undertake separately to afford the college course to the very few in each who might properly pursue it, Mr. Turner goes on to say:

"What he needs is a school expressly provided for him, and for others in his circumstances—a high school for the deaf and dumb.

"This high school should receive only those who had completed a regular course of study at the State institutions, together with those semi-mutes who had in other ways acquired an equal amount of knowledge. It should afford all its students a three years' course of instruction under two or more of the ablest professors of the art that could be obtained. In such a school, suitably endowed and judiciously managed, we might expect such a development of deaf-mute intellect as has not hitherto been witnessed in this or any other country. We might expect that its graduates would be fitted to partake equally with us of the enjoyment derived from reading and literary pursuits. We might expect to see them creditably filling stations for which their peculiar privation has been thought to disqualify them. We might expect to find them in families of cultivated minds and refined tastes, the chief ornament and attraction of the social circle."

In closing his essay, Mr. Turner urges the importance of early action in the following terms:

" When ought this enterprise to be undertaken ? We answer, immediately. If there is a demand for such an institution, its establishment should not be delayed. There are no more serious obstacles to be surmounted, no greater difficulties to be encountered, no more labor or self-denial required at present, than will be at any future time. Let the subject be carefully considered by this convention. Let the attention of the officers and patrons of all our institutions be directed to it. Let there be harmony of feeling and of views respecting it. Let there be unity of plan and of effort among the friends of the enterprise, and success is certain."

In the discussion which followed, Mr. Wetmore, a director in the New York Institution, said:

" He was struck very forcibly by the arguments presented. He had often regretted that pupils should go out from our institutions for the instruction of the deaf and dumb before their education is thoroughly completed. In the State of New York the term is limited, and the course of study cannot exceed seven years. In this short period it cannot be expected that the pupil should attain beyond a moderate point in his acquirements."

Dr. Peet, the distinguished and venerable principal of the New York Institution, who has spent a most laborious life in the work of deaf-mute instruction said:

" He had long felt the importance of carrying forward our institutions to a point far beyond that which is now attained.

" Our institutions ought to be institutions for the *education* of the deaf and dumb; and he desired that provision might be made, in connection with our present institutions, by which the education of the deaf-mute could be carried to a greater extent. If this could *not* be done in our existing institutions, he held that the subject should then be fully entertained of establishing a high school or an academy, or whatever we may please to call it, for the higher education of the deaf and dumb. We shall need some method to instruct them in the fine arts, in science, in the mechanic arts, civil-engineering, &c., &c., for all which they are fully competent."

Mr. Cary, principal of the Ohio Institution for the Deaf and Dumb, says:

" Thought the idea was capable of being realized. There were obstacles to be overcome, it was true, but they were not insurmountable, and he trusted that the project would be deemed worthy some practical attempt. He suggested that the inst tution be planned with reference to its national character. We have a Military Academy at West Point, supported by the Government. Why may we not apply to the National Legislature for aid to establish an institution where the deaf-mutes in the United States may receive a higher education ? He believed a sufficient number might be selected to make the institution of sufficient size."

Mr. Morris, an experienced instructor in the New York Institution, and Mr. Ayres, now the instructor of the high class in the American Asylum, favored the project, and believed public opinion was ready to sustain such an institution.

A committee, consisting Messrs. Turner, Cary, and Van Nostrand, was appointed to consider the subject, and report at the next convention, which was to meet at Columbus, Ohio, in 1853.

As a result of this debate, the institutions in Hartford and New York undertook separately to meet the wants detailed in Mr. Turner's paper, by establishing high classes.

In view of these efforts the committee above named, in a report made at Columbus, Ohio, at the convention of 1853, says:

" We fully believe that the results of this experiment will be most happy, not only upon members of the high class, but upon those of other classes also, and upon the institutions in which it has been commenced. We would not, therefore, as a committee, recommend the adoption of any measures, under existing circumstances, which should interrupt or interfere with the workings of this experiment ; but advise rather to wait for its full development, under the impression that it may be necessary, as a preliminary step to the establishment of a high school, and the realization of all our hopes and plans in regard to it."

The high class at Hartford was formed on the 15th of September, 1852, and Mr. Turner was appointed to instruct it. He says of the project, in an article published in the American Annals:

" Although this plan does not secure all the advantages of the proposed high school, and may not remove the necessity of its final establishment, it does, however, meet a present want, and, if successful, will prepare the way for the more extended and better plan."

An able article on a college for deaf-mutes appeared in the American Annals for April, 1854, written by Mr. John Carlin, himself a deaf-mute educated in part at the Pennsylvania Institution, but who has, in his maturer years, improved himself in science and letters to a most remarkable degree. I quote from his article:

" Taking in consideration the great variety of minds, arising from the physical formation of the brain, and the effects of climate, disease, parental negligence, &c., it would be at variance with the logical principles of physiology to suppose that all speaking and hearing persons have minds equally capable of superior culture, or that all the minds of the deaf and dumb are incapable of higher training. Yet, though there can be found no difference between speaking persons and deaf-mutes of the higher class, in imagination, strength of mind, depth of thought, and quickness of perception, it cannot be denied, however repugnant it may be to our feelings, that the deaf-mutes have no finished scholars of their own to boast of, while the speaking community present to our mental vision an imposing array of scholars. How is this discrepancy accounted for, seeing that the minds of the most promising mutes are eminently susceptible of intellectual polish? Does it not show that there must be in existence certain latent causes of their being thrown into the shade?

" Is it not within the range of our researches to solve the mystery in which they are enveloped?

" The question whether there is any possibility on the part of able masters to develop the intellect of their prominent mute scholars to its fullest scope, were their term of pupilage extended and their course of studies semblant to that generally pursued at colleges, may be answered in the affirmative; for with the gracious permission of my excellent friend, Mr. I. L. Peet, the able preceptor of the high class at the New York Institution, than whom, as one fitted for that arduous avocation, the directors thereof could not have made a better selection, I have made careful and impartial investigations of the progress his scholars have made in their studies.

" Notwithstanding their having been but one year and a half in the high class, they have, in their pursuance of the higher branches of education, pushed on with prodigious strides toward the goal where merit, honor, and glory wait to be conferred upon their brows.

" Besides those of the New York high class, I have learned with much satisfaction that the scholars of the Hartford high class have made such progress as to encourage our hopes of the ultimate success of that department of higher mute education.

" Notwithstanding the acknowledged excellence of that department and its system, which is arranged expressly to accelerate the progess of its scholars in knowledge, it is still but a step which invites them to ascend to the college, where they may enter upon a still more enlarged scale of studies and then retire with *honorary degress*. But, alas! no such college is yet in existence.

" Those of those who speak and hear have, indeed, produced eminent men. So will our ' National College' also. I do not pretend to say that the mutes will be equal to the speaking in the extent of their learning and in the correctness and elegance of their language, but if proofs be needed to give conviction of the truth of my assertion that mutes of decided talents can be rendered as good scholars as the Barneses, Macaulays, Lamartines, and Bryants, I will readily refer to Dr. Kitto, of England, the celebrated biblical commentator; Messieurs Berthier and Pelissier, of France, the former a successful biographer, and the latter a fine poet; our own Nack and Burnet, both excellent authors and poets; and Mr. Clerc, who is the only mute in this country enjoying the honorary degree of master of arts, to which he is fully entitled by his learning and long experience in mute education."

It is to the officers of the Columbia Institution one of the most gratifying features of the present occasion that Mr. Carlin, whose self-culture under adverse circumstances entitles him to high honor among literary men, is here to-day to receive the honorary degree of master of arts recently voted him by our board of directors.

From what has been stated as to the expressed views of distinguished deaf-mutes and those engaged in their instruction, it appears that the desirableness of affording this class of persons opportunities for high mental development is strongly urged. And it is as plainly shown that the organizations known as high classes, of which there are but two in the country, viz, at New York and Hartford, while performing a most important and useful work, do not meet the wants of the deaf and dumb in this particular.

Without occupying time in adding to those already brought forward, by some of the most distinguished men of our profession, further considerations to show that a college for deaf-mutes is demanded and would be a source of great good, I will proceed to detail the purposes which the Columbia Institution entertains of perfecting that " more extended and better plan," so strongly recommended in the convention of 1851, of establishing that " National College for Deaf-Mutes," for which Mr. Carlin so ardently aspired.

Our institution, by the provisions of its organic law, is not limited as to the extent to which it may carry forward the education of those placed under its fostering care by the United States. It is authorized to receive and instruct deaf-mutes from any of the States or Territories of the United States, on such terms as may be agreed upon by their parents, guardians, or trustees, and the proper authorities of the institution. By a recent act of Congress the institution is authorized to confer degrees in the arts and sciences after the manner pursued in colleges. It thus appears that this institution has power to open a collegiate department of study, and to offer to such deaf-mutes as may avail themselves of its privileges, academic honors equal in rank to those conferred on hearing and speaking persons by the highest literary schools in the land.

To fulfill these important trusts is the earnest desire of those to whom the direction of the institution has been committed, and it is their intention to spare no efforts, that here, at the nation's capital, may be successfully established a seat of learning which may extend its benefits to deaf-mutes from every State of our Union.

There are cogent reasons why the college for deaf-mutes—and I say *the* college, since many years must elapse before the wants of the deaf and dumb in this country will require more than one—should be built up at Washington; one of the most weighty of which is that it has already, by the highest authority in the nation, been ushered into life here with its functions complete, although they may not yet possess that power and endurance that the accretions of maturity alone can give.

Appropriations of public money as well as the benefactions of private munificence will be needed in the development of the National Deaf-Mute College, and while it would not be right to ask the representatives n any State legislature to tax their constituents for the support of an institution for the benefit of citizens of other States, it is eminently proper to solicit the aid of the national legislators, representing as they do the people of every State, in behalf of an institution that shall extend its humane and elevating influences throughout the entire national domain. Undoubtedly the assistance of the Federal Government would be most important in the establishment and perfection of a national institution for the deaf and dumb; and where would that aid be more likely to be afforded than to a school already established and supported by the United States, under the very eaves, as it were, of its Capitol.

While our institution confined its operations to residents of the District of Columbia, Congress accorded a ready support; when its scope was extended to embrace the children of our soldiers and seamen, the Government promptly increased its appropriations; and now that we propose to enlarge our sphere of operations so as to offer to deaf-mute citizens of every State and Territory advantages which they cannot obtain elsewhere, the law-makers of the nation have set their seal of approbation on our undertaking by the appropriation of larger sums than ever before, supplying the needs of the institution incident to the establishment of the college, and giving an earnest of their intention to aid in its extension hereafter.

It is a question that may very naturally arise in the minds of those interested in the various State institutions, whether the proposed development of the Columbia Institution into a college will interfere in any way with the operations of its sister schools. To answer such queries in advance, it may be stated that our collegiate department is not designed to conflict, nor need it do so, with any existing organization for the instruction of the deaf and dumb.

It is no part of our plan to attempt to supersede or interrupt the most excellent and useful " high classes " now in operation. On the contrary, we desire the speedy advent of that day when every institution shall have its high class.

In no institution for the deaf and dumb have degrees in the arts and sciences been conferred upon graduates. In no institution does the course of study come up to the standard which would warrant such graduation. We propose to leave untouched in their operations the high classes, and bidding them God-speed in their good work, and urging their multiplication, to occupy a field of usefulness hitherto wholly uncultivated.

The time is not distant when the United States will contain a population of a hundred million souls. There will then be a deaf and dumb community in the country of fifty thousand. At least ten thousand of these would be undergoing instruction at the same time, requiring the employment of five hundred well-educated instructors.

The existing opportunities for mental culture are only enough to fit deaf-mutes to teach classes of low grades, and, as a consequence, they must receive relatively low rates of compensation, while the higher classes in our institutions demand the service of liberally-educated men at relatively high salaries.

It is admitted that deaf-mutes could be employed to a much greater extent than now, as instructors of their fellows in misfortune, and would make much more valuable teachers could they enjoy the advantages of a classical education. One of the designs of our college is to furnish deaf-mutes the means of obtaining that mental training and those academic honors which may entitle them to consideration in the world of letters, and allow them to gain positions of much greater usefulness and higher emolument than they can now aspire to.

We propose at least to test the question whether what is valued so highly by hearing and speaking persons, as a preparation for entering the more elevated spheres of usefulness in life, may not in like manner result in opening to deaf-mutes positions and pursuits from which they have been hitherto debarred.

If education to a high degree is important to a man possessed of all his faculties, is it not of even more consequence that those who make their way through the world in the face of difficulties which but a few years since seemed almost insurmountable, should, now that their aptitude for learning is proved beyond a question, have every advantage that the ingenuity or liberality of their more favored fellow-mortals can furnish?

The work of deaf-mute instruction in America may not inappropri-
ately be compared to the erection of a stately building. Fifty years ago
its foundations were laid broad and deep among the granite hills of New
England, and a shaft of rare beauty and strength was reared thereon.
Year by year the noble work has proceeded until but the pinnacle-stone
is lacking to complete the structure; and, though it must be small in
size and may escape notice amid the massive and beautiful pillars and
arches on which it must of necessity rest, yet it is needed to perfect the
work, and the founders of the Columbia Institution would fain essay to
place it in position.

And so to-day, in this solemn and public manner, they inaugurate the
"College for the Deaf and Dumb;" looking to Congress for a continuance of its favor, to a benevolent public for its approbation, to sister institutions for their countenance and sympathy, and to Him who "doth
not willingly afflict or grieve the children of men" for His sustaining
Providence to bear up the enterprise to a successful consummation.

ADDRESS BY HON. JAMES W. PATTERSON,

Representative from New Hampshire and Professor in Dartmouth College.

LADIES AND GENTLEMEN: I must beg your indulgence—perhaps I
ought to say your pardon—while I address to the audience, fascinated
with the able and finished productions to which they have already listened, a few unpremeditated remarks. My interest in the occasion must
be my excuse for this intrusion.

A little time since I visited, by the invitation of the superintendent,
the deaf and dumb and blind institution represented in the exercises of
to-day. I was deeply interested, I may say surprised, at what I there
witnessed. A few rapid and graceful manipulations were made by the
teacher, and the deaf-mutes extemporized upon the blackboard compo-
sitions upon geographical, historical, and moral subjects that would
have done honor to the best instructed in our academic institutions.
Problems were solved and mathematical principles elucidated with unusual rapidity and accuracy.

On inquiring, I learned with pleasure that Mr. Gallaudet, whom you
have now inaugurated as president of the new Collegiate Institution
for the deaf and dumb, was the son of Mr. Gallaudet who founded the
institution at Hartford for this unfortunate class of our race, and who
had instructed two young men who afterward attended my first district school, taught in my native town in New Hampshire.

These things awakened in my mind an active sympathy and deep interest, and when invited to attend these festivities I could not forego
the pleasure, though entirely unprepared to participate properly in the
exercises.

Education, properly considered, is three-fold, and its divisions, like
the legislative, judicial, and executive departments of government, are
theoretically distinct but practically blended. Primary instruction includes the elementary branches, such as reading, writing, and arithmetic, by which, at a later period, we secure higher knowledge, and which
are the instruments we employ in discharging the practical duties of life.

The development and discipline of the intellectual powers, by which we are enabled to concentrate and bring into full and harmonious action, at will, the full strength of our faculties, is secured by close and continuous application to the higher and more abstruse branches of study. Intellectual philosophy, the calculus, and the ancient languages, are useful mainly, to the majority of students, simply as a discipline.

The third branch of education consists in the acquisition of knowledge. This is not limited to the years of pupilage nor to the school-room. Learning must be gathered from libraries and work-shops, from the works of nature and the productions of art, in season and out of season, from elastic youth to decrepitude of age. All seasons are its own.

A liberal and complete education combines these three grand divisions, but they are rarely properly united. Great intelligence may exist without the practical skill which is derived from a thorough training in the elements of knowledge. Not every President could pass as a first-class clerk, and it is equally true that facility in the forms and manipulations of business does not indicate extensive knowledge or a thorough discipline of the faculties.

These reflections show the necessity of educational institutions of different grades. Nor are they unimportant to the deaf, dumb, and blind. I remember well a blind man in college, who maintained a commendable proficiency in the whole curriculum of study. Upham speaks of a blind guide upon the Alps, who was one of the most reliable mountaineers engaged in that dangerous pursuit.

If these unfortunates are excluded from some of the practical duties of life, they are specially adapted, by the wonderful compensations of nature, to excel in the higher walks of literature and art. Music and poetry, painting and statuary, number some of this class among its proudest names. Prescott dictated his matchless histories in partial blindness. The finger of God sealed the eyes of Milton that he might look upon diviner beauties, and the bard of " Scio's Rocky Isle" sang the praises of Achilles and the wanderings of Ulysses with darkened vision. Such examples and the remarkable success which has attended the instruction of deaf-mutes in this country justifies the enterprise upon which we have to-day entered.

You have how founded the first college in this country for the education of the deaf and dumb. You have inaugurated, with unobtrusive but appropriate and touching ceremonies, as president of the institution, him who has entered into the labors of his father, and wears his mantle with peculiar grace and dignity. Are there any here disposed to distrust the auspices of this day, and to despair of the final success of this Christian enterprise which marks so clearly the character and the progress of the age, let them call to mind the history of American colleges.

The University of Cambridge, ancient and venerable, the *Alma Mater* of a long line of illustrious sons, who have gone forth from her halls, though now lifted into affluence by the munificence of a wise and grateful people, in its infancy was sustained by the neighboring husbandmen with liberal gifts of beans and corn, wheat and rye, and other products of the soil. Those were the days of small things to the institution, but faith wrought with her works until she finally triumphed. Dartmouth College, with which I have the honor to be connected, and whose bright record of *alumni* unrolls through nearly a hundred years; which has sent forth such men as Poor, and Goodale, and Wright, to erect the standard of Christianity on benighted shores; which has given to the bar and the State, among other imperishable names, a Webster and a Woodbury, a Choate and a Chase, and the venerable statesman whose munificence has founded this institution, and whose presence gladdens these festivities, was at the first only a tent pitched in the wilderness by the elder Wheelock, for the education of Indian youth.

But you have laid the corner-stone of your college in the midst of wealth and in the very capital of the nation, where, beyond peradventure, the treasures of a generous people will be poured out to supply the necessities of the institution that is eyes to the blind and ears to the deaf.

Your college cannot fail to succeed, and will yet, I trust, be a blessing to many generations of the children of misfortune. Gladly, sir, do I welcome your institution to the circle of colleges, and your faculty to the fellowship of scholars devoted to kindred labors. You have entered upon an enterprise that involves great responsibilities and years of toil. Often will your mind alternate between hope and fear. Often will you lie down to rest perplexed with care and saddened with wearisome duties; but remember, through all, that your works will follow when—

> "The stars shall fade away, the sun himself
> Grow dim with age, and nature sink in years."

ADDRESS BY LAURENT CLERC, A. M.,

Instructor in the Royal Institution for the Deaf and Dumb in Paris, and in the American Asylum at Hartford, Connecticut.

MY DEAR FRIENDS: The president-elect of your institution, Edward M. Gallaudet, has invited me to come and attend the inauguration of a "National College for the Deaf and Dumb" in Washington, the capital of the United States, to take place on Tuesday, June 28, 1864.

I have accepted the invitation with much pleasure, and here I stand before you to say that I feel a just pride in seeing that the American Asylum at Hartford, Connecticut, has been the means of doing so much good, and has produced so many evidences of intelligence and learning.

Our school at Hartford was the first of its kind ever established in America, not only through the exertions of the late Rev. Dr. Thomas H. Gallaudet, and your humble speaker, but also by the generous subscriptions and contributions of both ladies and gentlemen in Hartford and other towns of New England. It has broken that barrier which had separated for several centuries the deaf and dumb from those who hear and speak. It has repaired the wrongs of nature in enabling them to replace hearing by writing, and speech by signs. It has also enabled many among you to become the teachers of your unfortunate fellow-beings. It has qualified your kind principal, and many gentlemen and ladies who hear and speak, to teach deaf and dumb persons in this and other schools which have since sprung up in several other portions of the United States.

Now, my dear friends, let me ask, what is the object of the foundation of a college ? It is for the purpose of receiving such graduates of the other institutions as wish to acquire more knowledge in natural science, astronomy, mathematics, geography, history, mental and moral philosphy, and belles-lettres.

Science is a most useful thing for us all. It is one of the first ornaments of man. There is no dress which embellishes the body more than science does the mind. Every decent man, and every real gentleman in particular, ought to apply himself, above all things, to the study of his native language, so as to express his ideas with ease and gracefulness. Let a man be never so learned, he will not give a high idea of himself or of his science if he speaks or writes a loose, vulgar language. The Romans, once the masters of the world, called the other nations, who did not know the language of Rome, barbarians ; so, now that there are so many schools for the deaf and dumb in the United States, I will call *barbarians* those grown-up deaf-mutes who do not know how to read, write, and cipher.

Finally, a well educated man, a gentleman by example, ought to add to the knowledge of one or two languages, that of ancient and modern history and geography. The knowledge of history is extremely useful. It lays before our eyes the great picture of the generations that have preceded us, and in relating the events which passed in their time we are taught to follow what is good, and to avoid what is bad in our own time. It lays before us the precepts of the wise men of all ages, and acquaints us with their maxims. The crimes of the wicked are of no less use to us. Seldom does Divine justice let them remain unpunished. The fatal consequences that always attend them preserve us from the seduction of bad example, and we endeavor to become good as much through interest as inclination, because there is everything to lose in being wicked, and everything to gain in being good.

The degree of Master of Arts can be conferred on the deaf and dumb when they merit it; but, on account of their misfortune, they cannot become masters of music, and perhaps can never be entitled to receive the degree of doctor in divinity, in physie, or in law.

In closing, let me express to you, my dear young friend, Mr. E. M. Gallaudet, president-elect of this institution, the earnest hope that in the great work which is before you, you will be blessed and prospered, and receive for your efforts in behalf of the deaf and dumb such proofs of its benefits as will reward you for the glorious undertaking.

ORATION.

A COLLEGE FOR THE DEAF AND DUMB:
BY JOHN CARLIN, OF NEW YORK.

MR. PRESIDENT, LADIES AND GENTLEMEN: On this day, the 28th of June, 1864, a college for deaf-mutes is brought into existence. It is a bright epoch in deaf-mute history. The birth of this infant college, the first of its kind in the world, will bring joy to the mute community. True, our new Alma Mater has drawn its first breath in the midst of strife here and abroad; but as the storm now raging over our heads is purifying our political atmosphere, the air which it has inhaled is sweet and invigorating; how favorably this circumstance augurs its future success!

I thank God for this privilege of witnessing the consummation of my wishes, the establishment of a college for deaf-mutes, a subject which has for past years occupied my mind. Not that the object of my wishes was to enter its precincts with the purpose of poring once again over classic lore, but it was to see it receive and instruct those who, by their youth and newness of mind, are justly entitled to the privilege.

To begin its history, I find it a very pleasant task to introduce here its founders. Yale College had its Elihu Yale, through whose munificence it has lived long and prosperously, enjoying a position high in our esteem; Harvard and Brown Universities had their John Harvard and Nicholas Brown, whose memories are embalmed with perpetual fragrance in the hearts of their students. The *founders*, if I may so express myself, of this college are—allow me, I pray you, to carry your memory to the Federal halls of legislation. You remember it was several weeks ago—a month wherein you saw thousands and thousands of patriots passing through your streets on their way to the horrid Moloch of War —our good President, ably assisted by his Secretaries of War and Navy, labored most incessantly to insure Grant's success; Seward, with such a consummate diplomacy as has gained him a high reputation, and a courtesy that might be recommended as an example worth imitating to the quintessence of English courtesy, the editor of the London Times, managed the good old lady beyond the Atlantic, known by the name of Mrs. Britannia, and her next neighbor, so as to keep them quiet, as he has successfully done the same thing for these three years; Chase watched with a great financier's eyes the workings of our national currency, now and then stepping in to improve its machinery, or remove impediments found clogging its motion, thus rendering the financial condition of our beloved republic healthy and conducive to our weal; and the members of both the Houses were busily occupied in what their country expected to see—the salvation of Columbia. Was it to continue the sanguinary strife? Yes; to save our Union. Sacrifice thousands of lives and millions of dollars in order to save the Union? Yes; to preserve our liberty and religion. In the midst of their arduous labors of patriotism they paused a while to listen to a few humble petitioners. They considered the memorial; they probably remembered the unenviable condition of their unfortunate brothers, sisters, daughters, sons, and friends, and, notwithstanding the rapidly increasing debt, they did not hesitate, even for a moment, to grant the boon embodied in the memorial.

Such are the founders, so far as dollars and cents are regarded; for, without their co-operation in this laudable act of philanthropy, the labors, however great, of their private fellow-founders, would have come to naught. In behalf of the mutes I beg leave to tender to them my most hearty thanks.

So the mutes have obtained a college of their own. The tangibility of the boon is actual. How great is the blessing thus bestowed on them! They see and appreciate its future usefulness to them—how bright these prospects are! Penetrating the future, they gaze upon its graduated students moving through the vast temple of fame—

> With minds and hearts aglow with pride,
> And eyes with joy dilating wide.
> Proud of their Alma Mater's name,
> And conscious of her soaring fame,
> Some move mute Clays, and Websters grand,
> Whose pens the power of speech command;
> Mute Whitefields, high in eminence
> Who speechless preach with eloquence;
> And Irvings, Bryants, Everetts,
> Who, exiled like the anchorets
> From society, diffuse their witching song
> And prose effusions o'er the admiring throng.

Is this a mere dream—an extravagant vagary, emanating from a heated imagination? It looks like it. But if this visionary spectacle be divested of its extravagance and assume the least appearance of possibility, a question will be propounded: Is it likely that colleges for deaf-mutes will ever produce mute statesmen, lawyers, and ministers of religion, orators, poets, and authors? The answer is: They will, in numbers like angels' visits, few and far between. No doubt this assertion strikes you as unsound in logic, as it is contrary to the laws of physiology, since, in your opinion, their want of hearing incapacitates them for exercising the functions of speech in the forum, bar, and pulpit, and therefore the assumption that mutes, no matter if they are learned, will ever appear as legislators, lawyers, and preachers, is untenable. Be this as it may; I shall have only to remark that they, such as may appear with extraordinary talents, will be able to speak to audiences exactly in the manner my address is now read to you. At all events, as to the appearance of mute Clays and Websters—remembering the fact that every graduate of Dartmouth College, which produced a Daniel Webster, is not a Webster in colossal intellect—you will have too much sense to hurry yourselves to Mount Vesuvius this summer to witness its next eruption which may perchance take place on your arrival there. It may occur in ten years, or later, instead of this year.

Well, my friends, with regard to mute *literati*, Dr. Kitto, the great Bible commentator, himself a mute—rather semi-mute, for he lost his hearing in childhood—James Nack, of New York, and Professor Pelissier, of Paris, both semi-mute poets of high repute, and Professor Berthier, of Paris, a born mute author, fully demonstrate the possibility of mute poets and authors, with minds maturely cultivated at college.

The avenues of science, too, are now about to be opened to the mute in this college; and as these are not interfered with by the necessity of speech, its scholars will be enabled to expand their minds as far as their mental capacities can allow. Thus we may safely expect to see among the graduates a distinguished astronomer, scanning the starry field, tracing the singular yet beautiful courses of Ursa Major and Ursa Minor—measuring mathematically the exact, if possible, distance of the Nebulæ—ever and anon exploring the solar spots, and making deductions from his researches and demonstrations as to whether the moon is really a huge, rugged mass of white metal, utterly devoid of water, vegetation, and breathing creation; a chemist, in his smoky laboratory, analyzing unknown substances, ascertaining the exact qualities of ingredients embodied in each, and, with the industry and learning of a Liebig or a Faraday, setting forth works on his discoveries; a geologist, roaming, hammer in hand, the rocky fields, diving into the fossiliferous strata for a stray ichthyosaurus or a megatherium, or, perhaps, a fossil man, in order to sound the correctness of the Lamarckian (development) hypothesis.

Though by no means impossibilities, these and mute poets are rarities. So you will please remember Mount Vesuvius. But mute authors of respectable ability and clerks of acknowledged efficiency will be found here in a number quite as satisfactory as may be wished.

These observations being duly and candidly considered as correct, you cannot but feel the indispensability of this pioneer college to the advancement of intelligent mutes to the point from whence they will be able to employ their minds in still higher pursuits of intellect, or in attending their professions with credit. Such are its advantages, which cannot be afforded by our existing institutions, excellent establishments as they are for the initiated. Nowhere but in this college the field of knowledge, replete with æsthetic flowers of literature, can be roamed over with a full appreciation of the pleasure so freely given by its benefactors.

However flattering the prospect of its success, it must be borne in mind that, by reason of the peculiar character of the deaf-mute's mind, of which I shall by and by treat, and of the popular *modus operandi* of instruction now pursued at our institutions, which, it must candidly be admitted, is as yet far from being the *ne plus ultra* of perfection, he— now a college boy—cannot be expected to compete with the hearing college boy in the extent of literary acquirements and in the accuracy and fluency of language. This fact thus shown, what courses of study should he best pursue? The dead languages, as are usually taught at colleges? Homer, Thucydides, Virgil, Horace, and Cicero are delightful text-books; but the deaf-mute cannot grapple them all. Besides the English, which he must by all means master, one foreign language will necessarily contribute to his exercise of philology; such an one as should benefit him most in his after life. The Latin, however admirable in many respects—more especially as an etymological index—is not as desirable as the French or German, for the latter languages are by far the most popular in use, and are everywhere spoken, while the Latin is found practically useful only in medical and theological institutions. The French phraseology, always as graceful in thought as it is elegant in construction, is admirably suited to accelerate the progress of his philological study. Thereupon it will, it is hoped, be regularly taught here. The sciences—such as may be judged most proper for mutes to study—will of course keep company with that foreign language. I would be glad to see the German taught here, because of its affinity to the English as well as to the Latin and Greek; but there is reason to fear that the term of tuition allotted to its scholars will render its study impracticable.

As has been stated, I shall now unfold to your view the character of the deaf-mute's mind. In doing so, I shall first give an extract from a former article of mine in the American Annals of the Deaf and Dumb:

"Notwithstanding his loss of hearing, the nature of his sensorium is not in the least different from that of the hearing person's; but as all persons of all conditions cannot be expected to possess the same quantity of mind, nor the same susceptivity of senses, nor the same retentiveness of memory, his (the mute's) sensorial faculty possesses more or less strength, it depending solely on the physiological condition of his brain. It generally retains, for a long time, impressions which are so repeated on his memory as to procure a cohesiveness difficult to weaken, and loses others which need repetition, though it sometimes retains with tenacity impressions of uncommon objects made but once."

Seeing that there is no difference in nature and capacity between the mute's sensorial faculty and the hearing person's, you might, as it is naturally anticipated, ask—so far as their fluency of language is concerned—how is the difference accounted for which is manifest between the mute's mental capacity and the hearing person's? The answer is easy, and you will, doubtless, be able to see the whole ground on which the necessity of a college is urged for the furtherance of the intelligent mute's education. This is: the hearing infant's sensorium receives through the auricular nerve verbal impressions, recognizes them when repeated, and, by mere force of imitation, learns to articulate them. His oral fluency increases as he articulates more words and phrases. With his physical growth his mind keeps pace in intelligence. At school, if he studies *con amore*, he makes rapid strides in spoken as well as written language, insomuch that he will find it comparatively easy to pursue the higher walks of knowledge at college.

The mute's sensorium, in consequence of his deafness, is all blank— speaking of oral impressions. True, it receives impressions of all objects which he has seen, felt, smelt, or tasted. It continues so until he goes to the deaf-mute school-room at the age of twelve years; perhaps older than that. What a sad spectacle this poor child presents! Looking into the depths of his mind, whether he has any distinct idea of Deity, you are shocked to find him an absolute heathen. A heathen in your very midst. At home, his brightness of expression that seems to imply high yet dormant intellect, all affection which his kin can possibly lavish on him, and the Christian influence of religious persons with whom he uses to come in contact with, cannot deliver him from the thralldom of abject heathenism. Nothing useful or ornamental can ever emerge from his dark mind. Where no schools exist for the benefit of mutes, the unfortunates move in a most pitiful condition, and, in certain places, are believed to be possessed with devils. In India and elsewhere mute infants are murdered lest they should grow up deadweights on their kin; and even in civilized nations, where deaf-mute schools flourish, uneducated mutes are often regarded hardly above beasts of burden, and therefore are employed in the drudgeries of life. In short, an uneducated mute—an innocent outcast, with a mind semblant to a gold-nugget still imbedded in the earth, yet to be brought up and refined in the crucible—drags a miserable existence.

He enters school. Remember, as a general rule, young mutes are admitted to school at not less than twelve years of age. It may be worth while to say that the New York Institute, much to her credit, took, last fall, the courage to receive them four years younger than that. So much the better. It is much to be hoped that this example will be extensively imitated. Our youth's mind begins to develop its faculties—

the seeds of knowledge one after another take root—they now germinate in a manner warranting the success of a mode of instruction altogether different from that of the hearing.   See here what a triumph of art !   How ingenious, how wonderful, was the discovery of this art ! Whoever be its inventor let him be blessed now and forever !   Thomas H. Gallaudet and Laurent Clerc are none the less entitled to our gratitude for their introduction of the art into our midst.   Shall I expatiate here on their noble disinterestedness, their patient labors in the schoolroom, their devotedness to their welfare, and the affection and veneration of the mutes for them ?   This is hardly necessary, for you all know them.   Dr. Gallaudet is now asleep in Christ.   Ere he departed this life he, like Elijah of old, flung his ample mantle upon his two sons, Thomas and Edward.   This mantle is the love for deaf-mutes.   When it alighted on those sons it divided itself into two, and, pleasing to say, each of the two portions is equal to the original mantle in extent and depth of the sentiment.   And Mr. Clerc, the venerable father of American instructors, is still in the land of the living.   He is shortly to be an octogenarian.   O, may he enjoy many more golden days of peace and happiness in the midst of his loving friends.

To return to the youth.   In a month or two he ceases to be a heathen, though by no means familiar with the Scriptures, and through his term—seven years—he acquires sufficient for his general business of life.   Owing to the brevity of his term and the fact that knowledge does not reach him through one main avenue, his knowledge is exceedingly crude, his grammar wanting in accuracy, and his language not quite as fluent as that of a hearing youth of twelve.   Should he, if he be a bright scholar, enter the high class, (there are but two of this kind in our country, one at the New York Institution and the other in the American Asylum at Hartford,) he would certainly, with ambition stimulating his mind to make efforts, acquire as much literary treasure as his short term could afford.   Still his language is found to have come short of perfection, and his intellectual appetite is, therefore, not satisfied.   Like Oliver Twist, he is still asking for more.   In other words, he wants to go to this college.   He knocks at her gates for admittance.

Alma Mater—young and comely, and breathing with the most healthy vigor of life under the ægis of Columbia—behold this youth !   See how he thirsts after knowledge !   Open your gates wide, that he may joyously cross your threshold !   O, stimulate his heart to the pursuit of hidden beauties of classic literature !   Unfold to his eager mind the coveted prize—ripe scholarship !   Like Aristotle, instructing his scholars while rambling under the azure arch, you will lead him through the walks of sacred lore under the soul-delighting canopy of Heaven, formed of angels and cherubim, with their wings spread out watching the world and counting every pilgrim that seeks to be admitted to the Celestial Abode.   And, in fine, send him forth into society a *man*, to whom the world will give the respect due to him—a *gentleman*, whom all will delight in making acquaintance with—and a *student*, still enlarging his store of knowledge at home, always remembering you and your congressional patrons, to use Massieu's words, with the memory of the heart—gratitude !

LETTER FROM REV. DANIEL R. GOODWIN, D. D.,
PRESIDENT OF THE UNIVERSITY OF PENNSYLVANIA.

UNIVERSITY OF PENNSYLVANIA, *June* 24, 1864.

Mr. PRESIDENT : My inability to be present on the happy occasion of your inauguration and that of the new college, is to me a source of sincere regret. As I cannot be with you in person, I desire to send to the new institution, on this day of its joyful birth, or rather of its transformation to a higher form and state of being, most cordial greetings and congratulations, not only in my own name but in the name of the colleges and universities of the country, so far as I may be allowed to represent their wishes and sentiments. I regard the establishment, in your institution, of a collegiate department for the higher instruction of the deaf and dumb, as reflecting high credit upon the wisdom and enterprise of your board of directors, as adding new luster to your own name, already ennobled by its associations with this sphere of instruction and benevolence, and as an honor to the country which thus leads the way in a movement that cannot fail to propagate itself on both sides of the Atlantic.

The idea is peculiarly Christian in its character. Savages have been accustomed to expose or destroy all those among their offspring who were physically weak or of imperfect organization. Even classic civilization, with all its marvelous perfection of taste and philosophy, never dreamed of the thought of attempting to raise deaf-mutes to an equality of culture and knowledge with their more fortunate fellows. It would have shrunk from the immense expenditure needed for the purpose, and called it *waste*. It is a glory of Christianity that, like a loving mother, she has a peculiarly tender and clinging affection for her more suffering and unfortunate children, and counts no expenditure a *waste* which may contribute to their relief and comfort. Christ gave sight to the blind, hearing and speech to the deaf and dumb, directly, by a word of miraculous power. We do the same indirectly, by a laborious process which, whatever it may cost, more than repays itself in the consciousness of sharing the spirit of the Heavenly Master.

The form of your present undertaking is novel, but I have no doubt that experience will prove it to be practicable and wise. Those who are deprived of one of the senses, possess, in general, as great intellectual capacities, as good natural aptitudes, and oftentimes as strong physical powers, and, withal, as earnest a desire for knowledge and activity, as those who are blessed with the enjoyment of all the organic functions. It is right that they should have an opportunity to gain a full preparation for the highest employments that may be open before them, and should enjoy the happiness of the largest intellectual, moral, and religious culture.

I only add the devout wish that your enterprise may meet with some extensive imitation, and be crowned with more abundant success than in your most sanguine expectations you have been led to anticipate.

Truly yours,

D. R. GOODWIN.

EDWARD M. GALLAUDET, A. M.,
President-Elect of the Columbian Institution, &c.,
Washington, D. C.

ADDRESS BY REV. THOMAS GALLAUDET. D. D.,
RECTOR OF ST. ANN'S CHURCH FOR DEAF-MUTES, NEW YORK.

In making a few closing remarks upon this deeply interesting occasion, I desire to fix one grand thought in the minds of all whom I see before me: The venerable man who has resigned to-day the presidency of the institution over which he has exercised such fostering care; the youthful man who to-day assumes the arduous position thus made vacant; those who have engaged in the instruction of the pupils of this institution; all those who have contributed in any way to its success—aye, all who in God's providence have come together to-day to witness the ceremonies appropriate to the inauguration of a college for deaf-mutes. The thought is this: That in what we have done to-day, it is our privilege to feel that we have put forth efforts which are in harmony with the great mission of the Incarnate Son of God to our fallen race. He came to raise man in the scale of being. He came to minister to the temporal as well as the spiritual wants of every descendant of Adam. He took special notice of those who seemed to be laboring under special trials. He spoke the gracious word "Ephphatha," to those whose ears had been closed. The state, therefore, as well as the church, is specially blessed when it cares for all sorts and conditions of men. I believe that this movement, inaugurated to-day, to elevate our deaf-mute brethren still higher in the scale of being, to make them more and more like Him who implanted in man intellectual as well as moral faculties, will be blessed from on high, and that, by and by, great results will follow from this beginning. Again I say, as we separate, let us bear away with us the ennobling thought that in God's good providence we have done something to-day to extend upon earth the Kingdom of our Lord and Saviour Jesus Christ.

CONFERRING OF THE DEGREE OF MASTER OF ARTS ON JOHN CARLIN, OF NEW YORK.

After the distribution of diplomas to the members of the graduating class of the academic department, Mr. Carlin advanced to the stage, and was addressed by Hon. Amos Kendall in the following language:

JOHN CARLIN: For the first time in the world's history has an institution for the instruction of the deaf and dumb been authorized to confer collegiate degrees. By representations to the board of directors they were satisfied that, by your varied attainments, notwithstanding the deprivation of hearing, you are a proper subject for the first exercise of this power conferred upon them by Congress. Their decision has been justified by the ability and earnestness with which you have this day presented the claims of the deaf-mutes of our country to a higher grade of education. While we bestow upon you this deserved honor, we hope thereby to induce other deaf-mutes to emulate your example, and not rest satisfied with the attainments now available in existing institutions. And whatever it is practicable for us to do, you may be assured, sir, we will not fail to do, to realize for your brothers and sisters in misfortune all the blessings invoked for them in your address of this day.

I am happy, sir, in being the instrument of the board of directors in conferring upon you this honor, and handing you an appropriate diploma.

The exercises of inauguration were closed in an earnest prayer, with the benediction, by Rev. Byron Sunderland, D. D., pastor of the First Presbyterian Church, the use of whose edifice had been kindly granted for this occason.

APPENDIX B

Extracted from the Ninth Annual Report of the Columbia Institution for the Deaf and Dumb for the Year Ending June 30, 1866.

REPORT OF OLMSTED, VAUX & CO.

110 BROADWAY, NEW YORK,
July 14, 1866.

DEAR SIR: In accordance with your instructions we forward herewith a study for the general arrangement of your buildings and grounds.

As the school is of scarcely less importance than the college, we have thought it desirable to plan the entrance in such a way that each department of the institution may be easily approached from the principal gateway.

The chapel (which has a direct access for the public from the main entrance) and the dining halls of both school and college are located in the intermediate space between the college and the school buildings, with which they are proposed to be connected by an arcade. An artistic grouping may thus, it is hoped, be secured, and the chapel will seem to belong to neither department exclusively.

The principal college building is proposed to have a westerly frontage, chiefly because this arrangement allows of a comparatively large space being set apart as a lawn and ornamental ground, entirely distinct from the section devoted to the use of the school.

South of the chapel a terraced garden is proposed, of moderate dimensions, as indicated on the plan; this is suggested by the present formation of the ground, and its semi-architectural character is depended on to assist in bringing the different elements of the composition into one harmonious whole.

The arrangement proposed for the offices and subordinate buildings will be clearly seen on reference to the design.

It is very desirable that, in the general scheme to be adopted by your institution, provision should be made for the residences of the faculty and of the president.

It will, we think, be impossible to provide for these necessary features of a liberally conceived general design, within the exact dimensions of your present lot; but if two hundred feet of ground to the west can be procured, a sufficient though by no means over-spacious arrangement can be made that will include sites for six residences.

It is evident that in the development of an institution for the deaf and dumb which is to be national in its character and sphere of operations, considerable expenditures must be involved in the erection of the appropriate structures; and as it would be very poor economy to spare expense for necessary ground while

[236]

COLUMBIA INSTITUTION
for the
DEAF AND DUMB,
PLAN SHOWING PROPOSED ARRANGEMENT
of the
BUILDINGS AND GROUNDS.
Designed by
MESSRS. OLMSTED, VAUX AND C.º
NEW YORK.
Scale 120 feet to an Inch.

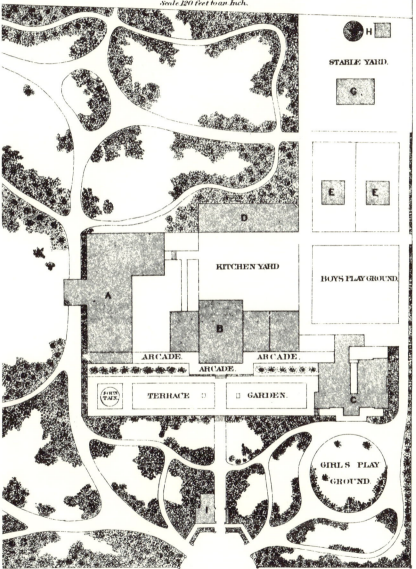

STABLE YARD.

BOYS PLAYGROUND.

KITCHEN YARD

ARCADE. ARCADE.

ARCADE.

FOUNTAIN TERRACE GARDEN.

GIRLS PLAY GROUND.

BOUNDARY STREET.

undertaking considerable outlays for necessary buildings, we have no hesitation in pressing on your attention the serious importance of adding to your site, at this time, at least the two hundred feet indicated in our design.

There seems, moreover, beyond the mere question of convenience, another reason why, in your institution, a liberal appropriation of space should be set apart for ornamental ground in the vicinity of the college buildings; the inmates of your establishment being unable to hear or speak, any agreeable sensation or delicate perception must depend on the development of other faculties.

In a well-regulated garden the senses of sight and smell are gratified in a most complete and innocent way, and there seems, indeed, to be no reason why the studies of horticulture, botany, ornamental gardening, and rural architecture should not be pursued to great advantage by your students if proper facilities are offered at the outset, and due importance is attached to that influential automatic education which depends entirely on an habitual daily contemplation of good examples.

The general plan for the buildings is a preliminary one; it embraces what has been already done, and shows how the idea can be developed in future so as to harmonize fully with our conceptions in reference to the general treatment of the design as a whole.

A road, twenty-two feet wide, is shown in addition to the two hundred feet proposed to be taken.

This, as you see, is a matter open for consideration. It will, however, if practicable, make the plan more complete, as it will furnish a private entrance to the houses on that side of the property.

Hoping the results of our study may be in accordance with your views, we remain, dear sir, very respectfully,

OLMSTED, VAUX & CO.

E. M. GALLAUDET, Esq.,
  President of the Columbia Institution for the Deaf and Dumb.

APPENDIX C

Extracted from the Tenth Annual Report of the Columbia Institution for the Deaf and Dumb for the Year Ending June 30, 1867.

REPORT OF THE PRESIDENT ON THE SYSTEMS OF DEAF-MUTE INSTRUC-
TION PURSUED IN EUROPE.

COLUMBIA INSTITUTION FOR THE DEAF AND DUMB,
October 23, 1867.

GENTLEMEN : In pursuance of the requirements of your resolutions of the twentieth of February last, directing me to examine the methods of instructing the deaf and dumb pursued in Great Britain, France, Germany, Belgium, Switzerland, and Italy ; to make memoranda of all facts of value elicited, and render an account of the same to you, I have the honor to report that, on the twentieth of April last, I landed at Liverpool and proceeded at once to prosecute the labor with which I had been charged.

Besides visiting the countries named in your resolutions, I have extended my personal inquiries into Russia, (including Finland,) Sweden, Denmark, Holland, and Ireland, being led to do this by statements which were made to me in central Europe of the interesting character of the more northern institutions for the deaf and dumb. I shall thus be able to present for your consideration a comparative view of the work of deaf-mute instruction, as carried on in fourteen countries, omitting from the family of European nations only Spain, Portugal, Greece, and Turkey. I allow myself to hope that this extension of my tour beyond the limits at first proposed will meet your approval in view of the greater completeness it has given to the examination instituted by your orders.

My programme of travel was arranged to avoid, as far as practicable, the vacations of the institutions I desired to see, and necessitated a somewhat circuitous route. I shall not, therefore, undertake to give the results of my observations in the order of my journey, but will rather divide the institutions I have visited into three classes, having reference to the fundamental principles on which the different methods of instruction are based. Each of these grand divisions may be subdivided when the less important differences of detail work are considered, but such distinctions will more properly be made to appear later in my report.

I. THE NATURAL METHOD.

I apply this term to the system founded by the Abbé de l'Epée, in France, in seventeen hundred and sixty, improved by his successor, the Abbé Sicard, and still further improved and introduced into America by Sicard's pupil, the first

Doctor Gallaudet, in eighteen hundred and seventeen. This system is based on a free use of the natural language of the deaf-mute that of pantomimic gestures; employing it, however, as a means only to the end in view, which is the induction of the mute to society by making him acquainted with the vocabulary, the grammar, and the idioms of his vernacular, thus empowering him to read understandingly and write correctly the language of the country wherein he resides.

The extent of education which may follow this great aim of the natural method, depends, of course, only on the means, disposition, and talents of the pupil.

Under this classification are to be grouped those institutions in which the study of articulation forms no part of the regular system of instruction, in which category are found all the American schools, with the single exception of one for quite young children, recently opened at Northampton, Massachusetts. In this establishment, so far as I have been made acquainted with the purposes of its founders, articulation is to be rigorously pursued, the exclusion of signs amounting to an almost absolute prohibition from the very beginning of the course of instruction.

II. THE ARTIFICIAL METHOD.

This system was founded nearly simultaneously by Samuel Heinicke, in Germany, and by Thomas Braidwood, in Scotland, in seventeen hundred and sixty. It has for its principal aim the development by unnatural processes of the power of speech, which exists unimpaired in all save a very few deaf-mutes, and the training of the eye of the mute to perform, as far as possible, the part of the palsied ear, by discerning the meaning of spoken words from the changes in position of the vocal organs. This division will include all those schools which began on what has been called by certain writers the "German method," with others that have adopted it, wherein signs are admitted only as a necessary evil, the continued use of them beyond the early stages of education being considered as pernicious in its effects on the deaf and dumb. Hence the natural language of the mute is, in schools of this class, suppressed as soon and as far as possible, and its existence as a language, capable of being made the reliable and precise vehicle for the widest range of thought, is ignored.

The extent of intellectual culture opened to mutes educated under this system is less within a given number of years than that afforded by the first method.

III. THE COMBINED METHOD.

Under this head I shall class those institutions which are endeavoring to combine the two methods just described, recognizing the utility of the sign language at every stage of the course of instruction, and at the same time including a greater or less degree of attention to spoken language. Here will be found many schools where the value and practicability of teaching articulation was once wholly denied and the system of "artificial speech" vehemently denounced; while, on the other hand, institutions organized and for many years conducted on the principles laid down by a man who declared "that all other methods than his own (that of articulation) were useless and pernicious, and no less than delusive folly, fraud, and nonsense," are now found recognizing and employing the natural language of the mute to a degree which assigns them a place in this third classification.

The old terms "German method," "French method," "English method," can now properly be used only in writing the history of deaf-mute instruction, to so great an extent have intercourse, discussion, publication, and an earnest purpose on the part of many instructors of the deaf and dumb to employ all serviceable means in the prosecution of their work, obliterated the ancient lines of division and even of dissension.

Should I undertake in this communication to give all the facts and incidents relating to the rise and progress of deaf-mute instruction that have come to my notice in central and northern Europe, to describe minutely all that has interested me in the many establishments I have visited, and to set forth the mass of valuable and suggestive statistics that have accumulated in my hands, it would be necessary to extend this report beyond all reasonable dimensions. I shall therefore limit myself to a statement of methods and appliances of instruction in the institutions which have fallen under my personal observation, together with a presentation of such comparisons, conclusions, and recommendations as shall seem to be warranted by the facts elicited in my tour; hoping to be able at no very distant day to lay before you and the public a report or volume embodying all the valuable matter I have collected, bearing upon the work of deaf-mute instruction on the other side of the Atlantic.

THE ARTIFICIAL METHOD REVIEWED.

In no school have I found the *theory* on which this method was originally based maintained at the present time.

Three teachers only, of all with whom I have consulted, claim success in artificial speech as attainable to the mass of deaf-mutes ; and these, admitting that experience has not yet sustained their view, ascribe the failure to the want of talent, patience, and industry on the part of instructors, thus assuming to sit in judgment on the great body of German teachers whose zeal, ability, and infinite good temper have received the applause of even their most decided opponents. But a single instructor, Mr. Hirsch, of the scores whose opinions I have sought, assumes to be able in the instruction of deaf-mutes to dispense with the language of signs. I have already quoted him as saying in a public address : "The act of seeing or comprehending and of speaking must be the exclusive principle of instruction, and neither the palpable alphabet nor the language of signs can have any connection with it."

And yet his utter inconsistency with himself is exhibited in the very next paragraph, where he says :

"It is true that the language of natural signs is the first means employed by the teacher to enter into relations with the pupils ;" adding the very indefinite statement, "but he does not make use of it for any length of time, and it is abandoned *as soon as it can be superseded by speech.*" (The underscoring is mine.)

How soon this supersession of signs by speech is possible with a considerable portion of the deaf and dumb may be gathered by a perusal of the following extracts from the valuable work of Canon de Hærne, to which I have already referred :

" In order to have a clear conception of the course at present pursued in the German institutions, it is important to study at the outset what has been advanced on the subject in conferences of teachers of deaf-mutes, especially in those at Winnenden, in Wurtemburg, in 1855, and at Zurich, in Switzerland, in 1857, as well as in the two conferences held at Esslingen, in Wurtemburg, in 1846 and 1864.

" The principle of articulation, as the basis of instruction of deaf-mutes, was admitted in these conferences, at which the most distinguished teachers of Germany and Switzerland were present. At these conferences the speakers gave expression to most interesting considerations, setting forth the fundamental idea of the German school, and making known the special methods appertaining to it. In the third sitting of the first conference, that of Winnenden, the following question was discussed : What are the necessary measures to be adopted in the case of deaf-mutes, inapt at articulation but capable of general instruction ? M. Wagner, director of the institution at Gmund, proposed to place them in a special class ; and M. Stucki, inspector of the canton of Berne, declaring that these pupils are not always the weakest in point of intelligence, warmly supported the motion. The assembly consequently pronounced in favor of " the erection of special divisions for the reception of children capable of instruction but unable to learn articulation, in order to be there trained, as much as possible, by signs and written language, to lip-reading and manual labor.' M. Henne, of Gmund, who was present at the conference, has developed, in the Organ of the Deaf and Dumb Institutions of Germany, the thought that had inspired this resolution, having first submitted his writings to the judgment of other teachers equally competent. He refers to four headings, the causes of the incapacity of certain deaf-mutes for articulation. Either, says he, the deaf-mute's weakness of intellect is such that the vocal organs which have remained inactive refuse to perform the exercises necessary to enunciation ; or these organs are so defective in a child otherwise capable, that we must foresee that it can never attain that clearness of pronunciation which is indispensable in oral communications with persons endowed with all their senses ; or the child, in consequence of the general debility of its nervous system, is affected with great physical weakness resulting from the feebleness of its internal organs—its lungs, &c., to such a degree that in spite of an ordinary intelligence and a normal conformation of the vocal organs, it is not in a condition to produce sounds even slightly emphasized ; or, in fine, the child has such weak sight that it is incapable of taking part in the instruction given to the pupils in general, since it can hardly read a single word on the lips of its professor, and is far from being able to seize a sentence of any length. If this defect manifests itself during the lessons, it will make itself still more strongly felt in relations with other pupils, or with strangers to the establishment. When several of these defects are found united in a greater or less degree, it is easy to understand how much more impracticable instruction becomes. M. Henne next proposes to teach the child incapable of articulation after the French method."

From this discussion it appears that prominent and able teachers who base their system of instruction on articulation admit that a sufficient number of their pupils to warrant the formation of *classes*, and even of *schools*, are found incapable of being taught on this plan.

I deem this calm and deliberate judgment of an intelligent body of practical instructors, fully committed to articulation as a valuable study for the deaf and dumb, taken in connection with the results of my own observation, of sufficient weight to lead me to reject the ideas on which the artificial method is based, as unsound in conception and impossible of execution ; in other words, that any system which assumes to rely on articulation as " the exclusive principle of instruction" must fail to educate a large proportion of the great body of deaf-mutes, or its supporters, if they would avoid this unhappy result, must vary their practice widely from their precept.

I would not, however, be understood as denying to the teachers representing this class of schools the merit of considerable success in the instruction of their pupils. I am inclined to believe that they are not always rigidly consistent with their avowed principles; hence those under their charge to whom the attainment of artificial speech is an impossibility avoid, in most cases, the unhappy consequences which would ensue were they absolutely deprived of that beautiful and effective means of communication which nature, in her seemingly afflictive dispensation, has still spared to them.

In schools of this class a large minority do certainly acquire a degree of speech and power of lip-reading that is of great value to them in their intercourse with the world. In exceptional cases, like that of young Polano, the success attained seems to amount almost to a miracle. But to argue from such an instance that all deaf-mutes can win equal success is no more reasonable than to infer from the attainments of a Humboldt or a Webster that all men have the power to rise to eminence as great as theirs, failure to do this being attributable entirely to outward circumstances.

THE COMBINED SYSTEM REVIEWED.

In drawing conclusions from the examinations I have made of schools where I found this system prevailing, it will be necessary to subdivide them into two classes—

A. Those institutions which make the sign language and manual alphabet the basis of their instructions, adding articulation to a greater or less extent.

B. Those institutions which make articulation the basis of their instruction, admitting signs freely to do the work which articulation fails to accomplish.

The use of pantomime and dactylology is, of course, much greater in schools of class A than in those of class B, while much more time, in the aggregate, is spent upon articulation in the latter than in the former.

I have made it a special endeavor in my investigations to compare general results in the schools of these two subdivisions, and think I am justified in stating—

1. That in schools of class A (where articulation is attempted with all the pupils, e. g., at Paris, Milan, Brussels, St. Petersburgh, and Stockholm) the percentage acquiring a really valuable degree of fluency in speech and lip-reading is quite as large as in those of class B.

2. That in schools of class B a considerable amount of time is thrown away in efforts to teach articulation to pupils whose use of speech and lip-reading can never extend beyond the narrow circle of their teachers and intimate companions, with whom signs or the manual alphabet might form as convenient and a more certain and extensive means of communication.

3. That in schools of class A a considerable gain is therefore experienced of time applicable to the real education of the pupils, raising the standard of attainment at graduation, after terms of study corresponding in length, to a higher point than in schools of class B.

4. That in schools of class B the sign language is more crude and imperfect, hence less valuable and precise when used, than in schools of class A.

5. That fluency of speech and readiness of lip-reading is not superior in the best pupils of class B to that exhibited by scholars of the same rank in class A.

6. That in schools of both classes the intellectual and moral development of the pupil is deemed to be the true aim in his education, the sign language being regarded as an instrument only to this, and articulation as a valuable means of communication between the deaf-mute and his hearing-speaking fellows, the imparting of which should be attempted in all cases when success is reasonably to be expected.

7. That in both classes the necessity of using the sign language in affording religious instruction is admitted.

8. That the presence among the deaf and dumb of intelligent children incapable of success in articulation and requiring to be taught by other methods is likewise universally recognized in the schools of the combined system.

The weight of the first five of these considerations leads me to accord to the schools of class A, under the combined system, the merit of imparting to their pupils a greater aggregate of benefit within a given number of years than those of class B, ascribing this result (1) to the greater discretion, which reduces the proportion of pupils receiving attention in articulation, and (2) to the fuller development and freer use of the natural language of the deaf-mute. In passing this judgment I wish to give all praise to the German teachers, under whose direction in every instance are found the schools of class B, for the position they occupy in regard to the cardinal points of the old French system, and to express the hope that they will go still further and meet their brethren from the other side of the Rhine, already far advanced towards mutual agreement on a common platform, adopting all the good and rejecting all the evil of the once rival methods, thus securing for future generations a combined system of deaf-mute education which shall afford the greatest possible advantage to the greatest possible number of that stricken class of our fellow-men, in whose behalf the hearts of Christendom move in a common sympathy.

THE NATURAL METHOD REVIEWED.

In collecting the testimony afforded by my investigations of the schools classed under this head, several considerations enter, not appearing elsewhere, which enhance the difficulty of the judicial duty I have to perform. It will be remembered that, with a single exception, in every continental institution which I visited* articulation is regularly taught, while it appears that in eleven British schools† three only give a limited attention to this branch of deaf-mute education, the others rejecting it in a very decided manner save for those few children who, before acquiring deafness, had laid the foundation of speech by the actual practice of it.

The testimony of such experienced instructors as those now conducting the eight schools declaring against articulation, coupled with the consideration that by a majority of them it has been successfully taught, is entitled to great weight; while the fact that it is where the English language is spoken that such strong ground is taken, should not be lost sight of by Americans. Those who have given attention to the study of phonology will understand that greater difficulties must attend the effort on the part of a person born deaf, to associate properly the written English words with their appropriate sounds than would be the case in German and its cognates the Danish and Swedish, or even with the Sclavonic languages, where the pronunciation follows the orthography much

---

* It is proper that I should state in this connection that in my selection of institutions for inspection it was my sole aim to see those reputed to be the most successful in the several countries I visited irrespective of the methods pursued. And I may add, that the idea of classification elaborated in this report has been wholly conceived and developed since the conclusion of my tour, owing its origin entirely to what passed before me in Europe, without reference to any previous opinions I may have had relative to the several methods of deaf-mute instruction.

† In the use of the term British schools I wish to be understood as including those of England, Scotland, and Ireland.

more closely than in English, and where the number of silent letters is much less than in our mother tongue. That our language presents greater obstacles than the French does not, however, so plainly appear, hence the success attained in the schools of France, where articulation is taught, would rather tend to remove the discouragements presented by the difficulties of English pronunciation.

On the other side of the argument, again, we have the historical testimony of the British schools, forcibly summed up by Professor Baker, as follows, in correcting an error into which I had fallen :

" You are wrong," says he, " in considering the *English* system as being based on articulation. I will go further, and state that, as a system, it never was based on articulation. The oldest treatises we have countenance the teaching of articulation, but these works seem chiefly to have arisen from a theory similar to that referred to by the learned Cardan when he says : ' Writing is associated with speech, and speech with thought, but written characters and ideas may be connected with each other without the intervention of sounds.'

" A few of the earlier experimentalists were content with producing *speech ;* such a thought as *education*, as we understand it, never entered into their heads ; those who attempted to convey *knowledge*, also, did not confine their efforts to articulation and labial reading, but also employed signs, writing, and the manual alphabet. Of this statement I could give good evidence. In the earliest days of the institution at Birmingham, taught by Thomas Braidwood, jr., it is stated that ' the children are taught to read and write, and in some instances to speak.' So that we may conclude that articulation was the exception in those days, (1815.) Three years after that time I was a resident in that institution, at which time, I can affirm from my own knowledge, that the teaching of articulation was only followed in comparatively few cases. The efforts of Holder and Wallis are directed exclusively, or mainly, towards speech ; but they were not teachers in our sense. The hereditary teachers of the London institution exalt Wallis at the expense of their relatives, the Braidwoods ; but, at present, in that institution articulation is by no means the exclusive vehicle of instruction ; signs, pictures, and other auxiliaries are employed.

" I have already alluded to the Birmingham institution dispensing to a large extent with articulation, in its early days, when under the charge of an accomplished teacher, whose family predilections were all favorable to its preference over all other modes of instruction.

" At that of Edinburgh, under Mr. Kinniburgh, articulation was the original basis, but to my certain knowledge it early gave way to means more universally applicable. Of the other institutions in these isles, (about twenty,) not one has adopted articulation, except in the cases of those pupils who could hear a little, or who had become deaf after they had acquired speech."

That under the natural method the *education* of deaf-mutes *en masse* may be successfully effected, rising with some even to a standard of high intellectual attainment ; that they, as a class, may be rendered to society self-dependent and self-sustaining ; that they may secure a precise and reliable, if not rapid, means of communicating with all persons knowing how to write, and this without the intervention of a lisp of articulation, has been most triumphantly proved in Great Britain and America, as well as in nearly every country on the continent of Europe.

Those schools, therefore, which have never made articulation any part of their regular system of instruction, satisfied with doing all that may be accomplished for their pupils within the bounds of the natural method, may justly claim to secure for the objects of their solicitude the *essentials* of an education; and this, too, in a far more effective manner than is possible under the artificial method as introduced by Heinicke and practiced by his successors for many years.

GENERAL CONCLUSIONS.

But in an age of improvement like the present, society does not rest satisfied with the achievement of mere essentials. The genius of civilization demands progress until absolute perfection is attained.

In the somewhat extended examinations already detailed to you of the leading deaf-mute schools of Europe, no one point has produced a deeper impression on my mind than the extent to which the teaching of articulation has been introduced into localities where it was formerly denied admission. The institutions of France, Belgium, Italy, Russia, Sweden, and Denmark, originally pursuing the natural method, now cultivate articulation vigorously and effectively. The attitude in this particular of the Paris institution, which was one of the first I visited, decided me to seek diligently for proof as to the real value to the deaf-mute of this accomplishment, for as such it must be regarded, * even in cases where it is successfully attempted.

The inquiry then must first be made, by what proportion of the mass of deaf-mutes, so called, including the semi-deaf and the semi-mute, can articulation be acquired. Not satisfied to form my opinions solely from the observations I might be able to make in a simple tour of inspection, I have taken pains to gather the views of many teachers on this point.

Mr. Hill, of Weissenfels, in answer to my queries, furnished the following, in writing :

"Out of one hundred pupils eighty-five are capable, when leaving the school of conversing on commonplace subjects with their teachers, family, and intimate friends. Sixty-two can do so easily.

"Out of one hundred, eleven can converse readily with strangers on ordinary subjects. Many others learn to do this after quitting school."

Professor Vaïsse, the head of the Paris institution, in answer to the same questions propounded by Mr. Hill, writes as follows :

"In my opinion nine out of ten can learn spoken language so as to derive more or less benefit from it; but only five or six will speak with sufficient ease to converse *readily* on all common subjects with their family and friends. As to the intercourse with their *teachers*, it extends to a larger number, to seven or eight out of ten. With strangers the intercourse is evidently much more limited. On some common topics it may extend, to be sure, to those seven or eight out of the ten I just mentioned; but on *all* subjects and with *ease*, it will not extend to more than two, and often no more than one out of these same ten deaf pupils."

Signor Tarra, of the Milan institution, estimates the number of deaf-mutes who may succeed in articulation at thirty per cent., this including many who could not talk readily with strangers.

Canon De Haerne says, of forty-six pupils with whom articulation has been attempted, twenty-two give sufficient evidence of progress to lead to the hope that they "will be able to converse readily with their family, teachers, and friends."

---

* M. Piroux is perhaps too severe when he says of articulation, "Its utmost value is that of an amusement for the drawing-room," and yet the danger of overrating its usefulness, even by those who teach it, is not small.

In the institution under his charge but two years have elapsed since this branch of instruction was undertaken, he being therefore unable, from observation at home, to form more decided or extended opinions.

Mr. Venus, of the imperial institution at Vienna, expresses himself as follows: "Eighty in one hundred pupils are capable when leaving school of conversing *readily* on common subjects with their teachers, their family and intimate friends.

"Fifty in one hundred pupils can do it with strangers."

Many other instructors have given me their views on these points, but these now cited may be taken as representing the various shades of opinion existing among teachers practicing the combined system.

But from what has fallen under my own observation I am disposed to believe that Mr. Hill's claims as to the results of instruction in articulation are fully sustained by facts.

Professor Vaïsse, it will be seen, coincides very nearly with his German fellow-laborer, while Signor Tarra and Canon De Haerne place the average lower. Mr. Venus in his first statement agrees so nearly with Mr. Hill and Professor Vaïsse that I am inclined to believe some misapprehension of my question (which was presented by letter in English) must have arisen; for nowhere have my own examinations exhibited results sustaining the view that fifty per cent. of the deaf and dumb can acquire a sufficient fluency in articulation to converse readily with strangers. That from ten to twenty per cent. can do this I have no manner of doubt.

The propriety of teaching articulation and lip-reading to this proportion of pupils diligently and continuously through their entire pupilage, admits, in my judgment, of no question whatever.

With reference to the additional forty to sixty per cent. who may aspire to converse on commonplace subjects with their teachers, family, and intimate friends, my mind is not so clear.

And yet Professor Vaïsse informed me that the practice of articulation had served to facilitate the acquisition of an idiomatic use of written language, even with those who did not attain to any very great success in speech.

"Here," he writes, "lies the greatest interest of the German system of tuition. It makes the child more conversant with the idiomatical forms of the language taught him. Indeed, I observed when I travelled through Switzerland and Germany that many of the deaf children uttered German but poorly, but at the same time I noticed that they had a very satisfactory knowledge of written language and used common colloquial idioms with more general ease than in the schools where speech was not taught. At the same time I must say they seemed to possess less general information.

'However it may be, I would by all means advocate the teaching of articulation in all institutions for deaf-mutes, though the use of the natural language of signs should by no means be given up." *

---

* All teachers of the deaf and dumb, whether basing their efforts on articulation or signs, agree in acknowledging the difficulty of imparting to their pupils the power of idiomatic and absolutely grammatical composition. The great loss of that daily and almost hourly tuition in conventional and exceptional forms of language received passively, but none the less effectively, by hearing children, is apparent in the deaf-mute at almost every stage of his education. That the difficulties thus occasioned may be increased by a too free use of the sign language at certain periods in the course of instruction is undoubtedly true; and if instruction in articulation can assist in removing these natural hindrances, it will accomplish a work by no means unimportant, even though the pupil do not attain the highest

In regard to the great value of articulation in those cases where it can be made a means of ready communication with the generality of speaking persons, there is, I think, no question, and I conceive it to be a duty devolving upon educators of deaf-mutes to instruct thoroughly, in speech and lip reading, the ten or twenty per cent. who are unquestionably capable of success.

In this connection I would call your attention to the fact that I have found not a few persons deaf from birth who have become fluent in speech and lip reading.

Thus it would seem that *attempts* in articulation should be made with *all* deaf-mutes, lest, unhappily, some possessing ability to acquire it, by neglect fail of doing so. I am inclined seriously to question the desirableness of continuing instruction in speech during a series of years, when no higher result can be expected than to enable the pupil to converse on commonplace subjects with his teachers, family and intimate friends, for with the instructor he has always the much easier and equally precise language of signs or the manual alphabet, while the family and intimate friends can with little effort acquire facility in dactylology, and this their interest in their mute friends will naturally lead them to do.

That German teachers, never having experienced the immense assistance to be derived from the use of the manual alphabet by the deaf and dumb, should continue to teach articulation in the cases I am now especially considering, is perhaps not to be wondered at, but I feel a good degree of confidence that, in the process of combination now taking place, they will in due time see the importance of this feature of the method of de l'Epée, and by adopting it relieve themselves and their pupils of a large amount of ill-requited labor.

It is hardly needful for me to say, after what has already appeared in this report, that nothing in my foreign investigations has led me to question the char-

---

success in oral utterance. The following from an experienced and successful instructor in one of the British schools will be of interest in this connection:

"I think our ideas upon the use of signs by the deaf and dumb in their ordinary intercourse with each other are not very dissimilar. My remarks are mainly directed against their use, or rather against the encouragement of their use, by the half-educated in intercourse with those who, by the correct use of written language, are able to materially assist them in the acquirement of ordinary phraseology. I cannot but think that signing, when carried to the extent that a half-educated deaf-mute would carry it, if he were encouraged in its use, would tend entirely to draw off his mind from the acquisition of that language by the agency of which alone he can raise himself to somewhat of a level with his fellow-creatures. When ordinary language is well acquired I do not think the use of signs in intercourse with those who understand them will have any detrimental effect.

"I have just been perusing the report of the Massachusetts State legislature on deaf-mute instruction. I have been much interested with that part which relates to articulation. I cannot go so far in my commendation of it as some of its advocates who were then examined; and I cannot understand how rapid and sure progress in ordinary instruction can be made only through its agency. I can readily believe that a conversation on ordinary topics, made up of sentences which have been repeated and rehearsed over and over again, may be carried on with merely the formation of the words, as shown by the lips, for a guide; but I cannot understand how the merely labial peculiarities of words can be sufficient to *explain* the difficult points of instruction to those whose affliction necessitates very clear and familiar explanation. No doubt, your observations on the German methods of instruction will throw some light on this. At the same time that I am unaware of any circumstances that should make me believe that articulation may be relied upon as the sole instrument of instruction, I think, as I have before expressed to you, that a great amount of good may be bestowed by a judicious course of instruction, supplementary to ordinary instruction by signs. With a good text-book, much may be left to the pupil's own exertions; *i. e.*, when he has acquired the elementary sounds. Having taught almost two hundred novices the elementary sounds, I think I may fairly lay claim to some knowledge of the general capabilities of the deaf and dumb in articulation."

acter of the foundation on which the system of instruction pursued in our American institutions is based. Our edifice is built upon the rock of sound philosophy; its corner-stone is universal applicability; its materials are cemented by consistency and practical success, while for its crowning beauty it has a dome of high educational attainment loftier and more grand than can be seen in the nations of the Old World.

And yet in the light of present experience it cannot be considered as complete. Stately colonnades may yet be added to enhance its beauty. Pillars and capitals have yet a place in the plan; not a few niches may be filled with rare works of art, and many pedestals stand ready to receive statues that shall reflect honor on their authors and enrich the architectural design.

It is plainly evident from what is seen in the articulating schools of Europe, and from the candid opinions of the best instructors, that oral language cannot, in the fullest sense of the term, be mastered by a majority of deaf-mutes. Its proper position, therefore, in the system of instruction, is not as a base or foundation, nor yet as the principal material in the superstructure, but rather as an adornment to certain portions of the building. Or, leaving this figure, it should be regarded as an accomplishment attainable to a minority only.

The number of those born deaf who can acquire oral language is small, and their success may justly be attributed to the possession of peculiar talents or gifts involving an almost preternatural quickness of the eye in detecting the slight variations in position of the vocal organs in action, and a most unusual control over the muscles of the mouth and throat.

Every one will understand that not all persons are endowed with a talent for music; that not every human being can succeed in art essays; that few men are capable of oratory, and fewer still of poetry.

So well established by the experience of ages are these conclusions that a teacher of youth would be thought little removed from insanity who should attempt to make all his pupils poets or orators, or artists or musicians, though all might learn to sing, to draw after a fashion, to declaim, and even to rhyme; and at the same time he who should endeavor to foster and develop talents for music, for painting, sculpture, oratory, or poetry, wherever among his pupils he found these choice gifts in existence, would draw forth universal commendation. Thus I conceive it to be with articulation among the deaf and dumb. To the mass it is unattainable, save in degrees that render it comparable to those sculptures and paintings that never find a purchaser; to books and poems that are never read, to music that is never sung; involving, it is true, much patient labor on the part of teacher and pupil, but exhibiting only that limited degree of success which honest criticism is compelled to stamp as no better than failure. And yet, when the congenital mute can *master* oral language, the triumph with both teacher and pupil is as deserving of praise as the achievement of true art, music, poetry, or oratory.

The actual restoration of speech and hearing to deaf-mutes may be looked for only at the hands of Him who when on earth spoke the potent "*Ephphatha*" as a proof of his divinity. But those who labor in His name in behalf of this stricken class should welcome every means of lessening the disabilities under which the objects of their care are found to rest.

You, gentlemen, and the government of the nation which has been ever prompt to approve and liberal in seconding your efforts, have done an important work for the deaf and dumb in the establishment of a college wherein the stores of literature, science, and art are laid open to minds till lately debarred the pleasures and advantages of high intellectual culture; and yet your action in ordering the investigations on which I have now the honor to report attests your unwillingness to rest satisfied with the ends already attained, and your desire to avail yourselves of every method and all appliances which may be likely to promote the welfare of the deaf and dumb, or any considerable portion of their number.

It is, therefore, with pleasure that I find myself warranted, from what I have seen in the deaf-mute schools of Europe, in suggesting the introduction of several new features into the management of our institution, which may, if adopted, prove important accessions to its already great means of usefulness.

RECOMMENDATIONS.

I therefore respectfully advise—1st. That instruction in artificial speech and lip-reading be entered upon at as early a day as possible; that all pupils in our primary department be afforded opportunities of engaging in this, until it plainly appears that success is unlikely to crown their efforts; that with those who evince facility in oral exercises, instruction shall be continued during their entire residence in the institution.

2d. That in order to afford time for this new branch, without depriving our pupils in any degree of that amount of training necessary properly to educate their intellectual and moral faculties, the term of study in the primary department be extended to nine years, and the age of admission be fixed at eight years, instead of ten as heretofore.

3d. That such additions be made to our staff of teachers as may be needed to secure thorough and effective instruction in this new line of effort.

You will remember that I found at Milan, in Italy, a normal school for the preparation of teachers of the deaf and dumb. The great good possible to be accomplished by this institution, both in the supply of competent instructors and in promoting unity of method, is apparent on very slight reflection.

In our own country the difficulty of procuring skilled workers in our peculiar field of labor has been felt in many institutions, and I conceive that one of the most important results of our college enterprise will be the furnishing of young men well fitted to teach the deaf and dumb.

But all teachers in our institutions cannot be deaf-mutes, and I would commend to your serious consideration the desirableness of making arrangements for the reception of hearing young men and women into our institution, who may wish to fit themselves for deaf-mute instruction.

I have met, in my European journey, more than one who desires to enter our institution with a view of acquiring the American method of teaching the deaf and dumb. Several applications have been received during my absence from persons in our own country anxious to learn our art, and I am confident great good would flow from the opening of our doors in these and similar cases.

With these recommendations, gentlemen, this communication, as an official paper, properly terminates.

I will, however, beg your permission to record my appreciation of the cordial greetings and hearty co-operation which met me everywhere from officers of institutions to which I sought admission for the purpose of critical examination. Every opportunity has been afforded me for full investigations, and in many places an interest manifested in my work and its results which betokened a strong desire to harmonize and combine the once conflicting methods of instruction.

For all these kind attentions on the part of my professional brethren abroad I return my most sincere thanks, indulging the hope that those from whose opinions I have been compelled in some degree to differ, will attribute to me no other motive than an earnest desire to arrive at the truth, and will believe me sincere when I express regret at being obliged to disagree with friends for whom I entertain a high personal respect and esteem.

To the representatives of our government abroad, whose assistance I had occasion to solicit, I must also express my obligations for their courtesy and efficient co-operation in my work.

To the honorable Secretaries of State and of the Interior, in like manner, I return thanks for having kindly furnished me in advance of my departure credentials which served in a most essential degree to facilitate the progress of my undertaking.

Above all would I acknowledge with humble gratitude the constant presence of that Being through whose providence sickness, disaster, and death have been forbidden to interrupt the prosecution of your commission, and by whose mercy the interests of the institution have been sustained and advanced during the period of our separation. Seeking from Him a continuance of that support from whence has sprung all our success in times past,

I have the honor to be, very respectfully, your obedient servant,

E. M. GALLAUDET.

The BOARD OF DIRECTORS
of the Columbia Institution for the Deaf and Dumb.

APPENDIX D

Extracted from the Twelfth Annual Report of the Columbia Institution for the Deaf and Dumb for the Year Ending June 30, 1869.

PROCEEDINGS AT THE FIRST COMMENCEMENT OF THE NATIONAL DEAF-MUTE COLLEGE.

These exercises were held in the First Congregational Church, corner of Tenth and G streets, on Wednesday, June 23, 1869, commencing at eleven o'clock a. m. A large audience was present, and the following gentlemen occupied the platform with the faculty and graduates : Hon. Amos Kendall, Rev. Dr. Starkey, Rev. Dr. Sunderland, Rev. Dr. Samson, president of Columbian College; William Stickney, esq., W. W. Corcoran, esq., Judge Sherman, General Howard, president of Howard University; Mr. Sidney Andrews, of the Boston Advertiser; Dr. C. H. Nichols, of the Government Asylum for the Insane; Rev. William W. Turner, ex-principal of the American Asylum for the Deaf and Dumb; and Mr. L. H. Jenkins, principal of the Kansas institution.

Rev. Mr. Turner opened the exercises by offering a prayer, in which he thanked God for the blessings of education that are now bestowed upon those who were once left to live in darkness and ignorance. He thanked God that such institutions existed, and invoked the blessing of Heaven upon the college and its graduates.

The prayer, and all other spoken exercises, were interpreted to the deaf mutes present by Professor Fay.

President Gallaudet then delivered the following opening address :

The occasion which brings us together to-day marks an era in the history of civilization. It stands forth without precedent, a bright and shining beacon in the higher walks of philanthropy and benevolence. The unreflecting and cold indifference that, because of their deprivation of a single sense, degraded a half million of God's rational creatures to the level of the imbecile, has given place within the lapse of a single century to the large-hearted practical philanthropy which first discovered the key at whose magic touch the mental prison-bolts should fly back, and has since declared in all the nations of Christendom that the deaf mute is no longer a pariah of society, but is entitled to the respect of his fellow-men, and is capable of a mental culture as full and as valuable to the community as that of his hearing and speaking brother. From the early days of imperfect results, wherein was claimed for deaf mutes only a development that might fit them to perform the humbler functions of intelligent labor, a growing estimate has been placed upon their capabilities, which to-day advances to the high position of according them the academic degrees of college graduation.

Where, in all the march of educational effort since time began, does a greater century stride appear? From mental midnight, starless even by reason of the thick clouds of prejudice and misapprehension overshadowing it, to the high noon of scholary honors, revealing bright pathways not a few, wherein the so-called imbecile of a hundred years ago may walk onward and upward to usefulness and influence and fame. From moral darkness, deeper even than that of heathen ignorance, wherein no proper idea of God or religion could germinate, to the full light of comprehended and accepted Christianity, stimulating the soul to the highest development possible in our world of many clouds, and revealing the glorious hope of ripened fruitage under the rays of the Sun of Righteousness in the land of eternal day. For no class of intelligent beings does education perform so great a work as for the deaf and dumb. The starting point is so much lower, the plane of attainment so nearly as high, and the time spent in school-training so nearly the same with the deaf mute as with the hearing and speaking, that the return purchased by education is actually far greater in the case of the former than that of the latter.

Many of the intellectual phenomena presented in the transition from a state of ignorance to the condition of enlightenment in which the training of the schools leaves the mute are unique, and, in not a few instances, intensely interesting to him who would study the operations of the human mind in its various processes of development. It is not, however, our purpose at this time to consider the education of the deaf mute from a philosophic, or even an economic, standpoint; nor yet to tell of the origin and detail the history of this peculiar work in the world; but rather to relate briefly the story of the particular institution which has invited your attendance upon its first commencement festivities to-day, and to show what grounds its friends have for thanksgiving to that Power which has crowned their labors with results exceeding in speediness of attainment their most sanguine expectations.

It will be remembered by a few here present that in the year 1856 an adventurer from the city of New York brought with him to Washington five little deaf mute children, which he had gathered from the almshouses and streets of the metropolis. With the aid of a number of benevolent citizens he succeeded in setting up a school and in collecting a half score of deaf and blind children belonging to the District of Columbia. His ostensible object was the establishment of an institution for the education of these classes of persons, and in this he was supported by a number of influential gentlemen, most prominent among whom, both in giving and doing, was the Hon. Amos Kendall, to whom belongs the honor of being named the father and founder of our institution. The sharp discernment of Mr. Kendall soon laid bare the selfish purposes of the adventurer, as well as his entire unworthiness and unfitness to direct the work he was aiming to inaugurate. Good, however, ultimated from his efforts in the formation of an association having as its aim the performance of that work, which he would fain have used as a cloak to cover his selfish ends.

On the 16th of February, 1857, an act of Congress was approved incorporating the "Columbia Institution for the Instruction of the Deaf and Dumb and Blind," and authorizing the education at the expense of the United States of indigent mute and blind children belonging to the District of Columbia. On the 13th of June following, in temporary buildings provided by the liberality of Mr. Kendall, the school was opened. During the progress of the first year it was discovered that the provision made by Congress fell very far short of being adequate to meet the objects for which it was granted, and on May 28, 1858, a supplementary act was passed supplying the deficiencies of the first law. This second act also extended the privileges of the institution to children of men in the military or naval service of the United States. In the spring of 1859, Congress up to that time having appropriated nothing for buildings, Mr. Kendall added to his former benefactions by erecting a substantial brick structure and deeding this, together with two acres of ground, to the institution.

Thus far the directors had limited themselves to the work of affording the deaf and the blind of the District of Columbia and the army and navy an education suited to fit them for mechanical and industrial pursuits. But in the annual report for 1862 a purpose was announced, which had been in contemplation from the outset, of extending the scope of the institution so as to include a collegiate course of study, the benefits of which might be enjoyed by deaf mutes from all portions of the country. This extension of the work was plainly suggested by the organic law of 1857, the fifth section thereof permitting the directors to receive pupils from any of the States and Territories of the United States, and no limit being placed in the act on the duration of the course of study. Early in the year 1864, it was determined to realize if possible this national collegiate feature of the institution, and the passage of a law of Congress was secured empowering the board of directors to confer degrees.

On the 28th of June, in this year, (1864,) the college was publicly inaugurated, and on the 2d of July Congress recorded its approval thereof by a liberal appropriation "to continue the work for the accommodation of the students and inmates of the institution." On the 8th of September following, the work of the college was commenced, with seven students, in a temporary building, which had been purchased, together with fourteen acres of land adjoining the original grounds of the institution. But one provision was now lacking to open the college freely to deaf-mute youth from all parts of the country, viz: adequate means for the support of those unable to pay for their education. To meet this want a few benevolent gentlemen were found willing to assume the support of individual students, and the college was enabled to receive all worthy applicants.

This private aid, though temporary in its character, was most important at this particular juncture, and the names of Amos Kendall, William W. Corcoran, George W. Riggs, Henry D. Cooke, Charles Knap, and Benjamin B. French, of the District of Columbia, with William Sprague, of Rhode Island, J. Payson Williston and George Merriam, of Massachusetts, and Edson Fessenden and Thomas Smith, of Hartford, Connecticut, subscribers of free scholarships, will be held in grateful remembrance by the young men who have received the immediate benefit of their generosity and by all the friends of the college.

But during the year 1866 an incident occurred, the effect of which was to secure the very end desired by the officers of the college, and this in a manner wholly providential—quite independent of any plans or endeavors of theirs. A young man, residing in Gettysburg, Pennsylvania, who had become totally deaf at the age of fifteen, hearing of the establishment of the college, applied to Hon. Thaddeus Stevens for aid in securing admission. Mr. Stevens, with his well known ready sympathy for the unfortunate, promised the young man his assistance, and addressed the president of the college on the subject. To his surprise he learned that there was no law authorizing the free admission of students to the college save from the District of Columbia and from the army and navy. "What," said he, with no little indignation in his tone, "have we been appropriating the money of the United States to build and sustain a college for the deaf mutes of the country, into which a deaf mute from my district cannot be admitted?" On being informed that such was the fact of the defective legislation on the subject, he said, "We will very soon remedy this error, and the young man from Gettysburg shall be as free to enter your college as he who comes from the District of Columbia." This resolution Mr. Stevens carried into effect, by procuring the passage, on the 2d of March, 1867, of a proviso attached to the appropriation for the support of the institution, that deaf mutes, properly qualified, not exceeding ten in number, should be admitted to the collegiate department of the institution from any of the States and Territories of the United States, on the same terms and conditions as had been previously prescribed for residents of the District of Columbia.

Thus did the silent appeal of the Gettysburg boy open the door for the higher education of his brothers in misfortune throughout the land. Thus did the veteran "leader of the House" of the fortieth Congress, in the midst of the heavy cares of state, which were exhausting his failing strength, find time and vigor enough to secure from the government of his country a boon for the deaf and dumb, the efficacy of which shall endure, as we trust and believe, till that day of joy and peace when the "lame man shall leap as an hart and the tongue of the dumb shall sing."

While private benevolence has performed an important part in the inception of our college work, to the Congress of the United States belongs the honor of establishing and endowing the institution in a manner worthy of the government of a great nation.

Our present distinguished minister to Great Britain, after describing, in his world-renowned history of the United Netherlands, the depression and distress which prevailed throughout the low countries in the closing year in the sixteenth century, records a notable event in the following words: "And thus at every point of the doomed territory of the little commonwealth, the natural atmosphere in which the inhabitants existed was one of blood and rapine. Yet during the very slight lull which was interposed in the winter of 1585-'86 to the eternal clang of arms in Friesland, the estates of that province, to their lasting honor, founded the University of Franeker; a dozen years before, the famous institution at Leyden had been established as a reward to the burghers for their heroic defense of the city. And now this new proof was given of the love of the Netherlanders, even in the midst of their misery and their warfare, for the more humane arts. The new college was well endowed from ancient church lands, and not only was the education made nearly gratuitous, while handsome salaries were provided for the professors, but provision was made by which the poorer scholars could be fed and boarded at a very moderate expense; the sum to be paid by these poorer classes of students being less than three pounds sterling a year. The voice with which this infant seminary of the muses first made itself heard above the din of war was but feeble, but the institution was destined to thrive, and to endow the world for many successive generations with the golden fruits of science and genius."

If the world justly applauds this act of the estates of Friesland in providing the means of higher education for the youth of the state in general, at a time when it was perhaps least to be expected, shall not more emphatic commendation be given in the pages of history to that government which, having in the first year of gigantic civil war furnished means for the rich endowment of colleges in every quarter of its domain, was ready, in the closing year of the exhausting struggle, while laboring under the pressure of enormous and unprecedented taxation, to assume the burden of maintaining a college for a class once deemed incapable of even the lowest degree of education?

In this college, designed to be national in the bestowal of its advantages, are already assembled students from every quarter of the land. From the Keystone State have come six; from New England seven; four from the Empire State; while the States of the West have sent seventeen; and eight have come up from the South. These, with six from the District of Columbia, form an aggregate of forty-eight youth, representing sixteen States of the Union, who have received the benefits for a longer or shorter period of the course of study opened to them.

To those who are disposed to inquire what range of acquirement in the liberal arts is open to the deaf and dumb, it may be stated that deafness, though it be total and congenital, imposes no limits on the intellectual development of its subjects, save in the single direction of the appreciation of acoustic phenomena. The curriculum, therefore, in our college has been made to correspond in general to what is known as the academical course in the best American colleges, with the design of combining the elements of mathematics, science, history, philology, linguistics, metaphysics, and ethics, in such a manner as to call into exercise all the leading faculties of the mind, and to prepare the way for whatever line of intellectual effort may be suggested by the varying tastes and talents of individuals.

To those who are inclined to ask what avenues of usefulness are open to well-educated deaf mutes, it may be responded that even before the completion of the course of the first graduating class have students of the college performed no inconsiderable service to literature by the translation of foreign publications. Already have some of them become valued contributors to public journals; already has an important invention in a leading branch of science been made by one of their number, while others have been called to fill honorable positions in the departments of the government and as teachers in the State institutions for the deaf and dumb.

But we do not on this occasion feel the need of verbal argument to prove the desirableness of collegiate education for the deaf and dumb.

The government of the United States, in that spirit of enlightened liberality which enacted the law for the endowment of agricultural colleges in the several States, has determined that the experiment of affording collegiate education to deaf mutes shall be tried. Funds necessary for the purchase of lands, the erection of buildings and the employment of competent professors, have been provided. Youth of the class designed to be benefited have eagerly sought to avail themselves of the offered privileges, and to-day, in the persons of our first graduating class, go forth the *living* arguments which shall prove whether the government has done well or ill in their behalf. They, and those who shall follow them year by year, must answer the question, "What can educated deaf mutes do?"—must show whether they can render to society an adequate return in the labor and influence of their manhood for the favors they have received at its hands during the formative and receptive years of youth.

In the belief that the result will abundantly vindicate the wisdom of Congress in founding and sustaining our college, shall we, its officers, go forward in our work—placing our trust in that Providence which has signally seconded our efforts thus far; and relying on the benevolence of an enlightened Christian people, making itself effective through the acts of their national legislators, to perfect and settle on foundations which may endure till time shall be no more the work they have nobly begun.

"It may not be our lot to wield
The sickle in the ripened field;
Nor ours to hear on summer eves
The reaper's song among the sheaves:

But where our duty's task is wrought
In unison with God's great thought,
The near and future blend in one;
And whatsoe'er is willed is done."

The several members of the graduating class then delivered their orations, Professor Pratt reading the papers for the benefit of the hearing portion of those present.

After the delivery of these orations the Hon. Amos Kendall spoke as follows:

MR. PRESIDENT, LADIES, AND GENTLEMEN: This occasion brings to me a train of interesting memories. About fifteen years ago an adventurer brought to this city five partially educated deaf-mute children, whom he had picked up in the State of New York, and commenced exhibiting them to our citizens in their houses and places of business. He professed a desire to get up an institution for the education of unfortunates of that class in the District of Columbia, raised considerable sums of money, and gathered a school of about sixteen pupils. Apparently to give respectability and permanency to his school, he sought and obtained the consent of some of our leading citizens to become its trustees. It soon appeared, however, that he had no idea of accountability to them, and only wanted their names to aid him in collecting money to be used at his discretion. On being informed by the trustees that such an irresponsible system was inadmissible, he repudiated them altogether.

In the mean time, an impression had gone abroad that he maltreated the children, and it led to an investigation in court, ending in the children being taken from him and restored to their parents, except the five from abroad, who were bound to him who now addresses you as their next friend.

The trustees then had a meeting to determine whether they would abandon the enterprise or go forward. Having in the mean time understood that there were from twenty to thirty of their fellow human beings in the District who, from deafness or blindness, were cut off from all means of education in the ordinary schools, they determined to go forward. They adopted a constitution, raised contributions, hired teachers, and opened a school in a house set apart for that purpose at Kendall Green.

At the session of Congress in the winter of 1856-'57 they procured an act of incorporation, containing a provision for the instruction of the indigent deaf and dumb and blind in the District at the expense of the United States. This act, by allowing the institution to receive pupils from all the States and Territories, and leaving all details as to the objects of study, the arrangement of classes, and the length of time the pupils should be taught, to the discretion of the directors, enabled it to expand, should it ever become practicable and desirable, into a great national institution, in which all the higher branches of science, literature, and art should be taught.

The institution was organized under its charter in February, 1857. In May of that year the board of directors were so fortunate as to secure the services of E. M. Gallaudet, esq., under whose energetic and prudent management, first as superintendent and then as president, the institution rapidly advanced to the front rank of similar institutions, not only in our own country, but throughout the world.

At his instance an act of Congress was passed in April, 1864, authorizing the institution to confer degrees and issue diplomas. The time seemed now to have arrived for carrying into effect a project vaguely entertained from the origin of the institution. The State institutions taught little else than those branches of knowledge taught in the common schools. The deaf and dumb in the various States, desirous of attaining or able to attain to a higher degree of culture, were not numerous enough to justify the maintenance of a college in each State for their instruction; but it was believed there were enough of that class in all the States to sustain one such institution. And where could that be so appropriately located as at the seat of the general government? Influenced by these considerations, and in the belief that there were enough of deaf mutes partially educated who panted for higher attainments, and would find means to pay for them, the directors, in the summer of 1864, organized a new department in their institution, denominated the "National Deaf Mute College." In the mean time they had been relieved by Congress of the charge of the blind, and authorized to take the deaf mute children of soldiers and sailors.

Thus has our institution been matured; the progress of the college has been most encouraging, and buildings for the accommodation of all its departments are springing up on the confines of your city, an ornament to your surroundings, and a testimony to the benevolence of our people and our government.

In ancient times it required the exertion of divine power to enable the dumb to speak and the blind to see. The restoration of sight and hearing was the subject of miracles in the time of Christ. It was a part of his holy mission to cause the deaf to hear. We do not claim that there is anything surpernatural in the teaching of the dumb in this our day; but is it not the fruit of that love to our neighbor which Christ taught his disciples, and that use of those faculties of the mind which God gave to man from the beginning?

What more noble invention has Christian civilization brought to man than the means devised to teach the blind and the deaf to read and write? And what more godlike charity can there be than in furnishing the means to enable these unfortunate children of darkness and of silence to receive the lights of knowledge and religion—virtually to enable the blind to see and the deaf to hear? And where shall our benevolence stop? Shall we be content to merely fit them for the animal drudgeries of life, or shall we enable those who have aspiring minds to soar into the heights of science and art, to solve the problems of nature and admire the wisdom of God?

But the subject is not merely one of benevolence; it is also one of public policy. How many hands are made permanently useful to society, and how many minds are awakened to aid in the progress of our age, by the deaf and dumb institutions?

It is an accepted proposition that, the brain being unimpaired, the destruction of one of the senses renders the rest more acute. If the sight be lost, the hearing becomes more distinct; if the hearing be lost, the eye becomes more clear and piercing. Why then may it not be, that persons deprived of hearing are more fitted to excel in some branches of learning than those in the full possession of all their senses? Silence and seclusion are conducive to study and meditation. In the silence of the night the astronomer can best study the heavens. In the silence of the desert and cave the hermit can best meditate on the vanities of life and the attributes of God. And is it unreasonable to hope that men whose atmosphere through life is silence, may, if allowed the benefit of a superior education, become prominent in all those branches of learning to the acquisition of which silence is conducive? Why may we not expect to find among them our most profound mathematicians and astronomers, our most clear thinkers and chaste writers, our most upright men and devoted Christians?

My dear young friends of the graduating class, although you have been well taught, not only in books, but in your duties to God and man, I desire to say a few words to you at parting.

There is an old book, seemingly considered almost obsolete in some of our colleges and seminaries of learning, and yet it contains the earliest record of the principles and precepts on which are based all order, all law, and all religion that deserves the name or is useful to man. That old book is the Bible. I beg you to read and study it, not merely as religionists, but as men seeking after truth. You will find in it, as you doubtless have found, much that you cannot understand, and some things that may stagger your faith; but you will find this great principle running through it from beginning to end, that obedience—obedience to law and rightful authority—is the only guarantee of human happiness, national and individual, here and hereafter. The lesson is first taught in the story of Eve and the apple—whether fact or allegory it matters not—the teaching is the same. It is repeated throughout the book, from Genesis to Revelation, in narratives, in parables, in promises, in threatenings, in songs, in prayers, in prophecies, in famines, in pestilences, in wars, desolations, and captivities. All, all are represented as flowing from disobedience to lawful authority. And is not this book (in some parts the first of all books) worthy of profound study, if it were only to see whence came that principle on which all order, law, and just governments are based, and to trace it through the ages down to our own day.

I know not what your religious opinions are. You go out into the world at an era when society is shaken as by an earthquake. So wonderful have been the inventions and discoveries of modern times, that men's faith in everything old seems to be shaken. Strange and absurd theories, reversing the order of God and nature, are broached and find believers.

Remember, young men, that whatever else may change, the moral principles inculcated in the Old Book are unchangeable, and if its religion be called in question, tell the caviler to hold his peace until he is prepared to offer a better. Sweet is the Christian's hope, and none but a devil incarnate would seek to destroy it.

Index

This book was typeset in 10/13 Janson by Harper Graphics, Inc. of Waldorf, Maryland. It was printed on 60 lb. Glatfelter by Braun-Brumfield, Inc. of Ann Arbor, Michigan. The text and cover were designed by Lisa Ann Feldman.

of rapid promotion, I had
my mind to secure a
training and was study-
a view of entering Trinity
as soon as circumstances
permit.

seventeen I entered the
class of that institution,
firm purpose near to
a business life. ~~start~~
thankful, however, to have
~~so~~ the training
used from my then
the bank, which proved
out help to me in the
which I was to enter

during my first year
the Principal of the
Deaf-Mutes in Hartford,
Rev. W. W. Turner,